Reclaiming Female Authorship in UK Television Comedy

Edinburgh Television Studies
Series Editors: Karen Lury and Amy Holdsworth

Titles:

Television/Death
Helen Wheatley

Reclaiming Female Authorship in UK Television Comedy
Laura Minor

Television and the Moving Body
Zoe Shacklock

Reclaiming Female Authorship in UK Television Comedy

Laura Minor

EDINBURGH
University Press

Edinburgh University Press is one of the leading university presses in the UK. We publish academic books and journals in our selected subject areas across the humanities and social sciences, combining cutting- edge scholarship with high editorial and production values to produce academic works of lasting importance. For more information visit our website: edinburghuniversitypress.com

© Laura Minor 2024, 2026

Edinburgh University Press Ltd
13 Infirmary Street
Edinburgh EH1 1LT

First published in hardback by Edinburgh University Press 2024

Typeset in 12 on 14pt Arno Pro and Myriad Pro
by Manila Typesetting Company, and
printed and bound by CPI Group (UK) Ltd,
Croydon, CR0 4YY

A CIP record for this book is available from the British Library

ISBN 978 1 3995 0301 3 (hardback)
ISBN 978 1 3995 0302 0 (paperback)
ISBN 978 1 3995 0303 7 (webready PDF)
ISBN 978 1 3995 0304 4 (epub)

The right of Laura Minor to be identified as the author of this work has been asserted in accordance with the Copyright, Designs and Patents Act 1988, and the Copyright and Related Rights Regulations 2003 (SI No. 2498).

Contents

Preface vii

Introduction: Unravelling the 'Unruly' Woman: New Perspectives on Feminism, Intersectionality and Authorship in Contemporary UK TV Comedy 1
1. Julia Davis, Dark Comedy and Defying Ageing Stereotypes: Analysing Older Female Stars in TV Comedy 27
2. Phoebe Waller-Bridge, Posh Humour and Political Correctness: Constructing the Upper/Middle-Classes in TV Comedy 53
3. Caitlin and Caroline Moran, Celebrity Comics and Classed Humour: Examining Overlooked Duos in TV Comedy 79
4. Michaela Coel, Colourful Comedy and Challenging the Status Quo: New Representations of Race in TV 101
5. Sharon Horgan, Comedy Screenwriting and Starting Merman: Recognising Authorship and Entrepreneurship in TV Comedy 121
Conclusion: Rethinking Women's Place in Contemporary UK Television Comedy 141

References 151
Index 177

For my mum, Roz – the most remarkable woman I know.

For my dad, Kevin – whose support made this possible.

And for my cat, April – who wouldn't let me write, but forced me to take breaks by following her around the house.

Preface

This book is borne from my PhD thesis, which I began writing in 2017, examining women in UK TV comedy. I am deeply grateful to my dedicated supervisors, Beth Johnson and Melanie Bell, for their invaluable guidance and unwavering support throughout this journey and beyond. Additionally, I extend heartfelt thanks to the Arts and Humanities Research Council (AHRC) for funding the PhD that laid the foundation for this work.

At the time of embarking on my research, series 2 of Fleabag had yet to be made (there was no hot priest discourse, can you believe?), and Michaela Coel's explosive dramedy, *I May Destroy You* had also not appeared. Sharon Horgan was creating TV series at a rapid rate. *Derry Girls* aired on Channel 4 in 2018, only a few months after I began my studies. A couple of years later, when perusing HMV, I was immediately struck by a mug emblazoned with the phrase 'I AM A DERRY GIRL', showcasing just how popular and marketable the sitcom had become. These developments across comedy, and women creating comedy, were rapid – and it was hard to keep up. This, in part, captures the complexities of writing an extensive piece of work that relies on contemporary texts, but it also highlights how female comedians flourished on UK television from 2010 onwards.

Though American TV comedy has typically been at the centre of such discussions (see, for instance, Kohen, 2012; Fields, 2017; Peterson, 2017; Moeschen, 2019), there has been a veritable explosion of female-centred and female-authored comedies in the UK that are equally as significant but have been overlooked in academic discourse. Original series by the likes of Ruth Jones, Jo Brand, Jessica Hynes, Kathy Burke, Bernadette Davis, Sarah Hooper, Daisy May Cooper, Diane Morgan, Kayleigh Llewellyn, Holly Walsh, Lisa McGee and Roisin Conaty have shaped contemporary comedy.

In writing this book and focusing on the contemporary significance of specific authors, I hope to ensure that women's comic voices are heard in the present rather than only acknowledged in hindsight.

Introduction: Unravelling the 'Unruly' Woman: New Perspectives on Feminism, Intersectionality and Authorship in Contemporary UK TV Comedy

As the first episode of Phoebe Waller-Bridge's BBC Three dramedy *Fleabag* (2016–19) draws to a close, the eponymous protagonist (played by Waller-Bridge herself) is in a taxi riding through London. The driver engages her in light conversation, anticipating small talk to make his night go faster. Fleabag tells him that she 'kind of' runs a café by herself, and the story of how she co-founded it is 'kind of funny, actually'. Intrigued by these vague musings, the taxi driver urges her to tell him more. The protagonist reveals that she opened it with her friend, Boo. 'Cute name', the driver interjects before Fleabag continues,

> Yeah. She's dead now. She accidentally killed herself. It wasn't her intention, but it wasn't a total accident. She didn't think she'd actually die; she just found out her boyfriend fucked someone else and wanted to punish him by ending up in hospital and not letting him visit her for a bit. She decided to walk into a busy cycle lane, wanting to get tangled in a bike, break a finger maybe. But as it turns out, bikes go fast and flip you into the road. Three people died (S01E01).

The car fills with silence. Fleabag laughs: 'She was such a dick'. Wordlessly, the taxi driver looks at her in his rear-view mirror. 'So yeah... Kinda on my own', Fleabag says with a touch of awkwardness before the camera closes on her. In an intimate close-up, she opens her coat, exposing a bra underneath. From her trousers, Fleabag pulls a sculpture of a woman with no arms that she stole from her god-awful godmother/stepmother earlier in the episode. Turning her gaze to the camera, Fleabag graces us with a smile, while the raw, guitar-driven theme song starts to play during the credits.

Here, Fleabag encapsulates Kathleen Rowe's notion of the 'unruly' woman. This figure, in comedy, is typically associated with spectacle-making – she is noisy, excessive and dwells close to the grotesque. As Rowe contends, 'the unruly woman points to new ways of thinking about visibility as power [...] [enabling a woman] to affect the terms on which she is seen' (1995: 11). Certainly, Fleabag's visibility is integral to the scene. She dominates the frame by breaking the fourth wall, grinning at us after her monologue draws attention to the complexities of her past. Only later, in the sixth and final episode of the first series, do we find out that it is she who slept with Boo's partner.

Given that the show explores themes such as guilt, loss, grief, disillusionment and loneliness, in many ways *Fleabag* is established as a 'classic' British comedy, simultaneously biting, witty and caustic. Executive producer Jack Williams says of the show: 'It does feel very British – the sense of humour, the wryness, the ability to go from very funny to very sad' (Williams, quoted in Youngs, 2019). Even the production and institutional contexts of the show are characteristically British. Episodes are produced in batches of six, compared with the American tradition of twenty-four to twenty-six episodes a season. Alongside this, *Fleabag* is writer-led, a British comedy practice associated with single authors, including Johnny Speight, David Renwick, John Sullivan and Roy Clarke, as well as pairs of writers, such as Jimmy Croft and David Perry, Ray Galton and Alan Simpson, and Dawn French and Jennifer Saunders. This differs from the American system of team writing. A historical focus on authorship – and male authorship, more specifically – is one that has been romanticised in Western culture and TV studies (Newman and Levine, 2012), particularly in Britain through the male playwright (Nelson, 1997). Yet, in line with television's fundamentally collaborative nature, Waller-Bridge does work closely with family, friends and colleagues. The edgy theme track that plays over Fleabag's smile was written by her sister, Isobel Waller-Bridge, demonstrating both Phoebe Waller-Bridge's authorial control and the contextual factors that have influenced what we see/hear on-screen. In other words, the comedic female 'unruliness' of Fleabag's character, the subversive laughter she incites through her transgressive words and actions, is mitigated by what happens *off*-screen through industrial and production practices.

This scene highlights two concerns of this book. The first is based around Rowe's influential notion of the 'unruly', a term that has been used since the 1990s and which needs updating to consider how women in/on comedy function beyond this homogenised model largely informed by second-wave and third-wave feminism. With 'unruliness', there remains a focus on visibility and hence performance, as opposed to the labour and contexts *behind* what we see on screen: Phoebe Waller-Bridge's writing and mastery of the monologue, the relationship she has with her sister/collaborators and how British humour has influenced her work. The second relates to ideas of nation and nationality. UK and US television tends to be conflated in discussions of the contemporary televisual landscape. Scholars argue that markers of taste are now transnational (Nygaard and Lagerway, 2020), with an increasing number of comedy programmes having both UK/US talent that reach 'quality' TV and non-traditional comedy viewers (Horton, 2016). However, as the contexts of *Fleabag* indicate, there remain important distinctions between UK and US television that need to be examined, with this book arguing that nationalised broadcasting systems have affected how feminine-gendered fiction is created and programmed. Thus, this book has two aims: to revise Kathleen Rowe's notion of the 'unruly' woman and to apply this updated concept to British and Irish TV writers and performers who have either been neglected in academic studies or analysed as part of larger transnational projects.

In order to address these two concerns, this book focuses on British and Irish writer/performers – and their respective comedy texts – from 2010 to 2020, a period in which women's comedy has thrived. In the second decade of the twenty-first century, we were, as Claire Perkins and Michele Schreiber note, experiencing 'a golden age of television for women' (2019: 919) because of the revival of feminist beliefs and ideals online (see Cochrane, 2013 and 2014; Munro, 2013 and 2014; Banet-Weiser, 2018; Jouët, 2018; and Favaro and Gill, 2018) as well as the widespread use of multiplatform distribution networks (Mittell, 2015; Strangelove, 2015; Lotz, 2017; and Jenner, 2018). These two important shifts have propelled Anglo TV production to centralise stories by women, for women, and/or about women. Indeed, in the 2010s, the popularity of mainstream feminism shifted the television industry's market logic to consider a diverse range of female creators and characters who were brought onto TV screens. This diversity has fought 'the long-held masculinism of quality television as a system of evaluation that prioritises darkly realistic dramas premised upon male antiheroes and the sexist and abusive treatment of women' (Perkins and Schreiber, 2019: 920). Moving away from this form of programming, darkly realistic dramas have not been the primary focus of television created by women, with comedy becoming the genre of choice.

In the following order, I therefore examine five case studies looking at women and their respective comedy TV series: the oeuvres of Julia Davis,

Phoebe Waller-Bridge, Michaela Coel, Caitlin and Caroline Moran, and Sharon Horgan. It is challenging, though, to describe the contemporary 'unruly' woman: to condense the intricacies and contradictions inherent in her character. In contemporary popular culture, a multitude of different labels have come to describe 'unruly' women on TV: nasty (Robinson, 2016), unlikeable (Rodgers, 2019), difficult (Pinedo, 2021) and antiheroine (Tally, 2016). For the purposes of this book, none of these have been suitable in outlining the impact women in TV comedy have had on the cultural imagination. Building upon Kathleen Rowe's existing scholarship, I therefore define these women as 'fastidious' to outline how comedians demonstrate delicacy, precision and control over their carefully crafted TV series. This is not to suggest that the 'unruly' woman conceptualised in the 1990s does not demonstrate these qualities; instead, the 'messiness' associated with these women must be analysed alongside the attention to detail that goes into creating female-authored comedy. 'Fastidious' women navigate the current televisual ecology to produce spaces where women's humour can thrive. While 'fastidious' is used here to describe how women (re)present themselves and their work, I also employ this term for its ambivalence and the ambivalence shown *towards* women – 'fastidious' may be used as a positive or negative descriptor, and this is reflected in the reception of contemporary female comedians. Traced back to the Latin noun *fastidium*, which means 'aversion' or 'disgust', the dual meanings of the term mirror the contradictory critical receptions that women in comedy, or women in the media more generally, often face.

With these understandings of 'fastidiousness' in mind, I examine two important threads throughout this book: the authorial authority of women in comedy and ambivalence surrounding them or their work. Addressing the former, the women that will be analysed throughout this book all serve as directors, writers, (executive) producers and actors in their texts, and though their characters may be 'messy' and transgressive – 'unruly' in Rowe's terms – they are also carefully crafted creations. This book thus recognises women's work and the labour that goes into producing comedy texts, mainly since female authorship has been treated as a different 'category' from canonical or even male authorship. That women have to work twice as hard as men – with one mistake causing them to be 'exposed' as frauds – is evidence that women do not have room for manoeuvre like their male counterparts. It is thus essential to recognise how the contemporary 'unruly' woman is not only rebellious, disorderly and uncontrollable on-screen, but disciplined, methodical and painstaking in her development of British and

Irish comedy television off-screen. The secondary focus on 'ambivalence' in analysing 'fastidious' funny women is significant in that it has been referred to in Kathleen Rowe's work. I similarly argue that it is integral when analysing the contemporary 'unruly' woman. As she argues, the 'carnival and the unruly woman are not essentially radical but are ambivalent, open to conflicting appropriations' (1995: 44). Though to a certain degree, the 'unruly' woman is now a well-established figure in the televisual landscape, she has a new set of expectations placed on her by the ever-growing and invasive neoliberal media as well as critics and audiences, thereby fuelling the ambivalence of the 'unruly' or 'fastidious' woman in the 2010s.

The writer/performers that I suggest as displaying 'fastidiousness' have been chosen for various reasons. The first chapter focuses on Julia Davis because she is an anomaly of sorts. While comedies by 'messy' millennial women now focus on self-expression, semi-autobiographical musings and a close examination of the personal, Davis's comedy has explored fictitious characters that demonstrate excessive and exaggerated forms of femininity in middle-class Britain. She has also been in the television industry since the 1990s, while most other authors to be analysed began gaining traction in the 2000s (and onwards). Though most famous for her macabre comedy *Nighty Night* (BBC Three, 2004–5), which tells the story of beautician Jill's obsession with her neighbour, since then, Julia Davis has produced, written, directed *and* starred in *Camping* (Sky Atlantic, 2016) – forming as principal showrunner – while also creating *Hunderby* (Sky Atlantic, 2012–15). The latter series won her a BAFTA Craft award for 'Best Comedy Writing'. Both shows aired on the cable channel Sky Atlantic, situating Davis's work as distinctly 'premium' in the UK. Davis has also created the UK–US televisual production *Sally4Ever* (2018), which aired on Sky Atlantic and HBO, further situating her series as 'prestige'. In these series, Davis has amplified and exacerbated key themes she explored in the late 1990s and early 2000s, with her work demonstrating the complexities and contradictions surrounding femininity, sexuality and class. Though overtly 'unruly' in her series, in interviews, she is reserved and unassuming, perceived as unusual compared with the loud and visible presence of other writer/performers who are considered stereotypically 'unruly'. It is this dissonance, I argue, that demarcates her as a 'fastidious' woman, as she is treated ambivalently by critics and audiences for this behaviour.

The second subject of this book is Phoebe Waller-Bridge, referred to at the beginning of the book, who cites Davis as one of the inspirations for her work (BAFTA Guru, 2017). Like *Nighty Night*, Waller-Bridge's standout series *Fleabag* has been situated as an 'edgy' and 'complex' show. Unlike Davis's work, however, *Fleabag* is a BBC–Amazon co-production described as the UK's answer to Lena Dunham's American comedy drama *Girls* (HBO, 2012–17) because of its focus on the self-destructive and emotionally chaotic millennial woman. This figure clearly interests Waller-Bridge, as she can be seen in her first TV series – *Crashing* (Channel 4, 2016) – which Channel 4 decided not to renew after its first season. Bridge's quiet introduction to comedy changed when the BBC picked up her play *Fleabag* after being performed at the Edinburgh Fringe Festival. First airing on BBC Three before transitioning to BBC Two, the sitcom's second season has been hailed as 'a near-perfect work of art' (Davies, 2019) and one of former President Barack Obama's favourite TV series of 2019 for its portrayal of grief and trauma with a comedic edge (Lampen and Arnold, 2020). In this chapter, I argue that Waller-Bridge has created a carefully crafted depiction of 'unruliness'. Ultimately, however, this 'unruliness' lies in her ambivalence, as Waller-Bridge's 'bad feminism' draws attention to the unequal structures that make her work both critically acclaimed and derided in a digitised feminist landscape concerned with intersectionality as well as a British TV industry that favours (upper) middle-class narratives. While *Fleabag* is a co-production between the UK and the US, the perception of Phoebe Waller-Bridge as 'problematic' stems from her Britishness, or more specifically, British TV comedy's reproduction of conventional classed and gendered discourses. This chapter suggests that Phoebe Waller-Bridge has showcased this national fixation through her comedic conceptualisation of women and class (via her character, Fleabag, and high-profile public appearances on *Saturday Night Live* [NBC, 1975–] and the covers of *Vogue*). Through the new 'fastidious' woman who creates tightly woven texts, I argue that class politics remains at the forefront of British comedy.

The works of Davis and Waller-Bridge have been described as 'nasty', which contrasts with the 'upbeat' semi-autobiographical comedy *Raised by Wolves* created by two sisters to be explored in the third chapter – Caitlin and Caroline Moran. *Raised by Wolves* follows in the footsteps of Channel 4 programming concerned with alternative representations of the working-class, such as *Shameless* (Channel 4, 2004–13). Though this is the first comedy Caitlin and Caroline Moran have created for TV, they both have significant careers and unique points of view that are important when considering women's foray into comedy – particularly in representing the underrepresented area of Wolverhampton. Of the two sisters, Caitlin Moran differs from this book's other writer/performers. Though she has had an enduring career like Julia Davis, she did not begin in TV comedy, but in journalism. Known for her celebrity feminism, I explore the ambivalence of Caitlin Moran's personal politics, as she is often seen to negatively represent 'white' celebrity feminism while simultaneously providing positive representation for the Midlands, Wolverhampton and the working-class. Alongside this, I interview Caroline Moran to offer a personal and reflective perspective on her work in comedy and the current state of the genre. Previously working in radio comedy, more recently, Caroline co-wrote the TV sitcom *Hullraisers* (Channel 4, 2022–) and created *Henpocalypse!* (BBC Two, 2023–), in which a group of women on a hen-do in remote North Wales face the world's end. As I suggest, in a similar vein to Julia Davis, Caroline Moran's quiet diligence helped *Raised by Wolves* become a reality, with Caitlin stating that her sister was the one who did most of the groundwork (Moran, 2013). Throughout this book, then, I contend that 'unruliness' is impossible without 'fastidiousness' – the unremitting attention to detail and care that is often overlooked.

Another writer/performer who explores the lives of working-class women is Michaela Coel – the subject of Chapter 4 – and in her debut for E4, *Chewing Gum* (E4, 2015–17), she takes a more intersectional approach by exploring the life of a working-class Black woman on a council estate in London's East End. Like Waller-Bridge, Coel adapted her TV series *Chewing Gum* from her one-woman play *Chewing Gum Dreams*. Airing on E4, the series is part of British youth television that Faye Woods argues is 'separate from prestige serials and topical single dramas, existing primarily in youth spaces on digital niche channels' (2016: 8). After *Chewing Gum*, Coel was no longer perceived as 'niche', and she became the youngest and first non-white industry figure to deliver the prestigious MacTaggart Memorial Lecture at the Edinburgh TV Festival, during which Coel revealed she had suffered racism and sexual assault while working in the industry. Since these experiences, Coel created, wrote and performed in the BBC series *I May Destroy You* (BBC One/HBO, 2020), which documents these incidents of abuse and questions notions of consent. Similarly to Waller-Bridge, Coel's popularity soared in a relatively short period of time, and her popularity too began with comedy – an important genre in kickstarting the careers of female writer/performers. This chapter explores how 'unruliness', as a concept, does not consider the ways in which Black women have historically been represented on-screen. The 'unruly woman' is 'associated with looseness and occasionally whoreish-ness' (Rowe, 1995: 35). However, in an analysis of *Chewing Gum*, I contend that Coel has shifted what it means to be 'unruly' in her deconstruction of stereotypical and offensive representations of Black women as sexually aggressive, with Coel creating sexually naïve and innocent characters. This chapter also focuses on her TV series *I May Destroy You* to examine production and industrial contexts. Here, I argue that Michaela Coel's 'fastidiousness' – being difficult to please and demanding – is a significant part of 'talking back' to a male-dominated industry, particularly for Black women and feminists in/on television.

The fifth chapter of the book centres on Sharon Horgan, an Irish writer and performer. While acknowledging the importance of her Irish heritage, the primary focus of this book is on 'UK Television Comedy', which serves as the predominant context for Horgan's work. As as an actor, writer, director and producer, Horgan has been described as 'the busiest woman in British television' (Harrison, 2019) despite her Irishness, and it is clear why. She has created multiple original comedies across the UK (and US), including *Pulling* (BBC Three, 2006–9), *Catastrophe* (Channel 4, 2015–19), *Motherland* (BBC Two/BBC One, 2016–present), *Divorce* (HBO, 2016–2019), *Bad Sisters* (Apple TV+, 2022), *Shining Vale* (Starz, 2022–) and *Dreamland* (Sky Atlantic, 2023–). Horgan began her comedy career by winning the 2001 BBC New Comedy award for sketch-writing with her writing partner Dennis Kelly. Since then, she has continually collaborated with others, and in 2014, she founded the production and entertainment company Merman with Clelia Mountford, producing TV shows such as *There She Goes* (BBC Four/BBC Two, 2018–), *This Way Up* (Channel 4, 2019–) and *Frank of Ireland* (Channel 4/Amazon Prime, 2021–). Both women also founded Mermade, a digitally focused sister company specialising in content for social, digital and on-demand broadcasters. This chapter argues that Horgan continually produces TV texts featuring 'unruly' women, but it also examines the importance of her work off-screen and the politics of gendered entrepreneurial labour (her 'fastidiousness'). In doing so, it explores the complexities and contradictions of the enterprising self: both empowering and socioeconomically desirable on the one hand, capitalist and corporate on the other. Reading Horgan's stardom through the lens of identity politics, this chapter further analyses how Horgan has traversed the current landscape as a white, Irish and middle-aged writer/performer.

In analysing these women, there is some purpose of determining the structural, narrative and ideological patterns in the TV series created by female comedy writers in the UK. However, this book is primarily concerned with the symbiotic relationship between creator, craft and context. To capture the complexities of the media landscape in which contemporary female writer/performers operate, I argue that the relationship between creator, craft and context is central in foregrounding their labour of production. In terms of the creator's role, I emphasise the symbiotic relationship between the female writer/performers and their work, highlighting how their identities, experiences, and perspectives shape the comedy they create. Craft refers to the meticulous process of creating television texts, encompassing writing, performance and production. I showcase how these women's attention to detail contributes to their 'unruliness' and success. Finally, context includes the institutional logics of television and the socio-political shifts of the 2010s. I argue that understanding the context in which these creators operate is essential to appreciate and understand the labour that goes into producing comedy texts. This triadic relationship is central to the book's analysis, foregrounding the nuanced interplay between the creator, their craft and the surrounding context. Therefore, a comprehensive analysis of Coel, Davis, Waller-Bridge, Horgan and the Morans, both on and off camera, is employed to analyse their place within UK TV production. However, such an examination needs to be contextualised, and I will now provide a theoretical background to women in comedy before analysing these authors in the forthcoming chapters.

Why 'Fastidious'? Theoretical Underpinnings of Women in Comedy

In the 1990s, a body of work examining the importance of women/humour emerged, traced by important female comedy academics Patricia Mellencamp (1992), Frances Gray (1994) and Kathleen Rowe (1995), key thinkers who have heavily influenced and informed this book. Patricia Mellencamp, in her book *High Anxiety: Catastrophe, Scandal, Age, and Comedy* (1992), examines women and the situation comedy – including figures such as Gracie Allen, Lucille Ball and Roseanne Barr – tracing their careers through the use and critique of Freud. Gray (1994) more specifically explores sitcoms and stand-up to argue how women are not only objects 'of the male gaze but of the male laugh – not just to-be-looked-at but to-be-laughed-at – doubly removed from creativity' (ibid: 9). Like Mellencamp, Gray examines the work of Lucille Ball and Gracie Allen but also creates an important space to discuss British sitcoms. However, it is Kathleen Rowe's theory of the 'unruly' woman that has persisted as the theoretical underpinning of studies on women and comedy since the 1990s. Rowe points out, through this figure, that women have been making spectacles of themselves for centuries – from medieval and early modern Europe to the present-day.

According to Rowe, there are eight key characteristics of the 'unruly' woman that can be traced back to early modern European culture of carnival (1995: 31). She dominates, or tries to dominate, men; her body is excessive or fat; her speech is similarly excessive; she makes jokes or laughs at herself; she draws attention to the social constructs of gender; she may be old or masculinised; her behaviour is associated with looseness; she may be pregnant; and she is associated with dirt, liminality and taboo. These traits are primarily concerned with the 'unruly' woman's visibility, which is why they have been instrumental in analysing film and television as forms of visual communication. In the first half of her book, Rowe's two primary case studies are the feminine yet domineering figure of Miss Piggy and the fat, white working-class writer/performer Roseanne Barr, before offering a revisionist history of romantic comedy films from the 1930s to the 1980s in the second half.

My main interests lie in the first half of Rowe's book, where she provides an understanding of comic female figures on television in terms of the body. Because of this, Melissa Williams suggests that Rowe overlooks the significance of social class: 'Barr's class identification is only significant to Rowe via physical signifiers, rather than via Barr's thoughts on gender and feminism. This is problematic primarily because Barr was one of the most prolific and outspoken working-class feminists in the United States in the early 1990s (2017: 112). Now, there is a great urgency for feminist television studies to challenge oppressive institutions and discrimination by exercising an intersectional approach, acknowledging the myriad of voices and identities in contemporary TV comedy.

Rowe herself has discussed shifts in 'unruliness' since the 1990s. As she wrote in 2017,

> a panel of feminist scholars at a recent international conference took up the question of whether unruliness, or the transgressiveness associated with women in comedy, has become the 'new normal' in our post-*Roseanne*, post-feminist world. The question is provocative. On July 25, 1990, Roseanne unleashed a firestorm when she combined a screeching performance of the national anthem with a parody of male gestures associate with baseball. Today such a performance – or at least the vulgar aspects of it – might elicit only a shrug. For me, this is

> not a sign that female comedy has lost its disruptive power, but of the reverse. Women's laughter has altered what we consider normal, and for the better. (viii)

If comedy has changed the baseline for women's acceptable behaviour and what is deemed 'normal', then 'unruliness' needs to be reassessed and reconsidered for the second decade of the twenty-first century and a new era of feminism.

Linda Mizejewski is one scholar who has considered these changes and made notable contributions to academic debates surrounding women and comedy since the 1990s. Her edited collection with Victoria Sturtevan – *Hysterical!: Women in American Comedy* (2017) – acknowledges the importance of Kathleen Rowe's work, with her volume including the aforementioned quote from the comedy scholar in its forward. Here, Rowe argues that 'scholarship on women and comedy has typically lagged behind the reality of women's presence in the genres of laughter' (2017: vii).

With the ever-growing popularity of women in comedy, there have been further contemporary studies. A few scholars have examined the issue of inequality in British stand-up comedy, as evidenced by the works of Quirk (2015, 2018), Tomsett (2023) and Sedgwick (2024). The field of television comedy has also been explored in relation to gender and sexuality. Two significant studies stand out in this area: Mizejewski's *Pretty/Funny: Women Comedians and Body Politics* (2014) and Rosie White's *Television Comedy and Femininity: Queering Gender* (2018). White's monograph is particularly noteworthy for its analysis of how British and American television comedies, despite being predominantly heteronormative, engage with the complexities of heterosexual identities. White argues that these comedies offer a space in which 'women may move beyond the normative bounds of heterofemininity' (2018: 15), suggesting that even within heteronormative contexts, there is potential for subverting traditional gender roles and expectations.

Rosie White's notion of 'queering gender' in comedy informs the concept of 'fastidiousness', as popular comic figures throughout the twentieth century have been described as performing both. Charlie Chaplin, for instance, has been described as an unrelenting perfectionist (see, for example, Neibaur, 2012 and Gehring, 2014), earning a reputation for having a demanding and 'fastidious' work ethic as both an actor and a director. Stan Laurel, of Laurel and Hardy fame, is also perceived as a perfectionist who wrote his scripts meticulously and loathed to appear in front of an audience unprepared (Valinoti Jr, 2010). In terms of female comedy writer/performers, Lucille Ball, who is often invoked in theories surrounding women and comedy, has also been described as a 'fastidious perfectionist' (Landrum, 2007: 231). For women in comedy, particularly those concerned with slapstick and physicality, Ball is often used as a point of comparison. For instance, when discussing the contemporary burlesque performer Little Brooklyn's subversive and comedic acts, Lynn Sally argues that '[l]ike the work of Lucille Ball herself whose comedic timing appeared effortless but was in fact the product of perfectionist-level rehearsals, Brooklyn's comedy is indebted to her fastidious planning and thoughtful referentiality' (2021).

Significantly, those described as 'fastidious' typically undermine and subvert gender binaries via their performances. Charlie Chaplin and Stan Laurel often act in drag roles, with Harry M. Benshoff and Sean Griffin arguing that both 'presented such convincing impersonations that their acts may have undermined the supposedly stable male-female gender binary' (2005: 22). Writing on Charlie Chaplin's comic figure 'The Tramp', Wibke Schniedermann contends that '[h]e occupies both rural and urban space and straddles the divide between freedom/masculinity/mobility and domesticity/femininity/immobility' (2020: 169). The gendered aspects of being 'fastidious' are demonstrated via excessive delicacy, with high standards in work(wo)manship contributing to the skill and control of the comic author. Eleanor Patterson, for instance, notes that Tina Fey is a comedian who straddles feminine and masculine spaces, with the front cover of her memoir *Bossypants* (2011) depicting an image of contradictions: 'Fey's petite head sits atop the torso of a sizeable (and hairy) ostensibly obese male, and her face leans on one hand with a look of dissatisfaction. Fey wears a black Charlie Chaplin–esque bowler hat and a white collared shirt and tie' (2012: 233). This image is significant because Tina Fey draws attention to Charlie Chaplin as a comic figure and, by blending binaries, continues a practice that transforms gender through talent and skill. Rosie White highlights how many of these techniques are embedded in theatrical, cinematic and television performance traditions. Still, when having a female actor deploy such skills, it 'remains an exceptional act rather than a gesture which confirms tradition' (2018: 10).

While White uses theory from the 1990s to support her critical reasoning, she contends that the 'complex landscape of television comedy and postfeminist popular culture in the twenty-first century challenges many of the grounding assumptions of early academic work on gender and comedy' (2018: 63). Faye Woods has specifically referenced the excessive use of

Rowe's 'unruly woman' and has argued that, though significant, it has become 'something of a theoretical straight-jacket. Overused culturally to the point of abstraction [...] it has become the wearing default frame through which to discuss women in comedy' (2019: 198). These reflections on scholarship around women and comedy signify an important conceptual shift in the current academic landscape – with Mizejewski and White's work forming a new canon. Contributing to this comedy scholarship, this book argues that Rowe's theory remains integral to contemporary analyses; however, there are changes in identity politics and feminism that have impacted how the contemporary 'unruly' woman performs and is perceived in the cultural climate.

Feminism, Intersectionality and Comedy

As such, an awareness of the social, cultural and political context of the 2010s is crucial in understanding women's place in UK TV comedy. Rather than outline specific behaviours that the new 'unruly' woman exhibits, this book recognises shifting power dynamics in the second decade of the twenty-first century that affect how gender interacts with class, sexuality, age and race – highlighting how the subversiveness of women (or at times lack thereof) is tied to the formation of their social identities. When examining romantic comedy, Linda Mizejewski similarly contends that '[f]emininity is a concept inherently racialized, historically configured, and weighted with specific class connotations' (2007: 5) and must be analysed accordingly. In other words, these social categories must be contemplated to understand the nuanced nature of women's lived experiences. In Brett Mills and Sarah Ralph's thematic analysis of interviews with women in British television comedy, for instance, they found that 'gender is simply one aspect of a writer's identity, with class and age also marking an individual as different from the "norm" within the comedy industry' (2015: 106). Each chapter in the book thus examines comedy and gender in relation to class, region, age and race, dissecting how 'unruliness' has been debated and shaped through these social categories (particularly since the 'unruly' woman is demarcated as deviating from the 'norm'). Via this analysis, interlocking social relations will reveal how various forms of stratification highlight the complexities of contemporary comedic women. Helen Davies and Sarah Ilott note that '[q]uestions related to comedy and the representation of gender, sexuality, ethnicity, religion, class, and disability are becoming increasingly prominent in contemporary political debate and news journalism' (2018: 1–2).

This focus is underpinned by the popularity of intersectional feminism in the second decade of the twenty-first century.

Intersectionality is often linked back to Black legal scholar Kimberlé Crenshaw, who argues that it is 'a prism for seeing the way in which various forms of inequality often operate together and exacerbate each other' (Crenshaw, quoted in Steinmetz, 2020). It has also been discussed, in many forms, by other Black feminists of the 1960s, 1970s and 1980s, such as Barbara Smith, Audre Lorde, bell hooks and Patricia Hill Collins, when they 'demanded an antiracist, antisexist, and anticlassist analysis of oppression' (Hunt, 2017). Throughout the 2010s, intersectionality has become important in creating solidarity among fourth-wave feminists whose movement focuses on digital technologies and social media (Munro, 2013 and 2014). According to Tegan Zimmerman, '[i]ntersectionality, with its consideration of class, race, age, ability, sexuality, and gender as intersecting loci of discriminations or privileges, is now the overriding principle among today's feminists, manifest by theorizing tweets and hashtags on Twitter' (2017: 54). Since intersectionality forms an essential strand of feminism in the second decade of the twenty-first century, it is my goal to examine how it has affected women who create comedy texts because of its increasing usage and popularity over the course of the 2010s.

However, there are some problems with using intersectional feminism as a pedagogical tool that potentially extends to this book. Sirma Bilge (2013 and 2014) argues that the overuse of the term and its international growth online have depoliticised intersectionality, with white feminism being criticised for rendering invisible the struggles of Black women through their broad application of the theory and privileging gender over other axes of identity such as race. The tendency to misrepresent and misappropriate this concept erases the contribution of Black feminists and their identities, which Bilge coins as the 'whitening of intersectionality' (2014). Part of this 'whitening' forms part of the neoliberal agenda, whereby 'institutions and individuals [. . .] accumulate value through good public relations and "rebranding" without the need to actually address the underlying structures that produce and sustain injustice' (2013: 408). Through this colonisation, consumption and co-option, the radical politics of intersectionality are effectively neutralised.

For Kathy Davis, this raises further questions of 'how we should view the transnational circulation of ideas and theories in a globalizing world and what this means for how critical feminist scholars ought to think about the ownership and uses of the knowledge we produce and disseminate' (2020: 144).

This self-reflection is indeed needed in feminist studies on intersectionality. Davis further states that she has 'often felt uncomfortable and, at times, unfairly maligned by the characterizations of European critics of intersectionality as white managerial feminists with a neoliberal agenda' (2020: 115). Rather than take a defensive stance in this argument, it seems more appropriate for me to recognise my own whiteness and acknowledge that white people have and are a race. In the 1980s, critical race scholarship witnessed a rapid growth in studies on whiteness, which began with essays such as Richard Dyer's (1988) ground-breaking work 'White'. As he argues, 'white power secures its dominance by seeming not to be anything in particular' (ibid, 44). That is to say, it is perceived as non-racialised, non-coloured and a form of (artificial) universality. For Dyer:

> [i]t is the way that black people are marked as black (are not just 'people') in representation that has made it relatively easy to analyse their representation, whereas white people – not there as a category and everywhere everything as a fact – are difficult, if not impossible, to analyse qua white. (1993: 143)

There are no neat or easy solutions to this analysis of whiteness and constructions of race. Still, it needs to be critically interrogated – both personally and in this book – to analyse the complex axis between identity and privilege. When analysing Phoebe Waller-Bridge, for instance, her whiteness is explored and examined through the lens of class, highlighting how her 'unruliness' is made possible because of her white middle/upper-class representations.

Taylor Nygaard and Jorie Lagerway's book *Horrible White People: Gender, Genre, and Television's Precarious Whiteness* (2020) argues that transatlantic TV programmes that emerged between 2014 and 2016 targeted affluent, liberal and, most importantly, white audiences, with Phoebe Waller-Bridge being a prime example. Bar Michaela Coel, the women analysed throughout this book are white, which points to the lack of women of colour who have been allowed to reach levels of celebrity/stardom in TV (comedy). Nevertheless, this book recognises the different social identities that have informed women and their work while simultaneously acknowledging the lack of diversity in the UK TV industry. Comedy is an important genre to examine these categories of difference because of its social function – its connectedness to interpersonal relationships, whether individually or collectively – and widespread popularity.

Though not all the comedies I examine can be described as feminist, the women who created them and their experiences through these shifting terms and definitions are essential in identifying women's various experiences in comedy (given that there is no singular template of normative femininity). There are inevitable crossovers, criticisms and inconsistencies evident in contemporary iterations of feminism, as well as difficulties in characterising this comedy in an era fraught with cultural tensions. In the 2010s, with the election of Trump, a Conservative stronghold in Britain and the withdrawal of the United Kingdom from the European Union, Armine Ishkanian argues that in the UK and the US, and indeed all over the Western world, 'right-wing populist movements have been on a rising trajectory, based at least in part on very similar sentiments of discontent with electoral politics and neoliberal policies [...] we are now living in the period of the "great regression" [...] which is also characterised as the "age of anger"' (2019: 151). As such, this new political environment has greatly affected how comedians create and respond to their own work (Quirk, 2018). These changes have also influenced how female comedians create comedy in the 2010s, particularly because we have seen a rise of 'gendered violence in the West, a problem that a postfeminist sensibility would deem "solved", [which] has not only persisted but has gained high-profile coverage in relation to a few key events over the past 5 years', according to Jessalynn Keller and Maureen E. Ryan (2018: 5). Such key issues include: the leaking of celebrity nude photos; the mainstreaming and exposure of 'rape culture' as a concept (in which rape is normalised due to patriarchal culture); the 'gamergate' controversy wherein women highlighted sexism evident in video game culture (as well as the harassment they received after); and the 'Me Too' (or #MeToo) movement, which exposed the widespread sexual-abuse against film producer Harvey Weinstein and, more broadly, sex crimes committed by powerful and prominent men (Cobb and Horeck, 2018). With these few examples, violence against women is both shown in the media and happening *through* the media – what can be described as a mediatised 'war on women'.

This activism belongs to a strand of feminism coined 'emergent feminisms' by Jessalynn Keller and Maureen E. Ryan. They argue that it is an 'expanded theoretical lens that can offer insight into a media culture that has changed dramatically over the past decade' (2018). Keller and Ryan offer a conceptual framework that broadens contemporary understandings of feminism and the pervasive nature of postfeminism that dominates scholarly debates (see, for instance, Whelehan, 2000; Tasker and Negra, 2007;

Gill, 2007 and 2017; McRobbie, 2004 and 2009). To understand the divergent aspects of feminism in the 2010s, we must first understand why postfeminism, as a concept, has persisted. According to Rosalind Gill, postfeminism highlights a 'specific sensibility: the entanglement of feminist and anti-feminist ideas' (Gill, 2007: 161) – but in recent years has had increasing negative connotations among feminists. This postfeminist sensibility situates femininity as:

> increasingly figured as a bodily property; a shift from objectification to subjectification in the ways that (some) women are represented; an emphasis upon self-surveillance, monitoring and discipline; a focus upon individualism, choice and empowerment; the dominance of a 'makeover paradigm'; a resurgence of ideas of natural sexual difference; the marked 'resexualization' of women's bodies; and an emphasis upon consumerism and the commodification of difference. (Gill and Scharff, 2011: 4)

As these criteria suggest, postfeminism is, by definition, incredibly ambivalent, and this can also be seen in depictions of postfeminist humour (see Swink, 2017 & Shifman and Lemish, 2010 and 2011) in which discussions of American texts such as *30 Rock* (NBC, 2006–13) and *Girls* dominate (see, for instance, Kaklamanidou and Tally, 2014; Watson, Mitchell and Shaw, 2015; amongst others previously cited). The components of postfeminism have inevitably shifted and developed over the years. As Rosalind Gill argues, 'one of the most important developments of the last decade has been the attempts to open up the term to intersectional interrogation, questioning the assumption that white, western, middle-class, heterosexual young women are the privileged – or indeed the sole – subjects of postfeminist discourse' (2017: 612). More specifically, she argues that postfeminism's classed dimensions and the relationship between gender and ageing have been examined with a renewed vigour.

Fourth-wave feminism can be perceived as an 'emergent feminism' because, as Nicola Rivers points out, 'postfeminism is not a static term – or indeed phenomena – and as such, the arrival of fourth-wave feminism may signal the transformation of postfeminism(s) and the need for continued interrogation, rather than its demise' (2017: 4). Beginning in the 2010s and gaining traction in academic circles (Munro, 2013; Phillips and Cree, 2014), fourth-wave feminism is a significant movement to conceptualise for this book. Kira Cochrane, in her book *All the Rebel Women* (2014), interviews UK-based feminist activists and concludes that fourth-wave feminism can be characterised by four key points: challenging rape culture, technology, inclusion/intersectionality and humour. She details the personal experiences that drove specific women from the UK to activism, and many of the feminist activists she spoke to said that:

> humour is a defining mark of the fourth wave, an idea that is potentially controversial. Feminism is, after all, a call for social justice, a challenge to the status quo, a set of serious political demands. In these terms, humour can sometimes seem like acquiescence, or complacency, clearly unmatched to the day-to-day work of pushing for equal pay, for justice for rape and domestic violence victims, the slow chipping away of male supremacy. (2013)

The prevalence of fourth-wave feminism, and its focus on humour, comedy and laughter, coincides with the increasing visibility of female comedians in the 2010s. Analysing American comics Amy Schumer and Sarah Silverman, Joanne Gilbert argues that '[i]t is only fitting that as a discourse intended to delight and disrupt, humor is both a tool of and a context for fourth wave feminism'. Much like other feminist scholars, she argues that the movement 'has raised awareness of sexism through online discussion and activism, gaining strength as a movement "defined by technology" and one characterized by "pragmatism, inclusion, and humor"' (2017: 218). However, she goes on to argue that 'Sarah Silverman and Amy Schumer are simply contemporary practitioners of a robust and enduring female comic tradition' (2017: 221). It is therefore significant to note how this new era of feminism and comedy is a *continuation* of what has come before. In the case of UK comedians – Carla Lane, Victoria Wood, Dawn French, Jennifer Saunders, Nuala McKeever and a host of other important women have paved the way for contemporary comedians such as Phoebe Waller-Bridge, Caitlin and Caroline Moran, Michaela Coel and Sharon Horgan. While I do not aim to reconfigure and reconsider the waves of feminism, I aim to reframe *national* understandings of feminism by analysing comedy via British and Irish writer/performers. As such, postfeminism and postfeminist comedy should not be conceived as all-encompassing concepts, and I follow Jessalynn Keller and Maureen E. Ryan's assertion here that 'Gill's deployment of postfeminism as a sensibility has since been applied by scholars with disregard to historical and geographic specificity, production contexts, and audience engagement, assuming that postfeminism functions as a widespread "consciousness" amongst all women' (2018). In other words, there needs to be a consideration of particular moments in time, slippages between movements and 'emergent feminisms' in contemporary comedy.

Female Authorship and UK Television Comedy

To consider the significance of comedy created by women in the 2010s, notions of authorship in the UK TV industry must first be addressed. In the contemporary climate where film and TV industries in the UK, US and elsewhere are profoundly unequal and dominated by men, some of whom enact violence against women, it is vital to recognise how women can produce feminist alternatives and possible futures. It has become commonplace to consider individual male identities and their accompanying art, to defend them and engage in what Stefania Marghitu calls 'auteur apologism' (2018). Yet, examining the controversies surrounding male artists and their work is not enough. Instead, we must locate other forms of pleasures and recognise the women producing them, in part because female creative participation in screen production, once a form of invisible labour, is now becoming both visible and popular (Perkins and Schreiber, 2019). Comedy has become a key site for these alternative pleasures, new configurations of the self and the televised revision of socio-political structures from 2010 to 2020. As the title of this book suggests, we must both reclaim and acknowledge the increasing recognition of female authorship. Writing on Roseanne Barr, Kathleen Rowe argues that her '*greatest* unruliness lies in the presentation of herself as author rather than actor or comedian, and indeed as author of a self over which she claims control. "Roseanne" is a persona she has created for and by herself' (1995: 65, my emphasis). Despite this focus on authorship here, when discussing the 'unruly' woman, scholars tend to focus on the (re)presentation of the female body and what can be seen over authorial control.

When it comes to authorship, as has been argued by multiple TV scholars, writers have typically been glorified in the shaping of televisual production (Newman and Levine, 2012; Mittell, 2015; Nochimson, 2019). Placing importance and emphasis on the author is based on a romantic theory of art that sees the writer as an individual genius. Brett Mills and Erica Horton more specifically argue that this categorisation is not an innocent act. It is instead a tool for hierarchising culture which 'sees an inevitable link between the creative individual and "quality" work' (2016). This hierarchisation, placing the writer above other roles, has been criticised due to the collaborative nature of television. Bill Grandberg more specifically argues that '[c]omedy at its basic form necessitates collaboration', evident through 'the unspoken bond between standup and audience, the onstage trust between improvisers, or the vast amount of writers, directors, and actors needed to bring a movie or show to life' (2011).

For some feminist scholars, there are distinct problems with authorship that revolve around gender. At the 'Doing Women's Film and Television History IV' conference, Yvonne Tasker argued that concern with the author is 'quaintly old-fashioned and pervasive' because maleness is perceived as the norm while women's presence requires a caveat. When focused on female-authored media texts, university syllabuses are often titled 'women and x' or 'x and women' to describe female authors and their work, marking them as *out* of the norm (2018). Other scholars, by contrast, have argued for the political necessity for defending female authorship. Nancy Miller is scathing in her suggestion that authorship is no longer seen as legitimate because '[t]he postmodernist decision that the Author is Dead and the subject along with him does not [...] necessarily hold for women, and prematurely forecloses the question of agency for them'. This conveniently shuts down discussions of agency for marginal subjects and those that 'do not occupy upper middle class, white, male, straight, able-bodied, cisgendered, Western positions' (1989: 6).

Corinn Columpar, to combat this masculine approach, coined the term auteure – the feminine equivalent of auteur – when examining Sally Potter and her cinematic output (2002). So Mayer also uses this label when analysing the Left Bank female filmmaker Agnès Varda, contending that 'the auteure, marked by a feminist difference, combines a quizzical reflexivity about her authorship with a foregrounding of the collaborative nature of creative practice, at once signing herself as creator and recognising her work as necessarily collective' (2018a). While Yvonne Tasker laments the 'othering' of women authors and their place within academia, Columpar's concept of the auteure encourages this difference in order to foreground the importance of feminised labour. Interestingly, Columpar and Mayer note the importance of collaboration to women (much like collaboration's importance to television), which can be seen in the relationships analysed throughout this book. For instance, Caitlin Moran created *Raised by Wolves* with her sister Caroline Moran; Phoebe Waller-Bridge has a strong relationship with her long-time partner and producer Vicky Jones; Sharon Horgan made *Dead Boss* with Holly Walsh, while Julia Davis has written her TV series *Hunderby* with Barunka O'Shaughnessy and frequently collaborates with Vicki Pepperdine.

Despite the numerous women collaborating in comedy, Linda Mizejewski argues that 'the female comedy auteur is increasingly visible but still a minority in a male-dominated field' (2017: 27), and it is this male-domination that makes the analysis of women's contribution to comedy TV even more pertinent and essential. Indeed, many media critics have been quick to notice the return of the comedy author. Sarah Larson argues that '[i]n the past decade, a new genre of highly personal TV comedies, starring the people who write the scripts, has flourished'. They further contend that the rise of streaming services and more experimental cable networks, the proliferation of web series and the most recent stand-up boom have contributed to this shift in recent years (2017).

This resurgence of the comedy author has not only been a trend but also reflects a broader cultural shift in how authorship is perceived. Sarah Larson's observation ties into a larger narrative where the concept of authorship is being redefined across the Atlantic. According to Elke Weissmann (2012), the UK and US value authorship as ownership, with UK discourses lionising a 'paternal model of creation' stemming from America (2012: 183). Through this cross-cultural emulation, they argue that the UK 'turn[s] to more masculine values of single authorship and creative ownership that television as an art form had actually made problematic' (2012: 183). It is my goal, then, to move away from these distinctly androcentric and Americentric points of view. Similarly, in her PhD thesis exploring women's humour in contemporary American television, Melinda Maureen Lewis argues that 'women's power over texts and gender representation has taken form in a variety of ways' that do not necessarily conform to previous models (2014: 16). Using examples from different female performers throughout American's comedy history, she outlines how there are various modes of authorship:

> Lucille Ball was not technically an author or a showrunner for *I Love Lucy*, however, she was identified by Madelyn Pugh Davis as fulfilling a similar managerial role through her positions as star and producer. Even Roseanne, who formed the narrative basis of *Roseanne* through her standup comedy persona, was not the showrunner. [. . .] Amy Poehler is not the creator or showrunner for *Parks and Recreation* (2009–), but the program attaches itself to her star power and aligns tightly with her outwardly expressed feminism. (2014: 16)

Lewis's thesis is useful in outlining how women – over the years – have displayed different levels of authorship and authority over the TV series they have created, written, directed, produced and/or starred in. The examples given here are particularly beneficial in examining how women in comedy deviate from male/masculine models, depending on how we define the term author. Given this book's national focus, too, it is worth reiterating that these varying American models cannot be replicated in other nations and should not be universalised.

Changes in authorship have also been impacted by the rise of global streaming platforms and video-on-demand services. For Claire Perkins and Michele Schreiber, the 'transnational flows of content they have enabled is also bringing to visibility the work of women from elsewhere around the world, most notably the UK, Australia and Europe' (2019: 919). Though the US has been the focus of 'quality TV' in the twenty-first century (McCabe and Akass, 2007; Newman and Levine, 2012), the visibility of UK TV comedy writers has emerged because of the transnational relationship between the UK and the US. Co-productions between both nations have become a more frequently used model for creating content, and technological shifts have changed how consumers watch television more broadly. For Claudia Bucciferro, Netflix's digital transformation, in particular, has:

> disrupted the traditional gatekeeping practices that regulated the production of film and television programs, by investing millions of dollars in creating original shows and signing up movie stars and directors (including older women and people of color, often sidelined in Hollywood) to lead numerous projects. (2019: 1054)

Bucciferro further contends that this has affected female authorship. Now, '[m]any series and films feature bold and independent women, and some are made by women, for women, offering narratives that shake old stereotypes. Some of these are even made in collaboration with production companies that employ primarily women' (2019: 1054). It would, however, be disingenuous to suggest that Netflix and other video-on-demand services broadly benefit those who have historically been marginalised in television production. While this may be true, the reasons for this are unclear and muddy. A company's altruism and dedication to diversity could be based on the capitalistic gain of audience demand rather than an attempt to create a democratic media ecology.

I argue, then, that it is perhaps more interesting to see how the advent of online streaming services has affected television broadcasting and the programming of nations. More specifically, for the purposes of this book, it is interesting to see how UK channels are responding to the increasing pressures of a mediated world. While individual authors such as Phoebe Waller-Bridge and Michaela Coel have become standout televisual stars from their presence on-screen and online, an increase in certain comics' visibility does not necessarily mean that there is an increase in the television industry's diversity overall. Put simply, individual power does not transform into structural power.

Indeed, Shelley Cobb, Jack Newsinger, and Clive James Nwonka argue that '[u]nder-representation of marginalised persons both on and offscreen remains a significant problem in the UK film and television industries, and governmental and institutional responses to this have had little to no effect' (2020: 5). Despite repeated instances of attempts to improve diversity in race and ethnicity, gender, disability and social class, recently published data from the Creative Diversity Network, through its new diversity monitoring system Diamond, found that diversity behind the camera is progressively worsening on original productions commissioned by the BBC, ITV, Channel 4, Channel 5/Viacom, CBS and Sky between 2019 and 2020 (*Creative Diversity Network*, 2021). More specifically, the General Secretary of the Writers Guild of Great Britain, Ellie Peers, argues that women in UK TV 'are being pigeon-holed by genre and are unable to move from continuing drama or children's programming to prime-time drama, comedy or light-entertainment' (Peers, quoted in Kreager and Follows, 2018: 4). While comedy in UK television has historically been a masculine space, this book examines women who have gained visibility in the televisual landscape while simultaneously acknowledging that there remain significant problems with diversity in the TV industry.

However, this has not always been the case in UK comedy. Female performers were particularly prevalent and popular in vaudeville and variety theatre. Sam Beale (2020), in their book *The Comedy and Legacy of Music-Hall Women 1880–1920*, analyses the legacy of women working on the music-hall stage, that is, British theatrical entertainment from the early Victorian era that involves a mixture of songs, comedy, speciality acts and variety entertainment. According to Beale, women's marginalisation from the twentieth and twenty-first centuries 'creates a perplexing disparity with the significant presence of women performing comedy on the music-hall stage. They appeared alongside male comics [...] and shared with them varying degrees of financial success, popularity, fame and longevity within the profession' (2020: 3). Women working between 1880 and 1920 performed irony, parodies of gender stereotypes and comically embodied grotesque femininity (Beale, 2020: 11). Performers such as Nellie Wallace, via their comic content on stage, can thus be interpreted through theories of the carnivalesque (Bakhtin, 1984) and Kathleen Rowe's 'unruly' woman (1995) because they disrupted accepted and acceptable versions of womanhood.

Between the 1930s and the 1980s, however, Laraine Porter argues that female comics encompassed a narrow range of stereotypes in film and television (2005: 69). In this period, women in UK TV comedy were exaggerated dumb blondes and dim-witted bimbos or desperate spinsters and hags who nag. Porter provides specific examples of this phenomenon, contending that '[t]arty, giggly blondes like Barbara Windsor, nagging wives such as Yootha Joyce, plump matriarchs like Hattie Jacques, [and] frustrated spinsters like Hylda Baker [...] formed the paradigm for female comic typecasting' (2005: 69). Women here are defined by their physicality, sexuality and gender roles in relation to male power, men as active subjects, and male heterosexual desire – which creates a stark contrast to female comics performing ironic, gendered caricatures on the music-hall stage. Moreover, authorship was limited for women writing in comedy during this period – with Carla Lane being the first woman in British television to become a 'name' through her comedies for the BBC, which included *The Liver Birds* (BBC1, 1969–79), *Butterflies* (BBC2, 1978–83) and *Bread* (BBC1, 1986–91). Despite Lane's popularity, Frances Gray laments that the media perceived her as a 'one-off talent, the exception that provides the rule about women's lack of comic ability' (1994: 89).

Yet another shift began to occur in the 1970s and 1980s with the advent of the alternative comedy scene. According to Elaine Aston and Geraldine Harris, the progress 'made by (white) women in British stand-up is an often-told story. Briefly, the burgeoning of an alternative comedy scene in the seventies and eighties resistant to the sexism and racism of mainstream comedy made space for women comics to crack the jokes rather than be the butt of them' (2012: 158). Performers such as Victoria Wood, Dawn French, Jennifer Saunders, Jo Brand, Jenny Éclair and Helen Lederer rose to fame in this era. These alternative comedians railed against the Conservative ethos spearheaded by prime minister Margaret Thatcher. Sam Friedman argues that they pursued a collective political project to increase public awareness of the economic downturn, growing unemployment and social inequality. The revolutionary notion for these comedians was that humour could be a radical means of communication to spark political action and energy, rather than only serving as a prosaic means of perpetuating 'false consciousness' (2014: 20).

Andrew Stott further contends that alternative comedy was overtly political from the off. Informed by a 'punk ethos that dominated British counter-culture in the mid to late 1970s, it defined itself against the expectations of mainstream performance, and encouraged people to write their own material, set up their own gigs, and perform without the need for agents' (2005: 112). This cultural climate allowed comedians to speak out against social injustices and provide 'alternative' forms of comedy to flourish in areas all over Britain (outside of middle-class London). It was an ideal time for women to write and perform. According to Jane Littlewood and Michael Pickering, women from this movement have been 'building on a distinctive female tradition of comic monologue that extends back to revue performers of the mid-century such as Joyce Grenfell and Hermione Gingold, and to character comedy as developed by music-hall artistes like Jenny Hill, Bessie Bellwood, Vesta Tilley, Nellie Wallace and Marie Lloyd' (2005: 306). The 1990s and 2000s saw several developments influencing women's work in UK television comedy. Comedians like Caroline Aherne, Catherine Tate, Victoria Wood, Dawn French and Jennifer Saunders became household names and moved from the alternative comedy scene to the mainstream. Successful sitcoms such as *Absolutely Fabulous* (BBC Two/BBC One, 1992–2012), *The Vicar of Dibley* (BBC One, 1994–2007) and *The Catherine Tate Show* (BBC Two/BBC One, 2004–15), as well as the all-female sketch show *Smack the Pony* (Channel 4, 1999–2003), were significant milestones in showcasing the talent and creative prowess of women in UK television comedy.

The role of women in comedy has had an extensive and important history, then, but Victoria Wood is perhaps the most well-known of these performers and has been discussed at length (see Littlewood and Pickering, 2004; Medhurst, 2007; Atakav, 2010). Other comedic women who flourished in this era remain important to scholars and their work. Jo Brand, for instance, has been interviewed by multiple academics over the years (Wagg, 1998; Sobott-Mogwe and Cox, 1999; Lockyer, 2015). Though women remain in the minority, a new generation of comedians has emerged who have yet to be analysed and examined in great detail compared with their predecessors. While Andy Medhurst argues that 'popular cultural history has been much more forgetful about funny women than funny men' (2007: 179–80), this book will not let this happen again. It will outline the importance of funny women *now*, given that there have been significant changes in the UK TV landscape.

The writer/performers examined throughout this book thus sit within longer historical traditions of women in UK comedy outlined here. From the 1800s to today, women have humorously reflected on personal issues via bold and bawdy performances in music-hall, stand-up and television. With the legitimation of TV in recent years, the medium has become a space to draw on music-hall and stand-up's 'unruly' style of comedy to appeal to a wide range of audiences. Contemporary female comedians experiment with genres, styles and formats, televising their subversive potential by radically criticising women's societal roles. Therefore, throughout this book, I argue that women have 'reclaimed' authorship because of the chequered history of female representation in UK comedy. Positive and progressive attitudes towards women have ebbed and flowed, but from 2010 to 2020 there has been another shift in audience and entertainment trends that has produced a more socially responsible attitude in/to comedy.

Overall, this book contributes to new understandings of comedy created by women in the 2010s, particularly in the context of the UK TV industry. It highlights the significance of intersectionality and authorship in understanding the 'fastidious' comic writer. Using Kathleen Rowe's concept of the 'unruly' woman, this book highlights important changes that have occurred since the 1990s in comedy and the televisual landscape.

1

Julia Davis, Dark Comedy and Defying Ageing Stereotypes: Analysing Older Female Stars in TV Comedy

This book first examines the writer/performer with the longest career, Julia Davis. Despite her longevity, she has remained a footnote in comedy – her name frequently squeezed between the men she has collaborated with. For instance, Richard Wallace uses Simon Cottle's notion of 'production ecology' to understand how Davis and a group of male comedians worked across different channels in the late 1990s and early 2000s. Production ecology is 'the idea that different groups of programme-makers working in the same field, but for different media institutions, inflect their programmes in different ways depending on a range of industrial factors', and Davis is perceived as belonging to 'a pool of talent including Rob Brydon, Steve Coogan [. . .] Armando Iannucci and Chris Morris and their associated production companies (most notably TalkBack Productions and Baby Cow Productions)'. As Cottle argues, these comedians 'created a number of mockumentary versions of established non-fiction television formats' and have collaborated frequently (2018: 12). Davis toured with Steve Coogan, appearing in, and writing for, a number of his series; she was cast in Chris Morris's dark comedy/horror hybrid *Blue Jam* on BBC Radio 1 (1997–9) and then starred in his most critically acclaimed TV series *Brass Eye* (Channel 4, 1997). However, the first TV show Davis created was *Human Remains* (BBC Two, 2000) with Rob Brydon, produced by Coogan's company Baby Cow and described as a 'macabre comedy masterpiece' (Nicholson, 2009). This series paved the way for Davis's critically acclaimed series *Nighty Night*.

Wallace admits that this list of comedians is overwhelmingly male, arguing that it 'raises particular questions about the gendering of the mockumentary' (2018: 12). Leon Hunt echoes these sentiments in his analysis of cult British TV comedy, specifically 'cringe' comedy (Havas and Sulimma, 2020):

> [i]f comedy is already, even now, a predominantly masculine field, then its darker, edgier corners are even more of a boy zone. While cringe comedy encompasses some engaging, rounded female characters [. . .], apocalyptic embarrassment somehow remains firmly in the fictional psyches of straight white middle-class men. Julia Davis is a particularly important figure then, not only for existing at all but by being regarded as able to match, if not surpass, the envelope-nudging of Chris Morris and others. (2013: 194–5)

This has not gone unnoticed by Davis. When interviewed about her comedy, the press has asked *why* she has come up with such dark ideas, and she, in turn, has wondered: 'Would a man be asked this? [. . .] It's almost like an accusation. Like, what's wrong with you?' (Davis, quoted in Gibsone, 2018). There are clearly topics that are deemed, or not deemed, suitable for women. That Davis was questioned about her motives for exploring dark, embarrassing and cringe-inducing topics reflects the gender divide in comedy. It implies that there are societal norms that women must abide by and serves to demarcate Davis's comedy as 'different'. Questioning her motives for creating this 'different' comedy, the media, consciously or unconsciously, showcase their own bias and discomfort in watching a woman on television who does not adhere to traditional iterations of femininity.

Although women in comedy are regularly side-lined, it is still surprising that little academic attention has been given to Julia Davis, mainly because she is one of the only women who has been acknowledged as being influential in the 'cringe' comedy category with a career that has spanned over twenty years. Instead, scholars such as Leon Hunt (2013) and Richard Wallace (2018) have recognised, through Davis's work, that women are woefully undervalued and their labour under-theorised in UK TV comedy. This analysis will therefore pay attention to three important elements of Davis's work in television – her oeuvre (via textual analysis), her persona (through extratextual analysis of interviews) and the television industry's role in commissioning and broadcasting her shows.

As this chapter suggests, the boom in semi-autobiographical comedies made by young millennial women has changed expectations of what women in comedy should look like, and both their personas off-screen and characters on-screen are now expected to be too loud and 'too much'. In comedy, there is typically an overlap between the two because, as Brett Mills argues, comedians complexly merge star and character (2018), and women are expected to adhere to postfeminist modalities of subjecthood – to display a level of 'authenticity', knownness and self-monitoring (Gill, 2007). However, I argue that Davis is perceived as 'fastidious' because she is ambivalent in this regard and does not marry these two expectations. Moreover, although Kathleen Rowe argues that the 'unruly' woman 'may be old or a masculinized crone, for old women who refuse to become invisible in our culture are often considered grotesque' (1995: 31), I argue that Davis's determination to play younger, overly sexual women is a subversive act to comment on the stifling and uncomfortable white middle-classes, as well as expectations placed on her to act her age. Finally, this chapter examines the authorial control of Davis through her collaboration and work with other women, such as producer Lucy Lumsden, arguing that this is a particularly important element of women's authorship in the second decade of the twenty-first century.

Dark Comedy, Industry Discrimination and Deconstructing Femininity

It is important to note that the dismissal of figures such as Davis is *slowly* dissipating, but this has proven difficult. Less accessible to female comics, 'crude' obscenities have been associated with masculine forms of comedy in a society currently dictated by a 'male dominance of all aspects of the comedy industry', as Brett Mills argues (2005: 111). This is distinctly related to the relationship between power and humour – who is *allowed* to speak. Frances Gray emphasises the importance of the relationship between power and humour when she contends that the majority of feminist work has focused mostly on silence and how to break it. Not only must oppressive areas be located, but they must also be given names because it is only via names that these issues may be made public. Probably the most fiercely guarded of all is the realm of comedic discourse, against female critics and female clowns. This is the reason why it is just as crucial for women to fill these roles and pursue careers in disciplines that are vital to the achievement of social change (1994: 12).

Guarding comedy and its 'edgy' areas ultimately constrains women comedians and the audience's engagement with them, thereby silencing both creators and spectators. The implication of perceiving comedians like Julia Davis as 'other', even in the 2010s, restricts the social change Gray longed for in 1994. According to Brett Mills, this has further implications in the media landscape because if 'society is unused to seeing women performing comedy and, when women do tell jokes, certain kinds of material are expected, it's difficult to see how programmes diverging from such content will be made or, if they are, how they will be intelligible enough to an audience to become popular' (2005: 112). This way of thinking is declining in the media and the television industry, with Julia Davis's squirm-inducing, scatological television series *Sally4Ever* winning a BAFTA for Best Scripted Comedy in 2019. However, the popularity of Davis has regularly been brought up by the print media, as some interviewers cannot understand why her peers have been *consistently* valorised throughout their careers and why she, by contrast, has not. Paul Flynn is one critic who has questioned the popularity of male comedians who explore similar topics to Davis, arguing that the 'thing that has happened to the British male comedy stars of the decade – that sprint from an imaginative, anarchic showcase on a terrestrial British TV channel to the peculiar professional high of Hollywood – has not happened to their female peers' (2010). Davis agrees with this sentiment, and when referring to colleague and long-time supporter Simon Pegg, she has said '"He is here," reaching her right hand up to the sky, "and I am there," resting her left hand on the table [...] "I mean, of course I should be living Ricky Gervais's life now"' (Davis, quoted in Flynn, 2010).

The professional success of Davis, compared to her male peers, raises larger questions about women and their experiences in male-dominated creative industries. In the UK, women's success in the media remains a problem. The CAMEo Research Institute for Cultural and Media Economies explored 'Workforce Diversity in the UK Screen Sector' in 2018, outlining and pulling together findings from various studies based on workforce diversity in the UK screen sector (specifically in film, television, animation, video games and visual effects between 2012 and 2016). The report found that there is an industry culture:

> in which gendered perceptions, gender bias, gender discrimination and gendered bullying are still widespread. Women are perceived to be more capable of caring, nurturing and communicating (Hesmondhalgh and Baker, 2015) and more suited to work on less serious topics such as children's programmes and quiz shows (O'Brien, 2014) and in production management and coordination (Global Media Monitoring Project, 2015). Women were perceived less suitable for senior and management roles (O'Brien, 2014) and for presenting topics that required gravitas: 'a producer told me that the documentary

would be taken more seriously with a male voice over' (presenter cited in O'Brien (2014)). These perceptions are not confined to men, as illustrated by the example of a female commissioner who told a presenter that she was 'too young and pretty to have any authority as an expert'. (CAMEo, 2018: 32–3)

There remain many issues to challenge and confront in comedy across different physical and psychological borders, as well as in the media on a larger scale. Nevertheless, Davis has had multiple comedy hits in the UK. An important figurehead in the industry for commissioning editors, the media and critics, Davis initially received attention as the creator of her series *Nighty Night*. It put her at the forefront of UK TV comedy and was lauded by audiences and critics alike for its devilish humour. David Renshaw, for instance, describes *Nighty Night* as 'a viciously funny, downright cruel comedy' (2014). Speaking of the show's main character Jill Tyrell, journalist and screenwriter Gareth McLean argues that she is 'an exquisitely vile comic creation' (2004), and Jasper Rees, writing for *The Telegraph*, similarly believes that Jill is a 'comic monster for our times' (2004). First airing on BBC Three, the show follows narcissistic sociopath Jill (Julia Davis), whose husband (Kevin Eldon) has cancer. Feeling sorry for herself, Jill decides to send him to a hospice to seduce her new neighbour, encouraging him to leave his wife, a disabled woman who has multiple sclerosis (Rebecca Front). This short synopsis sharply sums up Davis's comedic style – unnerving and unique in equal measure.

Leon Hunt has used Kathleen Rowe's concept of the 'unruly' woman to define Davis's character in *Nighty Night*, arguing that some of the qualities of this figure fit Jill better than others. As he states, Jill creates disorder by dominating, or trying to dominate, men. However, 'while the unruly woman can be associated with "looseness and occasionally whoreishness", Rowe distinguishes her from the "narrowly and negatively defined" sexuality of the femme fatale. But Jill is as much femme fatale as unruly woman' (2013: 196). Through this, Hunt questions 'whether Jill is a genuinely subversive figure or one who reinforces dominant notions of femininity by being "the very antithesis of what a woman should be", as Davis herself puts it' (2013: 197). Davis, however, refuses to answer such questions in her series. Though typically playing as well as writing cringe-worthy characters, she is the dominant, controlling figure in *Nighty Night* – both in terms of screen time and her role as creator and writer – with her sharp dialogue making the 'grossout' elements of her series all the more discomforting.

In Davis's oeuvre, this 'gross-out' humour is typically scatological and references the body. For instance, in *Nighty Night's* first season, her character Jill dances to Kylie Minogue with her legs spread wide open, she keeps bags of dog excrement underneath the sink, and in season 2, Jill has her asthmatic assistant Linda (Ruth Jones) artificially inseminate her at a hospital – with the ejaculate spraying over an elderly's women's dinner and face. These televised moments embody Kathleen Rowe's notion of 'grotesque'. For Bakhtin, this is a form of social critique, emphasising dirt, disease and death, but also, as Rowe explains, entails actions such as 'menstruation, pregnancy, childbirth, and lactation' (1995: 33) – thereby intimately linking grotesqueness with the *female* body. Human bodies are programmed to display social structures through their encounters with society, and for Bakhtin, this has specific classed connotations as opposed to gendered connotations. As Mary Russo and Kathleen Rowe contend, however, the female body is seen as uncontrollable, excessive, and, as Russo writes, 'extended, protruding, [it is the] secreting body, the body of becoming, process and change' (1994: 219). For feminist scholars, then, the female body is a source of political struggle because of its transgressive corporeal actions that are situated outside of cultural norms. For Rowe, this is an important element of 'unruliness', and Davis exemplifies this par excellence.

Mallory Young questions whether the use of such comedy and the representation of 'bad girls' is, in fact, subversive, much like how Leon Hunt questions whether Davis truly destabilises stereotypical notions of femininity:

> we might ask if the right to express bodily functions in public – and talk about them in equally coarse terms – truly exhibits a further step towards gender equity. Could these performances of bad-girl behavior even be obscuring actual inequalities by appearing to address pseudo concerns?'. (2013: 3)

I argue that these 'pseudo concerns', however, offer a critical assault upon perceived notions of female-centred comedy. When I refer to female-authored comedy, I am referring to comedy texts which 'position women as subjects of a laughter that expresses anger, resistance, solidarity, and joy' (Rowe, 1995: 5), as well as comedy that addresses topics specific or familiar to women. This comedy, I contend, is also different in that it typically involves female scriptwriters and features female protagonists, taking 'female subjectivity for granted' (Porter, 2005: 75). As Laraine Porter argues, this includes 'female stand-ups like Jo Brand, Rhona Cameron, Jenny Éclair and raconteurs such as Victoria Wood and female-orientated TV sitcoms such as *Absolutely Fabulous* (November 1992–95, BBC2/BBC1)' (2005: 75). Julia Davis also belongs to this troupe – but in drawing out the ugly characteristics of Jill and the women she portrays more broadly, Davis highlights the ridiculousness of femininity, sexuality and social class by centralising Jill's disgusting behaviour in the same way that I will argue Michaela Coel highlights the ridiculousness of racism through her 'over the top', excessive performance - taking 'female subjectivity for granted' in a way that both positions women as objects *and* subjects of comedy.

For instance, Davis mocks the performance of femininity in *Nighty Night*, with her character Jill invading a suburban home and the genteel niceties of her neighbour, Cath, by attempting to seduce her husband. She also mocks the restrained resentment of the show's middle-class couples in *Camping* (Sky Atlantic, 2016), a TV series based around friends reuniting for a camping trip to celebrate a fiftieth birthday. In the series, Tom (Rufus Jones) appears with his new girlfriend Fay (Julia Davis), an unexpected addition to the group whose overtly sexual appearance/behaviour and 'free' spirit are used to explore tensions, rivalries and failing relationships within the group, as well as midlife crises and what it means to be middle-aged. Through this, Davis offers a critical assault upon perceived notions of femininity via class and ageing. As Linda Mizejewski contends, 'gross-out' humour typically assaults 'good taste and middlebrow manners' (2014: 94–5), and this is particularly significant to Davis's work, as much of it satirises an oppressive class system.

Davis continues her deconstruction of femininity, sexuality and class in other series she has created in the 2010s, furthering the initial themes explored in *Nighty Night* throughout her oeuvre. Immediately after *Nighty Night*, however, Davis mainly took up acting jobs, starring in UK TV series such as *Gavin and Stacey* (BBC Three/BBC One, 2007–19) alongside Rob Brydon, as well as playing a small role in Chris Morris's BAFTA-winning film *Four Lions* (2010) – working alongside the men she had created comedy with since the 1990s. Between these acting roles, she was 'quietly producing hours of comedy' with *Spaced* (Channel 4, 1999–2001) writer Jessica Hynes 'for niche radio station Resonance FM' (Lamont, 2010). Although Davis has predominantly worked with male comedians, this 'quiet' collaboration led to both women co-creating the ill-fated but critically acclaimed TV comedy *Lizzie and Sarah* (BBC Two, 2010). Like *Nighty Night*, *Lizzie and Sarah* makes for uncomfortable viewing in its themes of spousal neglect, death, murder and various macabre subjects Davis is known for touching upon. *Lizzie and Sarah* was also broadcast on BBC Two, and, unlike *Nighty Night*, it was scheduled for the Saturday night graveyard slot at 11:45 pm, a time in which the television audience is very small compared with peak time television from 6.00 pm to 10.30 pm (Ofcom, 2015: 22). Series in the graveyard slot are shown late at night and early in the morning when viewers are typically asleep and consist of factual programming and repeats, as well as explicit/experimental television. According to Rebecca Nicholson, the BBC argued that this slot was 'the most appropriate time [for *Lizzie and Sarah*] given the nature of the content and the target audience', adding, 'we don't always transmit pilots but in this instance we wanted to give fans of Julia Davis and Jessica Hynes an opportunity to see their most recent creative collaboration' (2010). The BBC felt that the content was too 'adult' or 'disturbing' for an earlier time. Henry Normal, managing director of Baby Cow, said the show turned out 'darker' than the BBC had anticipated (Normal, quoted in Nicholson, 2010). The series subsequently, and unsurprisingly, did not perform as well as expected and was swiftly cancelled after the pilot episode aired – despite rave reviews, a Facebook campaign to save the show and endorsement from celebrities on Twitter.

However, Davis and Hynes have expressed their opinions to the media instead of fans. In an interview with *The Guardian*, both women assumed that it was aired at this unfavourable hour due to 'corporation angst bout the show's black humour', with Hynes stating that '[t]he BBC said they weren't keen on anything niche' (Hynes, quoted in Lamont, 2010). BBC Two, however, has always been home to niche programming. As Leon Hunt argues, 'prior to the arrival of BBC 3 (in 2003) and BBC 4 (in 2002), BBC 2 would be the most common home for cult comedy' (2013: 33), with surreal and eccentric series such as *The League of Gentleman* (BBC Two, 1997–2017) showcasing the channel's comedic ambition. The BBC's decision to axe *Lizzie and Sarah*, then, is still unclear – especially if it could have been housed on BBC Three or Four – but the frankness of this series and its focus on feminist issues have led Gerard Gilbert to ponder whether Davis 'may have simply been ahead of her time with [...] *Lizzie and Sarah*' (2015). Indeed, perhaps the BBC was not ready to explore topics presented in the show – it displays an *anger* that is absent in *Nighty Night* through its exploration and echoes of 'the political concerns of 1970s feminism in Britain and North America, by addressing questions of power, marriage and domestic labour in a white middle-class context', as Rosie White argues (2012: 416). Julia Davis's and Jessica Hynes's critically acclaimed but ultimately doomed series demonstrates how women working together behind the scenes is important in showcasing anger and 'unruliness' on-screen – their 'fastidious' attention to detail of socio-political issues in Britain illuminating feminist concerns that are ultimately constrained by network politics.

This is significant because, in the 2010s, angry women have become more visible. Helen Wood notes 'how many times the word "fuck" comes up in contemporary feminist protests against injustice' (2019: 609), arguing that the term 'sets in motion the urges to resist the regulatory norms that are meant to keep us in our place' (ibid: 610). Social media has affected representations of such anger. Simon Pegg and other comedians took to Twitter to profess their dismay over *Lizzie and Sarah's* cancellation, and women have used online spaces to share and disseminate their collective anger. What was once a private, internal struggle has now been cathartically externalised in public. The notion of collective anger (as opposed to individual) has been praised as a form of self-expression for women that was once unavailable and unattainable. Yet, as Jilly Boyce Kay suggests, there remains 'communicative injustice' in the current digital climate. Communicative injustice, she argues,

> relates to the multiple ways in which women, as well as LGBTQ people, people of colour, working-class people, disabled people and other 'others' are denied a voice that is sufficiently expansive, complex and meaningful so as to allow them a position of full citizenship and personhood in contemporary culture. The concept of communicative injustice refers to the ways that public speech is fraught with the difficulties of navigating contradictory and often irreconcilable gendered norms around speech and communication. (2020: 8)

As a reaction to the current socio-political climate, there has been a rise in feminist scholarship concerning anger (see, for instance, Wood, 2019; Chemaly, 2018; Traister, 2018). In an era where representations of complicated women on television have proliferated, Arielle Bernstein argues that this recent shift in the politics of anger offers something

> subversive: a focus on female empowerment, not female suffering [...] the sheer number of shows this season focusing on women fighting back is encouraging. It's a reminder that the angry women behind the scenes writing, producing and directing these shows are continuing to band together, and are nowhere near done. (2018)

Female suffering and female anger are not mutually exclusive, however, and can often manifest simultaneously. Phoebe Waller-Bridge's *Fleabag*, for instance, is a comedy exploring grief through a female lens. Though not as overtly bleak and shocking as *Lizzie and Sarah*, the decision to commission *Fleabag* and its subsequent critical attention points to a welcome change in television politics and commissioning policies. Now, broadcasters are willing to use comedy to examine challenging, dark themes about women and their lives.

Women as Commissioners and Producers of Television: Changing the TV (Comedy) Landscape

As the influence of these broadcasters indicates, it is easy to forget the importance of producers and commissioners in television, given that it is typically writers and performers who are central to the academic analysis of TV. This is particularly salient as women are dominating comedy commissioning in Britain, and in the 2020s three new commissioners have been appointed: Nana Hughes (Head of Scripted Comedy at ITV), Tanya Qureshi (Head of BBC Comedy) and Charlie Perkins (Head of Channel 4 Comedy). When discussing commissioning, production and gender, Ruth McElroy argues that 'feminist television scholars need to appreciate how internal professional structures and hierarchies, together with the ways in which women inhabit them, may contribute to how women workers themselves understand what gender, feminism and indeed television for women might mean' (2016: 42). What is expressed on the television screen is ultimately complicated by what happens *behind* the television screen. As McElroy goes on to argue, 'distinctions between how women working as writers, producers and commissioners might conceive of and articulate their work in relation to gender are an important reminder that the roles within television are diverse and distinct from, for example, the literary field' (ibid: 43). That is, when considering the difference between commissioners and writers, it is important to remember that they do not necessarily have the same goals in mind. In 2018, according to Nadia Khomami, more than '70 female TV writers [...] accused British drama bosses of failing to give them opportunities to write for the biggest primetime shows. In an open letter to commissioners, 76 women [...] said British drama was "overwhelmingly written by men"' (2018). Who are these commissioners, and what is their gender? Or, more specifically, what is their *agenda*?

According to the CAMEo Research Institute for Cultural and Media Economies, there has been strong evidence that decision-makers, such as commissioners and producers, associated risk issues with negative and gendered opinions of women. The film and television industries are characterised by unpredictable market success, and because project teams have to be assembled at short notice and there are tight production schedules, it becomes difficult to replace key creative workers. In this situation, men are viewed as 'a safer pair of hands', particularly those who have a history of working together. Women, on the other hand, 'are consistently perceived as "risky" in a way that men are not' (CAMEo, 2018: 33). From this study, it is unclear whether these commissioners are men or women. If some are women, it is also unclear if they are practising and projecting internalised misogyny by adhering to these ideas. Regardless, commissioners have problematic views that are distinctly gendered and shape the creative work of women.

Some female commissioners have recognised this, noting that their policies affect female writers and staff. For instance, ITV's Controller of Comedy, Saskia Schuster, has attempted to dismantle and disassemble this gender imbalance by increasing the number of female writers in comedy teams on ITV productions. In addition, she has agreed to 'create an independent database of female comedy writers which can be accessed for free, to set up mentorships and regular targeted networking for writers and producers', and has argued that this has nothing to do with 'meeting targets or quotas'; rather, it is about 'changing our comedy culture' (RTS Media, 2018). The decision to reinvigorate and revive comedy through these changes, she says, is because a 'disgruntled female writer crossly pointed out' that 'commissioners have the privileged opportunity to create change'. Schuster admits this scared her, demonstrating that the personal power of individual commissioners can incite transformation in the industry (RTS Media, 2018).

Differences between the collective and the individual, where TV commissioning is concerned, can be seen in Brett Mills and Sarah Ralph's thematic analysis of interviews with female comedy professionals in the British television industry. Both scholars found that:

> there is a mismatch between [. . .] large, institution-wide initiatives and the day-to-day perceptions and experiences of the individuals who are making programmes. We found that our interviewees did not see the institutions as places to turn to for help, and instead either drew on support from particular individuals they admired, or setup their own peer networks. Across many different types of organisations, mentoring relationships – whether part of a formal scheme or a more ad hoc arrangement – are an important resource for all employees, giving individuals a definite advantage over those without them, but

they are perceived to be an essential aid to women [. . .] Mentors – most effectively of the same gender – can advise female protégés on an organisation's structural politics, offer beneficial information on prospective roles or future projects, help to build self-esteem and provide useful feedback (Ragins 1999, 348). A number of these forms of support were given to Lucy Lumsden, Sky's Head of Comedy, during the early part of her career by key women occupying more senior roles [. . .] For Lumsden these women provided her with female role models whom she could admire, emulate and learn from. (2015: 110–11)

Multiple individuals, including Saskia Schuster, Brett Mills, Sarah Ralph and Lucy Lumsden, then, have found that the inherently personal and intimate nature of mentorship has benefitted women and their professional development in comedy. More specifically, as I contend now, Lucy Lumsden's relationship with female role models has had a trickle-down effect and ultimately impacted the creation of Julia Davis's programming. With Lucy Lumsden's oeuvre, Sarah Ralph contests that '[t]here's certainly a strong argument for presenting her as a contemporary television auteur' (2012).

While the BBC feared Davis and Hynes's 'niche' series about the dark side of women, *Lizzie and Sarah*, this led to Davis's later work being picked up by Sky Atlantic. Her next venture, the Gothic farce *Hunderby*, was turned down by the BBC, and for this reason, Davis said that she was 'lucky to go to Sky Atlantic', who were interested in her work (Chortle, 2015). The cable broadcaster provided her with an important televisual platform when Lucy Lumsden left her post as the BBC's Controller of Comedy Commissioning to become Sky's first-ever Head of Comedy in 2009. Lumsden speaks positively about her move from the BBC because, as an employer, she argues that Sky gave her 'uncluttered creative freedom' to work closely with writers and directors (Lumsden, quoted in Seale, 2012). According to Lumsden, Sky Atlantic's financial success has also affected the comedy genre's growth on the channel. Typically, the broadcaster emulates HBO and American quality TV more broadly in its acquisition of transatlantic TV series such as *Game of Thrones* (HBO, 2011–19). Elke Weissmann argues that 'Sky Atlantic's own brand identity relies completely on "edgy" and "must see" imports' (2012: 179) and 'imagines its viewers to know about and know what the US brand means [. . .] to develop its own strategy of addressing an affluent, young audience which appreciates the "quality" of its TV series provided by HBO, Showtime, and other US cable channels' (Weissman, 2012). This has led critics Imogen Carter and Andrew Anthony to question: is Sky Atlantic bad for British television? Will regionalised TV and other genres

– such as comedy – be marginalised? (2011). However, Lumsden admits that the opposite is true – money made from these series has been funnelled into comedy and positively impacted the channel, allowing new material to be made in a competitive marketplace.

Indeed, it is significant that women comedy writers and commissioners have been able to flourish on Sky Atlantic because programming on the channel – American 'quality' television – is typically classified and coded as 'masculine'. Dominated by male authors, showrunners and characters, quality TV in the twenty-first century focuses on masculinity behind the screen and in front of it. Their appeal, as Helen Piper argues, hinges on the successful marketing of 'quality' TV series 'as exceptions to the daily flow of broadcast or network television, the antithesis of its mixed generic menus and routine sociability, and of its 'feminized', populist and everyday output' (2016: 163–83). Yet the discussion of Sky Atlantic and its problematic properties revolve around the channel's importation of *drama*, as well as its male writers and male viewers. Lumsden, by contrast, is concerned with comedy that positions women as subjects of laughter, comedy that takes female subjectivity for granted and comedy that addresses topics specific or familiar to women. She has produced an overwhelming number of comedies created by and starring women, such as Ruth Jones's *Stella* (Sky One, 2012–17), Emily Mortimer and Dolly Wells's *Doll and Em* (Sky Living, 2014–15), Sarah Hooper's *Mount Pleasant* (Sky 1/Sky Living, 2011–17), Kathy Burke's *Walking and Talking* (Sky Atlantic, 2012), and Julia Davis's *Psychobitches* (Sky Arts, 2012–14) – an all-star sketch show featuring famous women from history and fiction who are seeking psychotherapy. 'Quality' is no longer synonymous with the 'masculine' or even drama, with female-created and female-led comedies occupying an important space in the Western broadcasting ecology.

Erica Horton argues that 'quality' comedy is no longer 'niche' or solely on 'cable channels and binge-watched on streaming sites' such as Sky Atlantic. Rather, this 'alternative comedy category' has 'shifted into a new normalised cultural space on British television', with Horton citing Sharon Horgan's *Catastrophe* as an important example of this shift (2016). While some female comedians such as Sharon Horgan, Michaela Coel and Phoebe Waller-Bridge have reached larger audiences because their series have been aired by public service broadcasters such as Channel 4 and the BBC, there have been a plethora of women (cited above) who thrive on 'niche' cable channels after working in 'mainstream' television, with Julia Davis shifting from the former to the latter – into the 'prestige' realm of 'quality'.

Sally4Ever (Sky Atlantic/HBO, 2018–) is a prime example of this shift. A series that explores love and sexuality, it follows Sally (Catherine Shepherd), a repressed woman trapped in a loveless marriage who is seduced by Davis's character Emma, a narcissistic lesbian intent on overtaking Sally's life. *Sally4Ever* is a joint broadcast from Sky Atlantic and HBO, with the latter being seen as the original home of 'quality' TV and 'an influential site of cultural legitimisation in defining contemporary television seriality as art and "high" culture' (Akass and McCabe, 2018). Shifting from public service TV to a 'premium' cable channel overseas, Davis has moved to an American 'quality' aesthetic, which is evident in some of *Sally4Ever's* key plotlines. Emma, Sally's girlfriend, is so narcissistic that she envisions herself as an actor, singer and dancer. In episode 4, she attempts to seduce Emma's friend's husband (Seb Cardinal) because he works in film/TV, and Emma is desperate to feature in a project involving *Game of Thrones* actor Lena Headey. The link between *Game of Thrones* and HBO as 'quality' is an important paratext that makes Davis's series more palatable for an American audience.

Julia Davis: The 'Pensive' and 'Bashful' 'Unruly' Woman

While 'bleak' and 'edgy' comedy has been a prominent feature of UK television, Sarah Larson argues that 'in the past decade, a new genre of highly personal TV comedies, starring the people who write the scripts, has flourished', and she names Phoebe Waller-Bridge and Michaela Coel as two standout writer-performers in this regard (2017). While telling these personal stories has allowed women to thrive and succeed both in front of the small screen and behind it, Sarah Hughes believes that 'the success of such personal tales has made it easier for TV executives to compartmentalise women writers, viewing them solely as tellers of intimate truths rather than writers of big-budget or mainstream shows' (2018). This is an important point, but Hughes does not examine the issue holistically. In Britain, there has been a lack of women writers being offered work (see, for instance, Khomami, 2018; Johnson and Peirse, 2021). While personal tales have indeed become increasingly popular in the twenty-first century, it has demonstrated that certain forms of 'feminized' TV – high-end or otherwise – are now being taken seriously in the contemporary televisual landscape. Writers of these narratives have gone on to create other original series because of how successful these have been. Phoebe Waller-Bridge, since *Fleabag*, has penned the critically acclaimed, BAFTA-award-winning drama *Killing Eve* (BBC America,

2018–2022), while Michaela Coel created the comedy-drama *I May Destroy You*. Other stories have been told without a personal or autobiographical edge – Sally Wainwright's dramas *Happy Valley* (BBC One, 2014–23), *Scott and Bailey* (ITV, 2011–16) and *Last Tango in Halifax* (BBC One, 2012–20), for instance, have become critical successes. While the compartmentalisation of female writers is undoubtedly troublesome, we should not focus on the pitfalls of semi-autobiographical TV series, which remain crucial to women's experiences. Instead, we should focus on how women create their own narratives. For instance, *Killing Eve*, according to Chitra Ramaswamy, uproots 'the tired old sexist tropes of spy thrillers' (2018), while *Happy Valley* unveils the misogyny and sexism that women police officers have to endure in their profession.

Personal tales are also significant because writers can perform as versions of themselves, drawing attention to their creative control. As Sarah Larson argues, however, 'not all TV auteurs write about themselves; some create roles that only they could play', for instance, American writers such as Rachel Bloom, 'a wit with Broadway pipes' created '"Crazy Ex-Girlfriend" [. . .] a delirious musical confection that gives her ample opportunity to belt' (2017). Davis does not write personal stories, and she *could* fit into this category of writers who create roles only they could play – however, she does not inject herself into her work so explicitly. Her complex characters are morally questionable and sexually motivated, which is why she typically gets offered roles as 'horrible people' (Davis, quoted in Gibsone, 2018). This conflicts with descriptions of Davis in the press as 'pleasingly, obviously, [. . .] nothing like most of her characters' (Nicholson, 2016). While contemporary writer/performers align themselves with their characters in some way, Davis eschews this. She is different in terms of self-representation and how her persona is (re)constructed by/in the media. There is an expectation on the contemporary writer/actor to perform as *themselves* in an 'authentic' manner – to tell 'intimate truths', as Sarah Hughes argues. Therefore, interviewers have felt the need to comment on the difference between Davis's persona and her characters. I argue that this is why she can be defined as a 'fastidious' woman. Critics treat Davis ambivalently for her refusal to conform to established ideas of the excessive 'unruly' woman who creates semi-autobiographical narratives.

Significantly, interviewers in UK broadsheets and magazines repeatedly stress 'shyness' in their description of Davis. Gerard Gilbert has described her as such but remarked that 'bashfulness doesn't get more beguiling than this' (2012). Rebecca Nicholson has also stated that Davis is 'pensive and slightly shy, and worries a lot about how she's going to be perceived [...] She's got a natural warmth that is at odds with the awkwardness a person must experience if they're spending a lot of time talking about themselves, when they clearly hate talking about themselves' (2016). Interviewers are often surprised by her shyness, but the adjectives used to describe this trait – 'beguiling', 'pleasing' and 'warm' – are interesting in their positive connotations. This, in turn, raises questions about femininity, sexual stereotyping, and how, in contemporary culture, the self needs constant vigilance. Women have historically been perceived as quiet, sympathetic, warm, sensitive and expressive, to name a few traits. In contrast, as Anne Helen Peterson (2017) and Kathleen Rowe (1993) argue, loud women are 'unruly' women and, therefore, a threat to the status quo.

When discussing such women in television, Joy Press contends that 'Shonda [Rhimes], Jenji [Kohan], Mindy [Kaling], Lena [Dunham], and Tina [Fey]' are influential TV writers with big personalities (2018: 3), and Peterson believes that such writers 'are too loud, too aggressive, too powerful, too revealing, *too much*' (2017: xii).

These writer-performers have been established as the primary perspective through which women in comedy are seen. Consequently, interviewers find it challenging to reconcile Davis's reserved demeanor with the bold and grotesque characters in her work. Yet this begs the question – why should she have to? The surprise expressed over Davis's personality is distinctly gendered because, as Rosalind Gill contends, women have been obligated to regulate aspects of the self in the media: '[d]o you laugh enough? How well do you communicate? Have you got emotional intelligence?' (2007: 156). These questions are imposed because of the media's constant surveillance, and, in Davis's case, there have been broader questions surrounding the dichotomy between creator/character and the public/private spheres, with these boundaries becoming blurred in a media landscape where women are seen, and expected to be, authentic to themselves and their 'unruly' characters. As I noted in the introduction to this book, to be 'fastidious' is to be both assiduous – disciplined, methodical and thorough – but also ambivalent. Julia Davis's ambiguity and ambivalence lie in her enigmatic and mysterious persona, refusing to tell personal, intimate stories. Her difference stems from being oxymoronic, with the quiet femininity she displays in interviews supposedly clashing with her characters' cringe-inducing traits. This highlights the complexities surrounding women in comedy and what is expected of them, with Davis showcasing how she is challenging to define in her 'unruliness'.

Brett Mills suggests that, for the comedy TV personality, 'there are [...] aspects of the star (the display of skill, the associations carried across texts) and there are aspects of the celebrity (the access to the self, the performance of identity); but the distinctions between these categories fall apart within the comedic realm as the performer moves unproblematically between the two' (2010: 200). Since there is a collapse of these boundaries, there are expectations placed on comedians from audiences – specifically for them to act and behave as their comedic persona. This has only intensified in the 2010s. Sarah Larson similarly proclaims that '[i]n the past decade, a new genre of highly personal TV comedies, starring the people who write the scripts, has flourished', and she clearly associates this type of comedy with 'high culture' or 'high art' when she further argues that '[w]atching their shows can feel more like reading a novel, or a collection of comic personal essays, than like watching "Cheers"' (2019). Here, she constructs a problematic dichotomy between literature/TV and the personal comedy/classic sitcom, elevating literature and the 'personal' essay while simultaneously denigrating both the medium (television) and the genre (comedy). In Larson's terms, then, Davis and her oeuvre would fit into the category of 'low art' or 'low culture' because she frequently uses the sitcom as a site of comedy and does not explicitly engage with the personal in her work. Her contradictory, complex and unstable stardom makes it difficult to neatly define her in the media. Though Davis displays the private through the public in her interviews, she refuses to do so in her work.

Davis's characters are often vacuous, manipulative and opportunistic. Still, in interviews, her persona is constructed as anything but – she is positioned as a quiet, thoughtful and quick-witted author interested in the politics of comedy and her anxieties surrounding life. Significantly, she is perceived as somewhat of an enigma: a technophobe who does not use social media, has never seen the US remake of *Camping* because she could not get the link to work and does not even know what the word 'spoiler' means, despite working in TV (Lusher, 2015). As such, the binary between her on-screen and off-screen performances has led Tim Lusher to describe her as 'otherworldly' (2015). Sandra Mayer argues that this intrigues audiences: 'the voyeuristic gaze of the public is invariably obsessed with the desire to recover the individual's "true" and "authentic" self behind the mask of the renowned public persona, and, paradoxically, the authorial pose of absence, elusiveness and inaccessibility thus only serves to increase the author's ubiquity and media exposure' (2018b: 56). Davis eschews Mayer's characterisation of the revered but invisible author – instead of increasing

Davis's media exposure, she has been mythologised as a writer-performer. Her work has reached 'cult' level, which is why she has been the subject of Leon Hunt's book *Cult British TV Comedy: From Reeves and Mortimer to Psychoville* (2013), one of the only academic works exploring Davis's work in-depth. Despite discussing her family, mental health, feelings about contemporary comedy, envy of other writers and other personal subjects, she is still perceived as elusive – most likely because she is rarely interviewed. The issue of access here is significant, as her whiteness, paired with her reserved nature, offers her a valuable and productive invisibility, a form of power within the production of knowledge and representation not afforded to comedic stars who remain underrepresented and overlooked.

In our 'hyper-surveilled celebrity culture' (Holmes and Negra, 2011: 7), where stars are more visible than ever, it is particularly interesting that Davis rarely gives interviews and does not appear on TV chat shows. As Davis herself has stated, 'I think most people, including me, like to read gossipy things about others; revealing things that I love to read, but I don't really want known about me' (Davis, quoted in Dickens, 2012). On the surface, this quote appears as a commentary on privacy and protection, but it also reveals Davis's fascination with others, particularly those who occupy the media spotlight. When exploring *Lizzie and Sarah*, Rosie White argues that 'it is not coincidental that the two sets of characters Julia Davis and Jessica Hynes play in the programme represent figures around which contemporary media circles, vulture-like, in the pages of celebrity magazines and makeover programmes—the middle-aged woman and the teenage girl' (2013: 422). Davis is particularly interested in middle-aged women, and this, too, is evident in *Dear Joan and Jericha* (2019–), a cringe-inducing satirical podcast where both Davis and Vicki Pepperdine play agony aunts on local radio, their unexpectedly filthy musings offering a hilarious take on 'tips and tricks' offered to women. While you could initially mistake their soft-spoken yet forceful voices as those on BBC's *Woman's Hour*, their ingrained and internalised misogyny shows through in their vicious attacks on the women asking for advice. Drawing attention to problematic constructions of the 'self', an area scrutinised in a postfeminist culture (Gill, 2007), Davis navigates a terrain where women are constantly pressured to mediate their worth. Her over-the-top, grotesque female characters – their amplified and exacerbated traits – mirror exaggerated representations we see in the media. Davis refuses to display any 'over-the-top' features herself, to be too loud or too much. Her 'fastidiousness' stems from her ability to create these characters in a society that demands her conform to other aspects of femininity routinely seen in the media.

Indeed, through these representations, Davis deconstructs the entanglement of feminist and anti-feminist ideas that Angela McRobbie argues is evident within contemporary representations of postfeminism (2004: 255–6), thereby highlighting the 'messiness' of femininity and its dominant depictions. This is particularly salient given that her characters privilege a perspective that is heterosexual, white and middle-class in her work, a key feature of postfeminism (Tasker and Negra 2007: 3). For instance, her character Jill in *Nighty Night* embodies a specific form of femininity from the 1990s and early 2000s, submitting to patriarchal norms in her focus on feminine beauty and heterosexuality. She wears pink clothing that would rival that of Britney Spears, French lingerie when jogging, and bares her flesh to accommodate the male gaze in a hilariously brazen manner. As Frances Gray argues, 'like sexuality, laugher has been sometimes highly valued, sometimes denigrated; but like sexuality – indeed with sexuality – laughter has been closely bound up with power' (1993: 6). Julia Davis's transformations of postfeminist ideals into the grotesque serves as a way of exploring gender and class, highlighting her capacity to challenge power dynamics and reflect on her position within these social structures.

This can be seen in her disavowal of technology. Just as she rejects expectations of women in the media, so does she reject technology, marketing and an online presence more broadly. Many women in the 2010s have used the internet as a powerful resource. Wallis Seaton argues that Lena Dunham is one comedic writer/performer who demonstrates 'how understandings of feminism are increasingly shaped by their virtual manifestations' (2018: 255). Other contemporary comedians similarly follow this route through their engagement with social media, as feminism is now defined partly by its focus on technology (see, for instance, Cochrane 2013 and 2014; Knappe and Lang 2014: 364). Though online platforms 'are utilised by feminists for their intersectional and transnational potential' (Seaton, 2018: 21) as well as their participatory function, Davis has been one author who has not used these artefacts. There is a refusal here – conscious or unconscious – to repudiate 'celebrity feminism', which, according to Jessalynn Keller and Jessica Ringrose, is a type of popular feminism recently brought to light by young celebrities who are eager to declare their feminist identities in public, which can be contextualised as part of the increasing prominence of 'neoliberal feminism', as defined by Catherine Rottenberg (2014). This brand of feminism acknowledges the disparities that exist today between men and women, but it rejects the social, cultural and economic causes of these differences in favour of the neoliberal ideals of free will, self-determination and individual initiative as the most effective means of achieving gender equality (2015: 132).

Julia Davis does not share this eagerness to claim a feminist identity publicly – nor has she ever. Though referring to the importance of women in comedy and how they need their own creative space (see, for instance, her interview with Icelandic singer Bjork by James Merry [2016]), Davis has feared 'backlash' and has never been outspoken online (Gibsone, 2018). While social media has been used as an important platform to disseminate contemporary feminism, Davis is an anomaly in that she refuses to be commodified, packaged as a product to be an 'empowered' woman in a marketplace wherein capitalism 'is fueled by the conditions under which feminism makes sense as politics', as Sarah Banet-Weiser and Laura Portwood-Stacer put it (2017: 886). Part of her feminist 'unruliness' is her refusal to engage with the personal. This, in part, is related to age and ageing. Plenty of articles have dissected the digital activism of young feminists (see, for instance, Jackson, 2018), but this rarely extends to middle-aged women and what their tools of feminist practice are.

Women, Ageing and the Media

'Fastidious' is an interesting term for women who are both assiduous and ambivalent because it has multiple meanings. To be primly 'fastidious' is to be 'old-womanish' or 'old-maidish', that is, having the characteristics of an old woman or being anile, fussy and finicky. To be an older woman is to be defined negatively, and there is also an uncomfortable relationship between ageing and representation in the media – particularly for women. As Kathleen Rowe similarly argues, 'the figure of the grotesque old woman often bears a masculinist culture's projected fears of aging and death' (1995: 63).

As a result of this fear, on television, Rosie White argues that 'older women have tended to inhabit the margins of mainstream programming as widows, grandmothers or eccentric spinsters. While soap operas and sitcoms have traditionally harboured visible numbers of older female characters, they have often been stereotyped as gossipy, asexual spinsters or as battleaxe figures feared by their husbands' (2014: 155). White analyses how television comedy 'has offered an arena for older women to behave badly' (ibid), but Josephine Dolan and Estella Tincknell continue this argument by arguing that stereotypes persist even in:

> contemporary 'woman friendly' shows such as *Miranda*, and make little space for alternative figures that represent different modes of aging. The black comedy *Getting On* is one significant exception – and it is screened on the 'minority' channel BBC Four for no discernible reason other than because of its cast and subject matter: older women. To date, no British television sitcom has offered the kind of positive, witty and subversive representation of older women found in the 1980s US show, *The Golden Girls*, or the gritty depiction of a working class middle aged woman found in the 1990s comedy, *Roseanne* [. . .] What these programmes powerfully illustrate is that, where there is sufficient will, it is possible to make interesting and widely accessible television programmes featuring active and likeable older female characters that attract a large audience. (2013: 3)

Ageing women, then, have been significantly marginalised in and on television. There have been few positive representations, with Dolan and Tincknell naming one positive example per decade here. Yet while these scholars explore the performance of 'older' characters – questioning how age is represented on television through men in drag (*Mrs Brown's Boys* [2011-]), women acting older than their years and the impact of programming featuring 'active and likeable' women – what are the effects of ageing women who present themselves as *younger*?

Julia Davis typically plays women who do not 'act their age'. As Sarah Hughes notes, in *Camping* 'it's interesting that she chose to play a pouting bombshell like Fay, who revels in her sexuality, flaunting it at all possible moments, at just the age when women are supposed to fade into the background' (2016). While it is 'interesting', it is certainly not unique. She plays this role in *Nighty Night* and *Sally4Ever*, clearly revelling in the part and using different representational strategies than those utilised in *Absolutely Fabulous* (BBC Two/BBC One, 1992–2012) or American TV series such as *Cougar Town* (ABC/TBS, 2009–15) and *Sex and the City* (HBO, 1998–2004). Debbie Rodan, Katie Ellis and Pia Lebeck argue that characters in the British cult sitcom *Absolutely Fabulous* focus on the 'young-old' (2014: 109), midlife characters Patsy and Edna, who are about to face old age. The show initially emerged from a sketch entitled 'Modern Mother and Daughter' in the *French and Saunders Show* (BBC2/BBC One, 1987–2017). The narrative skeleton of the show is based on how the mother acts like her teenage daughter and the teenage daughter acts like her mother.

However, the age of Patsy and Edna is evident in *Absolutely Fabulous* as the pair wobble around – unassured on their feet – physically embodying and comically reminding the viewer of their actual age. At the same time, in *Sex and the City* and *Cougar Town*, the main characters display unironic sexuality in their pursuit of younger men.

By comparison, according to Rosie White, there has been a recent proliferation of women:

> [w]ho employ a different technique, by dressing themselves as dolls — gender-appropriate women whose appearance offers further comic potential through the juxtaposition of femininity and outrageous behaviour or language. Sarah Silverman (*The Sarah Silverman Program* 2007–) in the US and Julia Davis in the UK (*Nighty Night* 2004 – 2005) exemplify this approach; attractive women whose language, behaviour, and dress employ stereotypes of femininity to fuel a comedy which is dark and challenging, provoking discomfort as much as laughter. Whether monsters or dolls, however, it is still about how the woman in comedy looks; about women performing difference. (2010: 357)

Though these two comics eschew the dichotomy between humour/looks by undermining the postfeminist embrace of 'girly' femininity, they nevertheless focus on what appearances are deemed acceptable or unacceptable in the Western imagination, thereby contributing to a culture that views women through the lens of physical suitability. While this may have been the case for *Nighty Night*, the representation of ageing has changed in Davis's work from the 2010s and onwards. For instance, Rosie White also compares Patsy and Edina to Julia Davis and Jessica Hynes's creations in *Lizzie and Sarah*, arguing that 'while Edina and Patsy's grotesque comedy is often based upon their battle to remain youthful with diets and surgical interventions, Lizzie and Sarah have lost that war and are already old, beyond redemption. Their bodies, clothing and unruly hair do not conform to the classical ideal' (2013: 417). While Davis typically plays older characters acting younger, dressing as a 'doll', *Lizzie and Sarah* shows how excess and the grotesque can satirise femininity from a different perspective. This subversion of gender roles is predicated upon the culturally moulded notion of what it means for women to 'act their age' as well as anxieties surrounding this.

White further argues that *Lizzie and Sarah* is remarkable for the way that it 'addresses categories which remain underrepresented in popular television comedy. When the middle-class, middle-aged woman does appear in contemporary British sitcom she is more usually confined to a marginal cameo role' (2013: 423). This figure remains central in the commissioned pilot of *Lizzie and Sarah*, but I would further this and argue that she is central to many characters in Davis's oeuvre - from Rebecca Front as Cath in *Nighty Night*, to Vicki Pepperdine as Fiona in *Camping*. Typically set in drab, grey and uninspiring pockets of suburbia that comment on middle-class relations, Davis's characters invade these communities, her youthful and brash aesthetic confronting uptight values of the middle-class and the poison that settles deep within them, too. While her appearance is certainly brash – she is not commenting on the superficial surface of her characters Jill, Fay and Sally, but rather, how those around her respond to the characters she has created, what it reveals about them and their place in society. This 'unruliness' thus has further meaning than simply showcasing excessive visibility on-screen and highlights how a deeper analysis of thought, intent and authorial assessment are fruitful in understanding contemporary comedy. Even with this class commentary, however, Davis has been probed about her motivation for dressing younger: 'I remember even when I did *Camping*, this man said to me something like, "Oh, and at your age you felt you could wear a short skirt like that" or whatever. Uh, a.) I was playing a character who would wear these clothes, and b.) Would you be asking a man?' (Davis, quoted in Read, 2018). Despite directing, writing and starring in *Camping*, the men around her still questioned Davis's decisions. This is unsurprising given that ageing women are not only disproportionately represented in front of the TV screen – but also behind it.

Semi-Autobiographical Comedies: The New Norm

In a different interview, Davis has also admitted that she experiences mixed feelings about her own work when watching intimate, semi-autobiographical comedies such as *Fleabag, Girls* and *Catastrophe*: '"I really like them and slightly envy them," she says. "I envy how they're more real. They're about real, [. . .] women, and I think I would find it hard to write that stuff. [My shows are] a bit too weird for some people" (Davis, quoted in Gibsone, 2018). Series created by and starring women have captured Davis's imagination, with her favourite comedies including Ilana Glazer and Abbi Jacobson's *Broad City* (Comedy Central, 2014–19) and Emily Mortimer and Dolly Wells's *Doll and Em*. The latter series made Davis want to create something in the same vein as she believes it 'captured something about women in a brilliant way' (Davis, quoted in Gilbert, 2015). The majority of these shows typically focus on millennials – which is perhaps one reason why Davis views them in a different light. This admiration goes both ways, however. In an interview with BAFTA Guru, Phoebe Waller-Bridge states that one of her most embarrassing moments is when she auditioned for a TV series with Julia Davis who she is a 'huge fan' of. During the audition, she could not help but hug Davis 'so tightly, a beat too long' and be 'weirdly intimate throughout the whole thing', despite Davis holding her hand out for a handshake (BAFTA Guru, 2017). Interestingly, this sums up both comedians – Waller-Bridge's open, embarrassing and personal style of storytelling, which contrasts significantly with Davis and her private, shy persona.

The majority of these comedies that Davis admires have been labelled 'precarious-girl comedies' by Rebecca Wanzo, who cites *Broad City*, *Girls*, *2 Broke Girls* (CBS, 2011–17), *How to Live With Your Parents (For The Rest of Your Life)* (ABC, 2013) and *Insecure* (HBO, 2016–21) as examples of this trend. These comedies, according to Wanzo, depict 'a perpetual girlhood produced not only by the greater economic insecurity faced by middle-class women post – Great Recession (that is, the period following the severe economic crises experienced worldwide in 2008) but also by the variety of social factors that generate feelings of immobilization and isolation' (2016: 28–9). The comedies that depict this alienation, immobilisation and abjection have solely focused on younger women, but what of older generations? David Lee has found that Generation X also experiences these feelings because life has become an extension of *you* as a marketable brand, with Generation X feeling the pressure to perform due to the move from analogue to digital culture (2019). It is telling, however, that Davis – and other ageing comedians – do not tell semi-autobiographical stories as frequently as millennials, and so this condition is not as visible in the media by comparison.

As a subgenre, semi-autobiographical comedy was not as popular in the 1990s when Davis first entered the British TV industry. This represents a shift in the types of storytelling that television has facilitated and selected over the decades, with an increase in the value of the personal story, confessionals and autobiographies. Comedy's generic evolution highlights the generational distinctions between Julia Davis and other modern female comedy writers, particularly figures like Phoebe Waller-Bridge and Michaela Coel. During the 2010s, she did not have to tell personal stories – both on and off-screen – for her original series to be commissioned and broadcast because of her history in television. Davis is inspired and impressed by contemporary women writers in the field, but she differs from others in the industry whose first series have adhered to a personal model of storytelling aimed at young women.

Despite this, Davis has moved from working with men in the 1990s – from the likes of Rob Brydon, Steve Coogan and Chris Morris – to working with women in the 2010s. This is evident in the TV series previously explored – *Lizzie and Sarah* was co-created with Jessica Hynes in 2010, while Davis's 2012 series *Hunderby* was co-written with Barunka O'Shaughnessy, a British actor, writer and producer who has worked on other comedies such as *Katy Brand's Big Ass Show* (ITV2, 2007–9), *Comedy Lab* (Channel 4, 1998–2011) and *School of Comedy* (E4, 2009–10). *Camping* is solely created and written by Davis, but Vicki Pepperdine's input affected the show greatly because of her history in female-led and female-authored comedy such as *Getting On* (BBC Four, 2009–12), and it is perhaps Davis's first original series where she is not perceived as the 'worst' character, with Pepperdine taking the lead role in that respect. As Sarah Hughes also argues, in *Camping* Davis leaves 'the most monstrous part to Vicki Pepperdine as control freak Fiona, a woman who spends her time lying to get her own way, bullying her hapless husband, and smothering her son with a terrifying motherly love. "That's the part that people expected me to play," Davis admits' (2016). Both Pepperdine and Davis are given equal screen time in *Camping* and have also worked together on *Sally4Ever* and *Dear Joan and Jericha*. In the former series, when Sally and Emma attend couples therapy, Pepperdine plays their therapist, and her toxic views mirror those belonging to Davis's character, Emma. Both characters insist that Sally will be a 'bitter old woman' if she does not have children with Emma immediately, a popular punchline that both women satirise in *Sally4Ever* and *Joan and Jericha*. Their subversive, collaborative efforts have cut across multiple media, with Davis's characters and the women who helped shape them, revealing the insidious and venomous depths of middle-class femininity.

These examples do not necessarily suggest that Davis is resisting through sisterhood or that her admiration of other women writers is a new phenomenon, especially considering she has worked with other women in the early 2000s, such as Ruth Jones – with Jones starring in *Nighty Night* and Davis starring in Jones's series *Gavin and Stacey*. Yet there has been a noticeable shift in the 2010s, with women playing significant roles on-screen and contributing to Davis's material off-screen, too which is a key feature of fourth-wave feminism (Bernstein, 2012 and Peroni and Rodak, 2020). The upsurge of women comedy writers and their recognition in the media has invariably affected Davis, how she views television and the creation of her own original series. Her focus on class and sexuality has been given greater recognition in the 2010s, with the 'legitimation' of TV, specifically comedy-drama and the proliferation of women writers in this era, encouraging her work to be picked up by cable channels.

While Davis was initially championed by male comedians in the UK televisual landscape, it is her relationship with women that has resulted in new stories being told in the 2010s. The quiet work of producers such as Lucy Lumsden and Davis's relationship with Vicki Pepperdine, for instance, highlights how being 'unruly' is not only about being loud and 'too much' but being diligent and collaborative behind the television screen. These women – and their work – showcase how 'unruliness' on-screen are mitigated by 'fastidiousness' off-screen.

Davis has also showcased her difference through her persona and how she is represented/presents herself in the media. As a writer and public figure, she rejects the relationship between the public/private as well as creator/character by refusing to inject the personal into her oeuvre – despite her projects being deeply personal in that she creates, writes and directs her own series. While comedy writers such as Lena Dunham, Tina Fey and Phoebe Waller-Bridge have been characterised as 'too much' and 'unruly' because of their loud, visible presence, this has led to a specific image of writer/performers becoming normalised and accepted in the cultural landscape. It is Davis's quiet, unassuming disposition that is perceived as out of the norm by contrast, particularly because she differs heavily from the characters she plays. Her 'unruliness' stems from her refusal to modify the self, as women are often pressured to in the media. As such, she is perceived as deeply 'fastidious' and ambivalent because she refuses to conform to comic stereotypes. The debate over whether Davis can be described as 'unruly' in Kathleen Rowe's terms, or as 'too much' due to her excessiveness, continues. Through this analysis, it is clear that she is difficult to pin down. Ultimately, Davis's work showcases the homogeneity of women in contemporary comedy.

2

Phoebe Waller-Bridge, Posh Humour and Political Correctness: Constructing the Upper/Middle-Classes in TV Comedy

Julia Davis has showcased the distinctiveness of women in UK TV comedy, and is different from the remaining authors in this book – Phoebe Waller-Bridge, Caitlin and Caroline Moran, Michaela Coel and Sharon Horgan – who take a semi-autobiographical approach to storytelling. However, Davis does exhibit similarities with Phoebe Waller-Bridge, the focus of this chapter. Both comedians craft 'edgy' characters infused with biting British humour. As a comic who began writing for TV in the 2010s, Waller-Bridge is an interesting figure to consider the changes in comedy since Davis began writing for television in the 1990s. First, this chapter starts by observing how, in a relatively short space of time, she has transformed from a minor to a major celebrity, a phenomenon which began with the creation of her one-woman play turned critically acclaimed comedy-drama *Fleabag*. Four years after the first series aired in 2016, Waller-Bridge was named among *Time* magazine's 100 most influential people, indicating how female authorship, particularly in an Anglo-American context, is now canonised by the media. More broadly, it reveals how television, for women, is becoming an increasingly important site for creative recognition and prestige as the rise of online feminism and online video services have allowed women to exercise control over their work and establish their own singular vision. As a result, by making women such as Phoebe Waller-Bridge visible to a large audience, Claire Perkins and Michele Schreiber argue that:

> conversations around women's television work also render the creators and their work accessible in an example of what Sarah Banet-Weiser calls popular feminism's 'feedback loop' (Sarah Banet-Weiser 2018, 10). This creates a situation whereby these figures are popular *because* they are visible, and the more visible they become the more self-evident the feminist content of their work is made to appear. (2019: 920)

This pattern has popularised women writers and/or comedy performers who have been celebrated and criticised for 'complex' representations of contemporary femininity. In female-authored American television comedies such as *Orange is the New Black* (Netflix, 2013–19), *Girls*, *Nurse Jackie* (Showtime, 2009–15), *GLOW* (Netflix, 2017–19) and *Transparent* (Amazon Studios, 2014–19), for instance, tensions have surfaced from their 'empowered' characters that are tinged with ideological ambiguity. In other words, they are 'unlikable'. Though 'unlikeable' women are typically examined through American TV comedies, this chapter is concerned with British writer/performer Phoebe Waller-Bridge, arguing that the new 'unruly' woman – what I call the 'fastidious' woman – is centred around the discursive contexts of what it means to be a 'bad' feminist and 'unlikeable'.

Often compared to Lena Dunham's *Girls* for their shared exploration of millennial 'messiness' and female sexuality, I propose that what distinguishes *Fleabag* from *Girls* is the portrayal and perception of social issues, which are deeply influenced by their respective national origins. While *Fleabag* is a co-production between the UK and the US (BBC and Amazon), the perception of Phoebe Waller-Bridge as 'problematic' to audiences stems from her Britishness, or more specifically, British TV comedy's reproduction of conventional classed and gendered discourses. The genre repeatedly favours (upper) middle-class narratives, and this chapter argues that Phoebe Waller-Bridge has showcased this national fixation through her comedic conceptualisation of women and class – specifically via her character Fleabag and high-profile public appearances on *Saturday Night Live* and the covers of *Vogue*. Through the new 'unruly' woman, then, I argue that class politics remains at the forefront of British comedy.

More broadly, this chapter considers commissioning strategies to suggest further that Waller-Bridge's 'bad feminism' draws attention to the problematic and unequal structures that make her work both critically acclaimed and derided in a digitised feminist landscape concerned with intersectionality as well as a British TV industry that favours (upper) middle-class narratives. This, I argue, renders her 'fastidious' in the way she is ambivalently treated by critics and audiences – critiqued for her social class but celebrated for her carefully crafted texts, with *Fleabag* being named the eighth greatest television series of the twenty-first century by *The Guardian* and ranking highly amongst male-authored, 'quality' texts such as *Breaking Bad* (AMC, 2008–13) and *The Sopranos* (HBO, 1999–2007) (Abbott et al., 2019).

Genre Classification, Context and Credibility

Waller-Bridge kickstarted her career after graduating from London's highly exclusive Royal Academy of Dramatic Art (with other alumni including Ben Whishaw, Ralph Fiennes and Alan Rickman). After her time at RADA, Waller-Bridge met her long-time collaborator and friend Vicky Jones during a Soho writers' bar night in London. Together, Waller-Bridge and Jones founded their theatre company DryWrite in 2007 to promote new writers and perform short plays. Waller-Bridge wrote several plays: one was adapted into the Channel 4 series *Crashing* and one was adapted into the BBC Three series *Fleabag*. Both TV series were released in 2016, but the former was quietly cancelled, and the latter dominated awards season with Emmy, Golden Globe and Sag wins in 2019. Waller-Bridge was subsequently recruited as the head writer for the highly successful crime thriller *Killing Eve*, a series that also won numerous television awards. Waller-Bridge's star power and recognition in the media is inextricably linked with the series, and after she left to pursue other ventures – most notably setting up her own production company to house her own Amazon projects in a reported 20-million-dollar deal – critics were dismayed, with one lamenting that '[w]ithout Phoebe Waller-Bridge's magic touch, this once adored drama has lost its sparkle, and become a poisoned chalice for each new writer' (Bennion, 2020).

It is *Fleabag*, however, that established Phoebe Waller-Bridge as an important author in the contemporary televisual climate. To put its popularity and critical acclaim into perspective, the series has joined big-named productions and 2019 Oscar winners such as *Parasite* (Joon-ho, 2019), *Knives Out* (Johnson, 2019) and *Joker* (Phillips, 2019) at The Drive in Cinema London's summer schedule in 2020, positioning it as a TV series associated with the 'cinematic' and therefore elevated to a higher cultural status in the contemporary televisual climate (Newman and Levine, 2012). Phoebe Waller-Bridge's association with cinema and the 'cinematic' has extended to her writing the newest James Bond film, *No Time to Die* (Fukunaga, 2021), and performing in *Indiana Jones and the Dial of Destiny* (Mangold, 2023). This association with cinema posits Waller-Bridge as extraordinary as opposed to television's supposed ordinariness (Mills, 2013: 62). As Helen Piper suggests,

> The medium of television has lately redeemed itself through association with a succession of internationally available 'cinematic' and complex texts, chief amongst them *The Sopranos*, *Mad Men* (AMC, 2007–15),

and, of course, *Breaking Bad*, each of which has been celebrated by various parties as the 'best television' ever. (2016: 163)

In these series, representations of white, middle-class males and their anxieties are seen as realistic, revealing and revolutionary, contributing to the perception of 'quality' TV as a complex genre while their male showrunners are heralded and romanticised as auteurs. As Piper further suggests, 'quality' TV series 'made their name internationally by being successfully marketed as exceptions to the daily flow of broadcast or network television, the antithesis of its mixed generic menus and routine sociability, and of its "feminized", populist and everyday output' (2016: 163–83), situating 'high art' as masculine and 'low art' as feminine. Phoebe Waller-Bridge's association with the 'cinematic' can therefore be seen as a form of male legitimation in the media landscape, much like how, in America, Lena Dunham's *Girls* was legitimated by the involvement of Judd Apatow 'to make safe potentially disruptive female comedy voices' (Woods, 2015: 41).

However, the binary of masculine/extraordinary and feminine/ordinary is currently being dismantled and deconstructed by contemporary female-authored TV comedies, which Jessica Ford argues began with the creation of *Girls*. As Ford suggests, a cycle of women-centric dramedies followed the landmark series, which can be classified as women's indie television. Rather than being defined by production-based spectacle like other 'cinematic' TV series, these dramedies showcase their feminist sensibilities through 'low-key styles of filmmaking that emphasise emotional spectacle' (2019: 939–40). As such, they converse 'with indie cinema, quality television and popular media feminisms' (2019: 928). In the new digital ecosystem, the creation of female-centred comedy-dramas has carved out a new space for considering crossovers between television and cinema. As is made clear by these conflicting definitions, Waller-Bridge is situated in-between these masculine and feminine spaces of cinematic TV and indie dramedies.

Because Waller-Bridge focuses on female protagonists and undermines male pleasures, she has inevitably been perceived as a feminist and her work is examined through the lens of feminism. Waller-Bridge has always been sceptical of this policing of her work, stating that 'if you go into the mainstream with a female perspective that seems to resonate with a lot of people, you have a political agenda imposed on you, you are told you are a feminist' (Waller-Bridge, quoted in Malone, 2017). However, at times, she contradicts this thought when discussing how the portrayal of her character Fleabag, or any believable female, is feminist (Waller-Bridge, quoted in Oyler, 2016). This complicated relationship Waller-Bridge has with feminist identity politics has further stemmed from her positioning as an 'unlikable' woman in *Fleabag*. As Svenja Hohenstein and Katharina Thalmann argue (2019: 113):

> the mid-2010s were pivotal in paving the way for a new kind of feminist TV culture in which women finally got to be what men had long been (and been celebrated for): complex, multi-dimensional, and even transgressive heroines of their own stories – in short, 'difficult women,' to borrow from the title of Brett Martin's *Difficult Men: Behind the Scenes of a Creative Revolution: From* The Sopranos *and* The Wire *to* Mad Men *and* Breaking Bad.

In the second decade of the twenty-first century, 'unlikeable' women are new antiheroines who, according to Suzanna Danuta Walters, 'are not merely criminal outliers who are villainized and extruded from the body politic but rather represent the development of a substantive – and new – imagery of female power and subjectivity as iterated through the trope of "antihero", a framing typically reserved for male characters' (2017: 200). In American television, this has been exemplified in comedy series such as *Orange is the New Black*, *Transparent* and *Girls*, while in UK comedy, it is *Fleabag* that has in recent years been made popular by its 'unlikeable' protagonist, unsettling patriarchal standards of appropriate feminine humour through the main character's morally ambiguous actions (and succeeding other important British TV sitcoms with 'unlikeable' women such as *Absolutely Fabulous* and the women Julia Davis plays in her oeuvre). However, Hohenstein and Thalmann do not 'define difficult women by the measure of their "unlikability" – a moniker that has often been used to dismiss unruly, uncomfortable, or unconventional women in fiction' (2019: 113). Significantly, they use 'unruly' here as a synonym for 'unlikeable', with other terms such as complex and transgressive being used as broad terms to (paradoxically) conceal the complexities of these women. However, I argue that these are not analogous terms; rather, that unlikability falls under the umbrella of 'unruliness': 'unruly' women can be 'unlikeable', but not necessarily.

This is evident in the various definitions of the contemporary 'unruly' woman herself. *Fleabag* falls within the 'precarious-girl comedy' subgenre, as identified by Wanzo (2016). Faye Woods observes that this subgenre diverges from the 'gently unruly' network sitcoms in the US that premiered between 2011 and 2012, including shows like *The Mindy Project* and

New Girl (FOX, 2011–2018) (Woods, 2019: 198). Elsewhere, Meg Tully develops the theoretical framework of 'trainwreck feminism', which she argues has recently been pioneered by contemporary American women in TV comedy, such as Abbi Jacobson, Ilana Glazer and Amy Schumer. Tully contends that these comedians 'adopt the trope of the trainwreck—excessive in need, sex, and madness—to demonstrate the disastrous consequences of growing up in postfeminist culture that both insists women are finally liberated and continues to police their choices' (2018: vii). In both cases, it is argued that women in comedy simultaneously embody and critique postfeminism. These new women comedians exhibit a similar 'unruly' spirit to their counterparts in the 1990s, yet they respond to distinct pressures in the second decade of the twenty-first century. For Taylor Nygaard and Jorie Lagerway, the visibility of female comedians such as Phoebe Waller-Bridge and other 'Horrible White People' who 'televisually foreground a supposedly precarious, threatened, middle-class whiteness', belong to a representational trend 'intimately tied to recession, the emergent mainstreaming of feminism(s), the unmasked visibility of racial inequality and violence, and changes in TV production and distribution models' in the age of Trump (2017). In the UK, however, different social, cultural and political conditions have informed the conceptualisation of the new 'unruly' woman.

The role of public service television, for instance, has influenced the rise of this figure. While the 'unruly' woman in America is typically situated on cable channels, in the UK she can also be found on public service broadcasters. Both comedies that Phoebe Waller-Bridge created – *Fleabag* and *Crashing* – are positioned on the BBC and Channel 4, two channels with specific remits and functions in the UK. Channel 4's statutory public service remit maintains that it must 'provide news and current affairs, appeal to a culturally diverse society, provide alternative views and perspectives, provide information and views from around the world, stimulate debate and inspire change, motivate participation in society, and include content for older children and young adults', to name a few relevant obligations (*Kantar Media*, 2017: 43–4). Indeed, Channel 4's former Head of Comedy, Shane Allen, reflects explicitly on the importance of female writers in the genre. Allen points out that 'authorship is key' and, while he argues that men remain at the forefront of comedy TV, women are becoming more prominent: 'recently you've got the likes of Victoria Pile, who created *Smack the Pony*, Jessica Hynes with *Spaced*, Sharon Horgan with *Pulling* and Ruth Jones with *Gavin and Stacey* . . . you've got really strong female characters through that' (Allen, quoted in Gilbert, 2010). The broadcaster's relatively recent emphasis on women has been significant for writers such as Waller-Bridge and her series *Crashing*, but it is BBC Three that aired her most popular and critically acclaimed TV series *Fleabag*. Over the years, the broadcaster has been characterised by young, new and talented comedy writers in contemporary Britain, such as Phoebe-Waller Bridge, Guz Khan, Jack Thorne and Kayode Ewumi. When it comes to hiring women, however, Woods specifically notes that in 2016, two of BBC Three's most significant audience and critical successes were produced by white female creators delving into the psyches of young women (2017: 144–5). These creators include Waller-Bridge, who created *Fleabag*, and Marnie Dickens, the maker of *Thirteen* (both aired on BBC Three). Their whiteness plays a role in shaping perceptions of which boundaries can be transgressed within television.

Fleabag achieved transnational acclaim overseas as it is a joint co-production with the American on-demand service Amazon Video. Though the UK and the US have had a long history of co-productions in the TV industry (and creative industries overall), *Fleabag's* long-reaching appeal increases the cultural and global value of Waller-Bridge since 'audiences [now] recognize US drama as increasingly qualitatively superior to much home-produced material' (Weissmann, 2012: 148). This has inevitably increased the credibility of series such as *Fleabag*, despite women typically being marginalised in discussions of authorship and 'quality' (see Piper, 2016). Waller-Bridge has noted this herself, stating that 'the American audience is so sophisticated in terms of the shows that are being made on HBO and Amazon and Netflix [. . .] I felt like the kind of qualities coming out of American TV, the idea of being in that gang, even if I'd muscled in across the pond, was really exciting' (Waller-Bridge, quoted in Kosin, 2016). A meaningful transnational relationship between America and Britain, coupled with the regeneration of feminism (and its digital turn in the 2010s), according to Sarah Cefai (2020), 'encourages a globalizing, if not transnationally produced, feminist media social discourse', which has inevitably affected Waller-Bridge's televisual output (and vice versa).

Amazon Video's acquisition of *Fleabag* is not only significant because of the increasing visibility of women-authored comedy, but because Waller-Bridge is British. As Christine Becker argues, there is a 'belief that all good actors are actually British, and the prevalence of this attitude in the United States plays into larger debates about cultural legitimation that influence the casting, marketing and reception of [. . .] series and their stars' (2018: 140–1). Notably, Becker believes this trend is only recognised in prestigious drama despite Britain's incredibly rich comedic legacy. This, she argues, stems from Britain and America's cultural differences, as comedy is more specific 'and tied to nationally specific language, mannerisms and timing and thus limiting the fit of a foreign presence' (2018: 142). While there is some truth to this observation, significantly, the women examined in this book *have* created series that have thrived overseas: *Chewing Gum* achieved worldwide acclaim after being picked up by Netflix; Julia Davis's *Sally4Ever* is a Sky and HBO co-production, while her TV series *Camping* was remade for American audiences by Lena Dunham; and Caitlin and Caroline Moran's sitcom *Raised by Wolves* is similarly being remade for American audiences by the director of films *Juno* (2007) and *Young Adult* (2011), Diablo Cody. Phoebe Waller-Bridge has had multiple hits in America: *Crashing*, like *Chewing Gum*, is available on Netflix Worldwide, *Fleabag* is co-produced by Amazon Studios with BBC Three and *Killing Eve* is on BBC America and BBC iPlayer.

Indeed, this relationship between UK and US television has impacted women's work. Waller-Bridge's humour, and her series *Fleabag* more specifically, have been likened to Lena Dunham and her American HBO comedy-drama *Girls*. Dunham herself is typically compared 'with New York male comedic auteurs – Larry David and Woody Allen – rather than contemporary female comedic writer-actresses such as Fey, Poehler and Wiig' (Woods, 2015: 40–1). As Faye Woods outlines here, women comedy writers in America, to be perceived as 'HBO-worthy', must be associated with the masculine rather than the feminine. With both being comedy-dramas, Waller-Bridge is perceived as continuing this tradition and belonging to a group 'dramedy queens: the women who built TV's new golden age' (Press, 2018). However, Waller-Bridge believes that such comparisons are unfounded when asked whether she has been inspired by series such as *Girls*. In one interview, she states, 'apart from the fact that it's about women of a similar age discussing sex and personal traumas and jokes, our work is really different! But I can totally see why people are drawing comparisons between three women writing about women—there aren't that many' (Waller-Bridge, quoted in Oyler, 2016).

While *Fleabag* and *Girls* exhibit distinct similarities, the academic and media responses to these comedies highlight that they face varying expectations. These expectations stem from their national origins and the broader historical context of the comedy genre. Media discourse surrounding *Fleabag* has focused on Phoebe Waller-Bridge's upper/middle-class subjectivities. At the same time, *Girls* has been heavily criticised for its representations of race, or lack thereof, beyond whiteness (see Watson, Mitchell and Shaw, 2015). When discussing the US adaptation of the hit UK sitcom

The Office (BBC Two, 2001–3), Alexandra Beedon and Joost de Bruin argue that '[t]he British class system is an integral and fundamental aspect of the country's psyche and is a theme that has been greatly explored by the sitcom', while 'the issue of race informs a number of American sitcoms' because of the country's history with slavery and civil rights. As they further suggest, these '[d]ifferences between the British and the American sitcom have been apparent since the 1950s, and many of these have remained in contemporary programs' (2010, 7–8). What sets American and British television comedy apart are these traditional concerns outlined in their specific social, cultural and political differences.

These concerns can be seen in the plot of *Fleabag* itself. The show revolves around the title character's (Phoebe Waller-Bridge) personal and psychological issues as she grieves over the accidental suicide of her best friend Boo (Jenny Rainsford) after Fleabag slept with her boyfriend. Alongside her sister Claire (Sian Clifford), Fleabag is coming to terms with her mother's death, too, as well as her father marrying her former godmother (Olivia Colman), who is not a wicked stepmother from a fairy tale, but, as Fleabag puts it, a 'cunt' (S01E01). Through these characters and events, *Fleabag* offers viewers a rumination on neoliberal individuality and isolation, the politics of millennial womanhood – being young, childfree and single – alongside the harsh realities of personal trauma. Visual glances and verbal asides to the camera construct an ongoing relationship between Fleabag and the viewer, sometimes complicit, sometimes confessional and often comedically tragic. The series blends generic and televisual conventions to situate itself as a 'tragicomedy' or 'dramedy' through the eyes of an upper-middle-class woman in Britain.

Classed Comedy in the UK

It is important, then, to discuss *Fleabag* and its relationship with representations of the (upper) middle-class in UK TV comedy. When discussing alternative comedy of the 1980s, Gavin Schaffer argues that 'alternative comedians tended to offer a middle-class critique for middle-class audiences' (2016: 394), and Sophie Quirk believes that comedy in the second decade of the twenty-first century has been subject to similar critique, stating that '[i]n spite of the professed hopes of its practitioners, debates around the cultural significance of comedy are charged with class struggle. As an industry, comedy seems more often to support than subvert this' (2018: 110).

This issue has been discussed countless times and examined with renewed vigour in the 2010s. In 2018, the British Film Institute (BFI) launched a season of screenings and discussions on 'Working Class Heroes' at the South Bank in central London – with guest speakers including Maxine Peak and Vicky McClure – exploring how the UK has 'class divide at its very heart' (Draper, 2018). Controller of BBC1, Danny Cohen, has asserted that too many TV comedies are about the middle classes (Cohen, quoted in Hilton and Ferguson, 2011), and multiple headlines have pondered the same question, with one bluntly asking, 'When did comedians get so middle-class?' (Logan, 2010). It is not just a case of *when* – but *how*. As Nick Butler and Dimitrinka Stoyanova Russell argue when discussing the emotional dimensions of a stand-up's labour, the creative industries 'are characterized by individual strategies for finding work and coping with uncertain, often informal, labour markets' (2018: 1668). This means that the comedy industry remains dominated by the privately educated and those with important networks. There are a few exceptions in the UK's televisual landscape, including Daisy May Cooper, who wrote and starred in the rural, working-class comedy *This Country* (BBC Three, 2017–20) alongside her brother Charlie Cooper. There's also Sophie Willan, who won the BBC's Caroline Aherne bursary which helped to support and develop her sitcom *Alma's Not Normal* (BBC Two, 2020–) (Minor, 2023). However, such success stories are infrequent and unique.

This class disparity is evident in comedy and the acting profession as a whole. Sam Friedman, David O'Brien and Daniel Laurison, drawing on both quantitative and qualitative data, found that 73% of performers in Britain are from middle-class origins, which they argue stems from the unequal distribution of cultural, social, and economic capital. In particular, there are 'profound occupational advantages afforded to actors who can draw upon familial economic resources, legitimate embodied markers of class origin (such as Received Pronunciation) and a favourable typecasting' (2017: 1). Working-class actors are also subject to visual discrimination, from the ways in which they conduct themselves to the clothes that they wear. In my interview with Caroline Moran, I asked her about how, as a working-class woman, she learned to navigate the world of comedy. She replied by discussing the unspoken rules you need to learn when entering the industry: 'If you come from a different background, rules have been trained in you from the very beginning. Rules like, when I learned that when you go for dinner, you're supposed to put your cutlery together to show that you've finished eating'. As Moran outlines here, seemingly simple actions can affect the working-class actor and their ability to integrate into an (upper) middle-class media environment.

In the UK, there is an ongoing discussion about the limited opportunities available for emerging talent in the modern television industry, a topic that has been addressed by veteran actors. In an interview with working-class actor and former *Coronation Street* (ITV, 1960–) star Julie Hesmondhalgh, Christopher Hogg asks whether her Accrington (Lancashire) accent has informed the roles she has been given. Hesmondhalgh remarks that she knows 'actors who routinely get cast as sex workers or teenage mums or young grandmothers on council estates' because of their regional dialect, concluding that 'there is definitely an established stratum of TV casting in terms of accents, the connected perceptions of class and social identity, and the associated roles being offered' (2020: 304). Speaking further of this problem, Hesmondhalgh joined fellow actors Maxine Peake and Christopher Eccleston in the 2017 documentary *The Acting Class* (2017) by Mike Wayne and Deirdre O'Neil, warning that Britain needs to address a lack of inclusivity in the arts. She argues that if working-class people 'can't get the access to the jobs that enable them to write or in those stories then we're going to have a future which has stories only about the elite and that is a major problem for our society' (2017). If this is not addressed, Hesmondhalgh further suggests in the documentary that this 'will create even more of an apartheid. An apartheid between the rich and the poor, the people who have access to things and the people who don't' (2017).

Actor, comedian, and working-class star Julie Walters has expressed similar sentiments, stating that '[p]eople like me wouldn't have been able to go to college today. I could because I got a full grant'. One reason for this, she argues, is that 'the theatre is dying out'. Now, young people 'can't get a grant to go to drama school, and soon 'the only actors are going to be privileged kids whose parents can afford to send them to drama school' (Walters, quoted in Hattenstone, 2015). In 2015, to combat this issue, the BBC broadcast 11 programmes that revealed stars returning to their roots in local theatre in an ongoing campaign to protect and preserve regional theatre from the dominance of London and the (upper) middle-classes. As Hannah Furness states, the documentaries 'showcase the challenges facing regional theatres, from cuts to their funding to the demise of repertory theatre, which used to give working-class actors greater access and a training ground before they entered the London stage' (2015). The nature of these documentaries is inherently political, and shutting out low-income households from acting became an official and outspoken problem in UK politics when, in 2017, The Labour Party urged drama schools to cut their audition fees to create opportunities for disadvantaged actors. Tracy Brabin, a former actor and MP who led the inquiry with fellow MP Gloria De Piero, has stated that [t]he systematic eradication of arts education in schools, sky-high drama school audition fees, chronic low pay and a lack of diversity behind the scenes are all contributing to a diversity crisis on our stages and screens' (Brabin, quoted in Brown, 2017).

Phoebe Waller-Bridge is a writer/performer caught up in this cultural and political debate. While Julia Davis satirises the middle-classes, Waller-Bridge is perceived as representing a privileged group of comedians and someone who has benefitted from these institutional and structural forms of discrimination. She was privately educated, descends from titled nobility on both sides of her family and attended the Royal Academy of Dramatic Art in London – one of the most prestigious institutions in the UK. It has been pointed out, online and in the broadsheet press, that Waller-Bridge is 'posh', with Ellen E. Jones of *The Guardian* arguing that '*Fleabag* is a work of undeniable genius. But it is for posh girls' (2019). The term 'but' here has specific connotations. It suggests that her 'poshness' poses a problem in the current landscape, the predominant reason being that Waller-Bridge invites identification with her character through direct address. As a result, her voice is touted as a universally authentic and shared experience. As Jones further states, they cannot help but remark Waller-Bridge's casual inclusion of upper-class language, tastes and values in the series: 'You want to listen attentively to Fleabag's latest anal sex anecdote [. . .] then she turns into a front garden and it's: "Christ! Her dad's house is massive!" Or you're moved to tears by a scene of sisterly bonding [. . .] before the sister casually drops in her million-pound promotion' (2019).

This criticism has not only been directed at Phoebe Waller-Bridge. Rosie White argues that Miranda Hart's eponymous sitcom *Miranda* (BBC Two/BBC One, 2009–15) has 'come under public scrutiny for its "middle class constituency"' (2015: 119), and *Fleabag* has been compared to the show on numerous occasions. Both protagonists are single, thirty-something white women from (upper) middle-class backgrounds; they run their own shops and cafés – *badly*; use direct address as a televisual device; have strained and dysfunctional relationships with their (step)mothers; a best friend who supports their ventures; and as is always the case with comedy, find themselves in entertaining and humorous predicaments (Franklin, 2019). The differences between them predominantly lie in their preferred genres:

Miranda, the 'old-school' slapstick sitcom, and Phoebe Waller-Bridge, the contemporary, 'edgy' comedy-drama. With Hart's unassuming and bumbling persona on television and in the media more broadly, as well as her 'humility and authenticity – that is, a lack of middle-class pretentiousness – and her "universal" appeal', White argues that she is positioned as 'outside social categories; as, simply, a star who transcends the everyday' for viewers (2015: 136). As both Miranda the 'character' and Miranda Hart the 'person', she is presented as unproblematically likeable, posing no threat to the status quo. Though stereotypically 'unruly' in her body and presence – being 'too' fat, 'too' loud and as a result, 'too' much – conforming to Kathleen Rowe's definitions conceptualised in the 1990s, as White argues, '*Miranda* and Miranda Hart represent a timely configuration of comedy and celebrity, offering audiences a seemingly de-raced, de-gendered and de-classed entertainment in a period of widespread austerity' (2015: 137). This is not to suggest that *Miranda* is simplistic. Rather, it is a sitcom that *presents* itself as simplistic. By contrast, Waller-Bridge's outward appearance is not 'unruly' in her conventional display of middle-class attractiveness, but she is seen as more 'complicated' in her politics because of her characterisation on (and off) *Fleabag*.

The contrast between Fleabag and her sister Claire exemplifies this complication in terms of class politics. Claire is constantly striving for perfection and is seen as uptight, a go-getter, a workaholic – but she offers a nuanced portrayal of the overlooked sister, the one who holds everything together despite not having everything together herself. As she tells Fleabag, 'You'll always be fine. You'll always be interesting, with your quirky café and your dead best friend. You just make me feel like I've failed' (S02E03). This sweetly bitter and bitterly sweet portrayal of sisterhood is often told through the series' self-knowing and self-reflexive commentary about London. For instance, in series 1, episode 2, Claire is concerned with her sister's café and its failure to attract customers. To compensate for her lack of funds, Fleabag overcharges a customer for a cheese sandwich – at a ridiculous £12.55. 'London prices', she shrugs nonchalantly. When the café *does* do well after Fleabag introduces 'Chatty Wednesdays', Claire is perplexed by its success, sharply exclaiming 'No!' to the unlucky customer who attempts to engage her in conversation. 'Loneliness pays', Fleabag shrugs nonchalantly again. The success of *Fleabag* in this context is humorously linked to its critique of neoliberal culture. According to William Waller and Mary V. Wrenn, neoliberalism teaches that each individual should be accountable to themselves, which diminishes accountability to others and, as a result, collectivity as a whole. Thus, the emphasis on individual accountability and responsibility naturally transitions into the power of the individual acting alone, and society is made up of self-interested, atomistic people pursuing their own agendas (2021: 8).

For scholars such as Orlaith Darling, the personal networks in Fleabag's café (Chatty Wednesdays) take precedence over monetisation and a competitive edge in the marketplace, particularly when compared with Claire's continuous effort to strive for this lifestyle. Darling contends that 'Fleabag's perceived failure to attain status by adherence to neoliberal norms ultimately exposes the shortcomings of neoliberal value systems, suggesting that Fleabag's "messiness" subverts neoliberalism's privileging of self-reliance over interdependence and individualism over connectivity' (2020: 2). Simultaneously, however, Fleabag commodifies this supposed 'connectivity' through her café and displays levels of individualist achievement in the process. Consequently, 'class divisions are obscured [by] the omnipresence of the successful female and the focus upon individualism, equal opportunities and meritocracy' (Gerodetti and McNaught-Davis, 2017: 356), with the accomplishments of the café being presented as humorous but at the same time reasonable, understandable and common sense. While the café is a significant backdrop to the series, its success is barely registered as significant. As an audience, we also know that Fleabag comes from wealth and is constantly offered money from her sister and father, contributing to the idea that '[m]iddle-class young women's problems are likely to be seen as temporary and remediable, while their working-class counterparts may be constructed as innately bad, or unfixable' (Gerodetti and McNaught-Davis, 2017: 361).

This complex adherence to and subversion of the postfeminist and neoliberal condition is reflected in Phoebe Waller-Bridge's relationships offscreen. A reflection on 'girl power' and individualism has been a significant facet of creative collaboration for Phoebe Waller-Bridge and many other female creatives in the 2010s. Women must create communities of their own and carve them out in a male-dominated industry to tackle these issues, and Waller-Bridge has done this with her long-time partner, Vicky Jones. As Waller-Bridge puts it in an interview with Emma Jacobs, Jones is her 'first love', best friend and creative collaborator. Comparing the personalities of both women, the interviewer goes on to describe Waller-Bridge as 'all theatrical gestures, comic pauses and the occasional thigh-slap', with Jones being more 'reserved'. Despite their evident closeness, the pair bring Jacobs into the 'gang', sharing jokes and the details of their relationship rather than making them 'the audience to their double act' (2016).

Other important female bonds affected the creation of the series, too. Waller-Bridge met Sian Clifford (who plays her on-screen sister Claire) at RADA and have been friends since, with Clifford stating: '[o]ur friendship and support of one another's pursuits remained steady. We have supported each other through our ups and downs' (Clifford, quoted in de Casparis, 2020). Olivia Colman, who plays Waller-Bridge's on-screen stepmother/ godmother, befriended the *Fleabag* creator when they met on the set of the *The Iron Lady* (Lloyd, 2011), where Colman requested that Waller-Bridge cast her in her future projects (Levine, 2019). Isobel Waller-Bridge, Phoebe's sister, composed the music for the *Fleabag* soundtrack, while their mother played a feminist lecturer in the first episode. These examples showcase how creative control is firmly in the hands of women and can consequently be perceived as a positive change in the industry, much like Julia Davis's collaborations. Yet for scholars such as Taylor Nygaard and Jorie Lagerway, these close bonds seek to mask racial (and class-based) problems in society. They describe comedies such as *Fleabag* as 'Horrible White People shows: bleak comedies or satires that feature middle-class, self-professed liberal white people, most often women. These characters' self-obsession [. . .] contributes to a cultural milieu that re-emphasizes the complicity of white liberal cultural products in supporting and maintaining white supremacy' (2018). In these series, the 'close, supportive, sometimes even joyful female friendships and self-aware humor [. . .] are an expression of emerging feminism, but also let white women off the hook for participating in and benefitting from white supremacy' (2018). This control keeps a small and very particular circle of creative workers in the media industries, thereby perpetuating and preserving a specific class milieu in contemporary television. Again, this seemingly positive act of connectivity has nepotistic/individualistic intentions and outcomes in comedy TV, with choice, power and independence appropriated for neoliberal ends.

This reflection on neoliberalism is not exclusively confined to *Fleabag*. It has been more broadly perceived as an essential element of contemporary women-centred TV comedies and dramedies, such as *Girls*, *Crazy Ex-Girlfriend* (The CW, 2015–19), *Insecure*, *Broad City*, *Jane the Virgin* (The CW, 2014–19) and *The Mindy Project* (FOX and Hulu, 2012–17). As Amy Shields Dobson and Akane Kanai argue:

> [t]here has been a noticeable affective shift in mediated femininity concurrent with the onset of recessionary culture, and some questioning and reflection on the cultural mythology of neoliberal

girlpower is taking place within such television, created by and about young women. We perceive in these shows narratives, premises, and affective tones that crack the shiny veneer of girl powered neoliberal mythologies of women's career 'success' as accessible, meritocratic, and 'chosen' by individuals through cultivating feelings and performances of confidence, self-esteem, and empowerment. (2019: 777–8)

Meg Tully specifically contends that 'women in comedy demonstrate how adhering to postfeminist tenets turns women into true trainwrecks and offer their own feminist antidotes to postfeminist culture' (2018: 151). Waller-Bridge's character, Fleabag, can be perceived as belonging to this group of women who showcase the pitfalls of neoliberalism and postfeminism through 'messiness', disorder and 'unruliness'.

This can be seen in the last episode of *Fleabag's* first series. For a TV series that includes sex as one of its main schemas, it is only fitting that this episode occurs at Fleabag's god/stepmother's 'sexhibition'. In a clinically open space overlooking the Thames, she displays an odd collection of sexual artefacts, including a wall of 12 penises (which Waller-Bridge now keeps in her hallway), a sculpture of Fleabag's father's genitalia and a full-body cast of Fleabag's ex-boyfriend. Commemorating her sexuality through what is essentially a vanity project is Fleabag's god/stepmother's attempt to hold power over her. However, when Fleabag is forced to hand out drinks and is rudely called over by her god/stepmother, who clicks her fingers impatiently, Fleabag smiles calmly and drops a glass on the floor – before dramatically dropping the whole tray. Her sister Claire demands, 'What the fuck was that?' blaming Fleabag for the incident and then claiming that she kissed her husband, Martin (Brett Gelman). An emotionally intense exchange between the sisters takes place when Fleabag denies this:

> Claire: 'How can I believe you?'
> Fleabag: 'Because I'm your sister!'
> Claire: 'After what you did to Boo?'.

Dramatic, sombre music plays as Fleabag looks at the camera in sadness and shock. Scenes flash rapidly in succession of Boo crying in emotional distress, revealing the events that led up to Fleabag sleeping with her boyfriend and the eventual suicide of her best friend. As the audience learns of this transgression and betrayal for the first time, Fleabag attempts to escape from the camera as it lurches forward at her accusingly – and almost aggressively. Grief and pain exacerbate the shock of this scene, and the visual impact of breaking the fourth wall further intensifies and ruptures the relationship between the audience and protagonist.

Though the glossy exterior of an expensive and lofty art gallery in London showcases a neoliberal aesthetic of identity, freedom and autonomy, Fleabag's outburst and descent into internal chaos here indicates how she cannot be contained in these suffocating structures, or rather, how these suffocating structures incite chaos. The combination of comedy/drama in this scene forms an important backdrop in offering a 'sardonic depiction of a society steeped in neoliberal dogma [which] serves, not to obscure the harms of neoliberalism, but to foreground and critique them', as Orlaith Darling suggests (2020: 14). The aesthetic and textual complexities of this scene are evidence of the 'fastidious' woman and her attention to detail. Through the 'messiness' of this scene, Waller-Bridge's character Fleabag is aligned with the 'unruly' woman in that she defies and disobeys '[t]hrough body and speech', since 'the unruly woman violates the unspoken feminine sanction against "making a spectacle" of herself' (1995: 11). Here, Fleabag truly makes a spectacle out of herself – transgressing the norms of femininity in which she should serve (literally, given that she is serving drinks) and behave. Yet this is a carefully choreographed depiction of 'unruliness' and one that would not be possible without the tightly crafted and 'fastidious' detail that has gone into constructing Fleabag's character, dialogue and use of direct address in making us, as spectators, feel ambivalent towards her character.

Although Darling argues that Waller-Bridge critiques the very structures of neoliberalism in *Fleabag*, paradoxically, Waller-Bridge only critiques what has affected her as a character – the individual – and has, in fact, reproduced conventional class discourses on other television series and in the media. For instance, at the height of her popularity in 2019, Waller-Bridge hosted the American late-night live television sketch comedy/variety show *Saturday Night Live* (S45E02), a series that has been airing for over forty years and holds great cultural weight in the US. Her Britishness was clearly an important component of the episode's humour. In a promotional video, self-proclaimed feminist singer Taylor Swift (the show's musical guest) attempts a British accent alongside Waller-Bridge: 'It's gonna be mental innit, like a randy hen'. Swift pauses momentarily before accusingly remarking: 'Did you write this?'. 'Yeah, sorry. It's too British isn't it?', Waller-Bridge replies. The pair turn away from each other, their cultural differences becoming a source of embarrassment for the purposes of the show. Though indicating how such differences can cause humorous tension between Swift and Waller-Bridge, the *Saturday Night Live* team's shared humour can be seen in a sketch parodying the British reality TV series *Love Island* (ITV2, 2015–). Visually exemplifying and mocking the 'Essex girl' stereotype via her physical transformation as well as her performance, in this sketch, Waller-Bridge proudly proclaims: 'Me dad's a boxer and me mum's a pub' (S45:E2). Critics have been quick to point out the problems with this depiction of class and gender. For Aimee Cliff:

> [t]he segment left a bitter taste, mainly due to the fact that Waller-Bridge isn't descended from a pub, but from English nobility on both sides of her family. It may have been playful (and definitely a case of something getting lost in translation overseas), but to a British viewer, there's a nasty double standard underlining the sketch. When Waller-Bridge writes a TV show – *Fleabag* – about an upper-middle class woman who uses casual sex to self-soothe and avoid dealing with her trauma, she's 'creating the most perfectly perverse character on TV' and 'gloriously affirming every woman's right to screw up' – resulting in a 'near perfect work of art'. But when working class women date and have casual sex on *Love Island*, they get mocked by Waller-Bridge (2019).

This skit points to more significant issues in comedy and how it continues to foster and maintain specific class dynamics. While parodies often tiptoe the line between commemoration and condemnation, it is Waller-Bridge's privileged position that calls into question the politics of her performance. As Cliff points out, this is something that bothers British viewers as opposed to American viewers. When discussing *Fleabag*, Waller-Bridge argues that '[t]o criticise a story on the basis of where the author has come from, or how privileged the author is, undermines the story' (Waller-Bridge, quoted in Day, 2019), while others in the mainstream press and media have argued that to judge Waller-Bridge's social class is the 'kind of inverse snobbery [that] threatens creativity' (Lawrence, 2019). However, there is a sense of hypocrisy here, given that Waller-Bridge readily mocks distinctly classed stereotypes on *Saturday Night Live*, yet does not want her own social status to define her work. With her *Saturday Night Live* character's long, dark and wavy hair – starkly contrasting with the trademark bob Waller-Bridge is known for – oversized fake lip fillers, false eyelashes and tanned skin, the creator of *Fleabag* performs a distinct form of femininity reminiscent of a British woman who hopes to reach reality star levels of fame, or, as the voiceover narrator puts it, is one of 'the hottest people from the worst towns'.

This mocking of working-class based femininity, in some ways, bears similarities to Matt Lucas's depiction of Vicky Pollard in *Little Britain*

(BBC Radio 4/BBC Three/BBC One, 2002–6), a 'chav[ett]e' who according to Sharon Lockyer 'has particular social and cultural resonance' because she 'taps into the contemporary stream of abuse of white working-class groups and individuals' (2010: 129). However, Lockyer also argues that, in some respects, Vicky Pollard's character can be deemed important because (s)he articulates and negotiates class identities, with Pollard drawing attention away from middle- and upper-class representations. She may also 'be interpreted as offering a contemporary manifestation of Kathleen Rowe's (1995) "unruly woman" whose body resists and challenges middle-class control and decorum' (2010: 131). Lockyer positions Vicky Pollard as a potentially progressive and transgressive character, 'unruly' in the way that her appearance works against the postfeminist ideals of self-beautification and self-improvement. Yet Waller-Bridge's character is not stereotypically 'unruly' in that her body does not challenge these media expectations. This is further complicated by Waller-Bridge performing on *Saturday Night Live* *because* of her stardom, personality and celebrity status – she is known for her middle-class and stereotypically attractive version of womanhood. This binary, for audiences, is a potential source of humour – and the skit tapped into this at the same time Phoebe Waller-Bridge was disavowing her privilege as being connected to her creative excellence.

Of course, in some ways, it is unfair to compare *Little Britain* with Waller-Bridge's appearance on *Saturday Night Live*, given that this is a three-minute sketch that Phoebe Waller-Bridge did not create nor write. As Imogen Tyler and Bruce Bennett argue, the classification of celebrity 'operates unequally along gender lines, with male celebrities less exposed to the inquisitive attention directed at women, and more able to ascend the scale of celebrity value' (2010: 377), meaning that Waller-Bridge is under intense media scrutiny for her choices as a woman. Nevertheless, it remains significant to examine her comedic choices and performances given that, as Tyler and Bennett further suggest:

> celebrity figures play an increasingly central role in the mediation and communication of class differences. Celebrity is a key vehicle through which value is distributed in public culture and is instrumental in practices of distinction-making between individuals and groups in everyday life. (2010: 389)

Sojourner McKenzie is conflicted in this regard, questioning how to praise Waller-Bridge: 'How much can we celebrate someone who is very much a product of their own privilege? As feminists, where do we draw the line between praise on talent and over-encouragement of upper-middle class wealth?' (2019). I suspect this question is unanswerable, but rather than making the individual answer to these questions and inequalities in the TV industry, we need to examine the institutional and structural issues at play here. That is, we have to question whether the new 'fastidious' woman is allowed to display behaviours that others cannot.

Phoebe Waller-Bridge, Postfeminism and Performativity

There are two reasons why Phoebe Waller-Bridge has been a source of contention and ambivalence. As I have pointed out, her gender has affected perceptions of her persona both inside and outside the confines of the text. For Stéphanie Genz, '[f]emale celebrities, in particular, have taken up the work of being a "private" self which reinforces the idea that the production of closeness and the public display of once-private feelings are intrinsically gendered activities, linking the personal to the conception of female celebrity' (2014: 552–3). This is particularly evident for comedians who are seen to play some estimation of their 'true' self. Since *Fleabag* is both semi-autobiographical and confessional in nature, this inspires specific expectations in audiences who feel as if they know Waller-Bridge and her persona/personality. This is despite Waller-Bridge refusing to partake in social media practices (for instance, she doesn't have her own Twitter or Instagram accounts), much like Julia Davis. Laura Portwood-Stacer (2013) defines this as a form of 'media refusal' – 'a kind of conscious disavowal that involves the recognition that non-use signifies something socially or politically meaningful about the non-user' (1042).

Nevertheless, the intimacy, familiarity, and revelatory aspects of being under the spotlight mean Waller-Bridge is subject to powerful scrutiny. Rhiannon Lucy Cosslett has more specifically discussed how the burden of representation has fallen on the creative woman, stating that 'she becomes a shorthand for contemporary femininity, and the diversity and innovation of the art of other women starts to fade into the background (then people get angry with the woman, whose work becomes similarly flattened)' (2019). This is particularly evident in the reception of *Fleabag* and Phoebe Waller-Bridge. Discussing her subjective and immersive experience of watching *Fleabag*, Rebecca Liu argues that the series reinforces the notion that 'we no longer watch television so much as we participate in it […] I had never heard, read, or seen so much about a television show I had yet to watch' (2019).

Though it would be assumed that the collective or communal social experience of television viewing has decreased in the second decade of the twenty-first century, much like the concept of linear TV, digital fan practices have fostered new ways of participating in its consumption. The convergence between the internet and television has produced specific online spaces for viewers to deconstruct and discuss their favourite TV shows, and the intensely positive and popular reception of *Fleabag*, for Liu, has resulted in fatigue. This is not what John Ellis coins 'choice fatigue', a consumer's inability to choose as the result of being presented with endless options (2000: 169), but the fatigue of the interminable, repetitive praise and visibility of specific TV series by women that are routinely heralded as works of art.

Liu is specifically referring to the acclaim and attention Waller-Bridge received from the media and audiences following the show's second series, with *Fleabag* often being described as a work of genius, transformative and the creator herself as a 'master of the monologue' (see, for instance, Hunt, 2019). This acclaim and attention have not only elevated Waller-Bridge's status but also sparked a trend in the media industry. Many articles have compared *Fleabag* to other contemporary TV series – particularly other UK comedies created by women. 'Could Aisling Bea and Sharon Horgan's new Channel 4 comedy be the next *Fleabag*?' proclaims one critic from *The Radio Times* (Carr, 2019). 'The Next "*Fleabag*": Inside Daisy Haggard's Sensational New Series "*Back to Life*"' headlines another (Fallon, 2019). Critic Shannon Mahanty, meanwhile, situates Michaela Coel's *I May Destroy You* as 'The Most Exciting New TV Series Since "*Fleabag*"' (2020). Positioned this way, *Fleabag* can be seen as an 'event serial' which David Rolinson and Faye Woods define as 'high-profile, high-budget (often co-productions) "authored" serial texts that are often BAFTA-nominated' (2013: 187). The fatigue of Waller-Bridge appears premature, but it is an example of how the visibility of women and the proliferation of fan practices has created an echo chamber in which singular authors are revered and others overlooked.

The second reason why Waller-Bridge has received backlash is that she does not fulfil, satisfy or grasp what contemporary feminism – or fourth-wave feminism more specifically – stands for in the second decade of the twenty-first century. She is not perceived as an intersectional feminist or even a feminist more broadly. As a theory, intersectionality has become commonplace within fourth-wave feminism to claim that multiple, intersecting systems of oppression construct women's lives. That is, oppression cannot be captured through single-axis thinking by examining gender alone. Intersectionality has gained popularity beyond feminist scholarship and activism, becoming a 'buzzword' – predominantly online - so it no longer reflects the theory itself. The concept is diluted, misappropriated, and white-washed, with the potential to neutralise the term originating from key Black feminist thinkers. Critics have been quick to use intersectionality in response to white women's work on television because, as Kathy Davis argues, it 'addresses the most central theoretical and normative concern within feminist scholarship: namely, the acknowledgement of differences among women' (2008: 70). As such, its popularity and perceived ease of use make it ideal for critics and media pundits to disseminate contemporary TV series by women and critique how inclusive certain women are (or are not). In this way, intersectionality is invoked 'to claim the intellectual, political, or moral virtue the term has come to imbue, without supporting the work of intersectional resistance' (Harris and Patton, 2018: 353). While useful in articulating how contemporary TV series should be including new voices and underrepresented groups in their roster, it has also been used to denigrate the work of women who are, to be blunt, expected to do better – again, an expectation that has not been placed on men.

There are, however, truths to some of these criticisms of Phoebe Waller-Bridge. In an editorial with *Vogue* (Collins, 2019), she is photographed posing elegantly on a bus in designer clothes, smiling exuberantly among drab-looking citizens seated around her – most of whom are of colour. This was perceived as a media performance insensitive to contemporary thinking regarding intersectionality. The issues surrounding Phoebe Waller-Bridge's limited engagement with intersectionality mark her as 'fastidious.' This is reflected in the mixed reactions to her series: on one hand, there's acclaim for her diligent focus on textual/authorial precision, and on the other, there's criticism for her perceived shortfall in feminist awareness. She is somebody who straddles the line between commemoration and condemnation in the contemporary media climate.

This complicated relationship Waller-Bridge has with what makes a feminist, or indeed, what makes a woman, is surmised by Stéphanie Genz as tumultuous, tempestuous, and often conflicting:

> women of the new millennium have been the subjects/objects of countless enquiries (fictional, political, media and academic alike) that have come to a number of conclusions: the 'new women' of the bimillenary are hapless 'singletons' looking for Mr. Right; confident 'chicks' who wear their lipstick with pride, political eye candy (Blair's Babes); 'power feminists', third wave feminists who relish difference and

> diversity, postfeminist traitors/saviours (depending on your viewpoint). Indeed, we seem to be trapped in a labyrinth of re(significations) and we can no longer say with confidence and certainty what it means to be female, feminine and feminist in the twenty-first century. (2009: 4)

This complexity extends to how Phoebe Waller-Bridge is presented both off and on-screen. Though Fleabag has been situated as one of the twenty-first century's 'unlikable' women, she is well-loved by audiences. Guy Webster argues that 'Waller-Bridge makes it easy for audiences to project the love they have for her character directly unto her [...] It is interesting that Waller-Bridge is so damn likeable when the construction of likeability – especially as it relates to women – has always been front and centre in her writing' (2019). Her 'bad' feminism, that is, Fleabag's vulnerability, openness and honesty about female-related matters, has manifested in one of the most popular lines from the TV series: 'I have a horrible feeling that I'm a greedy, perverted, selfish, apathetic, cynical, depraved, morally bankrupt woman who can't even call herself a feminist' (S01E01). Waller-Bridge expressed similar sentiments on *The Andrew Marr Show* (BBC One, 2005–21), stating:

> I think it's a feeling that a lot of women [...] feel like they could fall into a trap of being a bad feminist, which is somebody who doesn't tick all the boxes of what it is to be a perfect feminist or a perfect spokesperson for the cause. (Waller-Bridge, quoted in Petter, 2019)

Waller-Bridge draws attention to and breaks down the structures of what it means to be a 'bad' feminist in her work, which she achieves more specifically by breaking the fourth wall: as a character and as a celebrity, intratextually and extratextually. Both are laboriously constructed postfeminist personas that she strives to demystify via her comedic use of direct address.

In her acceptance speech at the Screen Actors Guild Awards (when winning the Best Female Actor in a Comedy Series), for instance, Waller-Bridge draws attention to the artifice and pursuit of the ideal celebrity body when she comments on her abs being contoured for the show: 'I have to say from the bottom of my heart, thank you for being so supportive of our show on these shores, with all the chaos of the outfits and the interviews and the six-pack that my makeup artist drew on me this evening' (Waller-Bridge, 2020). Deconstructing the postfeminist ideals of self-improvement and bodily discipline through the elements of comedy in her speech, Waller-Bridge nevertheless conforms to the mainstream image of femininity by having these fake abs sketched on her body in the first place – much like how she undercuts and comments on the pervasive elements of neoliberal ideology but also uses her powerful class position to 'punch down' in her jokes.

Letting the audience in on this celebrity 'secret' through her honest, vulnerable and humorous speech seeks to mask the very mask of (post)femininity itself. As Marjorie Jolles argues:

> one of the ways that the postfeminist's successful femininity is achieved and supported is through the subject's paradoxical relation to cultural norms: relying upon them to perform middle-class respectability and self-regulation, but self-consciously flouting them to display uniqueness in postfeminism's logic that reads defiance as self-invention. (2012: 48)

Uniqueness and self-invention are (re)presented through the conflicting expectations of femininity/womanhood, and this theme is evident in *Fleabag*, too. For instance, a flashback to Fleabag's mother's funeral reveals that she looked exceptionally and inexplicably beautiful that day (S02E04). 'Oh what the hell, you look incredible', remarks Claire. 'No matter what I do it just keeps falling in this really chic way', Fleabag retorts, attempting to mess up her hair exasperatedly. Though it seems disrespectful or even unfair to look this good while in mourning, her appearance has not, in fact, changed, other than her lack of red lipstick.

This light-hearted and comedic commentary on Fleabag's looks is significant in that Phoebe Waller-Bridge has often been discussed in terms of her appearance, and she self-reflexively draws attention to this in her series. Her chic, bouncy bob and striking red lipstick are often admired in the media (Mooney, 2019). When considering Rowe's work on the 'unruly' woman, Linda Mizejewski contends that mainstream narratives produce bodies that are 'petite and pretty, small-breasted, classical. The transgressive body has dropped out of the conversation' (2007). In television comedy, too, the body has become beautified and glamorised. However, the essence of Phoebe Waller-Bridge and her character Fleabag lies in this combination of binaries: emotionally 'messy'/physically immaculate. The tension instead lies in the question: does Phoebe Waller-Bridge merely adhere to neoliberal and postfeminist ideologies, as she is often criticised for, or does she structurally undercut them by drawing attention to the problems inherent in these concepts, what she is often commended for? The slippages between Phoebe Waller-Bridge (the persona) and Fleabag (the character) have contributed heavily to this. Though she has been positioned as a groundbreaking and revelatory author in her confessional outlook, her lack of intersectional foresight has opened her up to intense criticism online. Similarly, Waller-Bridge has been perceived as inclusive in how she champions women in her work, but it has predominantly been close family/friends who have benefited from this, pointing to the exclusivity and nepotism involved in (upper) middle-class media. This reveals the tensions between postfeminism and fourth-wave feminism in the 2010s, between individualism and collectivism, separateness and intersectionality, and pre-social media and digital activism.

The contemporary feminist media landscape has struggled to overcome these tensions in Waller-Bridge's work, and it is these tensions, I argue, that renders her 'fastidious'. This is exemplified by how British TV comedy, specifically *Fleabag*, articulates and negotiates classed and gendered identities. The biases and discrimination faced by Waller-Bridge as a woman result in her being more frequently critiqued compared to her male colleagues, who encounter such criticism less often. Kathleen Rowe argues that the 'unruly' woman 'points to new ways of thinking about visibility as power' (1995: 11), and the sheer visibility of Phoebe Waller-Bridge has led to extreme backlash, while comedians like Julia Davis avoid the spotlight. If to be 'unruly' is to be unmanageable, uncontrollable, deviant and disorderly – that is, unable to be controlled – then Waller-Bridge's inability to hide in the shadows and live up to specific feminist ideals have shifted what 'unruliness' means for feminist media scholars in the second decade of the twenty-first century. Moreover, if the 'unruly' woman is stereotypically 'excessive, or fat, suggesting her unwillingness or inability to control her physical appetites' and/or an 'old or a masculinized crone', then Phoebe Waller-Bridge would certainly not fall under Rowe's rubric of 'unruliness' (1995: 31). In the 2010s, 'unruliness' is more complicated than being excessive in appearance or speech, it can be the 'messiness' of expectations placed on women by other women as opposed to the 'unruly' woman of old who was resisting expectations of femininity placed on women by men.

3

Caitlin and Caroline Moran, Celebrity Comics and Classed Humour: Examining Overlooked Duos in TV Comedy

Introduction

Much like Phoebe Waller-Bridge, Caitlin Moran has been caught up in debates around class, gender and feminism in the 2010s. An English journalist, author, and writer for *The Times*, Caitlin Moran is known for her work in print media, as well as for her feminist memoirs *How to be a Woman* (2011) and *How to Build a Girl* (2014). However, she has also been hailed as 'the UK's answer to Tina Fey, Chelsea Handler and Lena Dunham all rolled into one' (Bernstein, 2012) – TV comedy-auteurs who have gone on to write their own authored memoirs. Moran is distinctive because she has charted a path contrary to that of her peers; she began her career in journalism before transitioning to television, where she created her own comedy series, the central subject of this chapter, *Raised by Wolves*.

Given that Caitlin wrote the series with her sister, Caroline Moran, it would be unfair to focus only on Caitlin because she is a celebrity feminist. An interview with Caroline will be interwoven throughout this chapter to demonstrate empathy, intimacy and mutuality for creative workers and Caroline as a writer. Indeed, she has an important history of writing for stage and screen. Her one-act play *Prepper*, performed at the National Theatre in 2015, was developed into a BBC 4 radio sitcom and won Best Radio Comedy at the Writers' Guild Awards in 2020. More recently, she collaborated with Northern comedian Lucy Beaumont to co-write the Channel 4 sitcom *Hullraisers*. She also created the BBC comedy *Henpocalypse!*, where five women venture to a cottage in rural Wales for a bachelorette party, only to be interrupted by the end of the world. Caroline's interest and experience in comedy were integral to the creation of *Raised by Wolves*. As Caitlin Moran herself argues, '*Raised by Wolves* is written by me with my sister Caroline

Moran, who is actually the one who wrote all the funny bits while I sat on the desk going, "What shall we wear to the Baftas? Let's wear Ghostbusters jumpsuits, and see if we can get off with Ant and Dec"' (Moran, 2013). The description of Caroline as a studious writer and Caitlin as an off-the-wall distraction mirrors the characterisation of both women in *Raised by Wolves* – a modern-day reimagining of their real childhood on a Wolverhampton council estate. Germaine (based on Caitlin) is a loud-mouthed teenager who, throughout the series, muses on topics that typically focus on bodies and the abject – sex, periods, vaginas, spots. Her sister, perceptive introvert Aretha (inspired by Caroline), objects to the filthy language of Germaine and instead tries to stay focused on intellectual pursuits in the face of her sister's antics.

Here, we can also see how Caitlin's reference to acclaimed TV personalities Ant and Dec is significant. Understood as a culturally powerful and influential male double act in Britain, Karen Lury argues that 'the key characteristics of Ant and Dec's personae are their strong regional identity (both come from Newcastle and retain their distinctive Geordie accents and a notional 'working-class' association) and their genuine friendship' (2005: 176). The same can be said for Caitlin and Caroline, working-class sisters from the West Midlands who share a close familial bond. Observing the pair in an interview, Rachel Aroesti argues that on set, 'Caitlin and Caz [Caroline] riff off each other like a veteran double act. The pair say their hive mindset – developed over years spent living on top of each other – was a gift when it came to writing the show' (2015). There is methodological currency surrounding the male double act, particularly in Britain (Roberts, 2018). Female double acts, however, are rarely subjected to close analysis.

This chapter, therefore, focuses on both the on-screen and off-screen personas of Caitlin and Caroline Moran. It argues that semi-autobiographical comedies have become a significant platform for portraying the working-class. The television sitcom *Raised by Wolves* is highlighted as a key example of a show that represents new forms of femininity and an underrepresented social class. Alongside this, I contend that Caitlin Moran embodies Kathleen Rowe's notion of the 'unruly' woman – being too loud and too much, excessive in body and speech, with her celebrity status reifying her behaviours and persona. Her 'unruliness', however, is complicated by her sister's restrained and diligent personality – her 'fastidiousness' which helped *Raised by Wolves* become a reality. While figureheads such as Roseanne, Miss Piggy and Caitlin Moran are important personas in showcasing the importance of women's visibility, it is their work and relationships with others behind the screen that are integral to the craft of comedy television. Through the politics of Caitlin Moran and her status as a celebrity feminist – one who has been lauded and condemned in equal measure for her lack of intersectionality – I also argue that she is 'fastidious' in her ambivalence. Though she is a socio-political activist, showcasing her feminism through her on-screen comedy and off-screen commentary, Caitlin Moran's complexities arise from her 'brand' of feminism/comedy, which is not always perceived as inclusive, and defines her as 'not feminist enough' by feminist magazines/websites and fans alike (much like with Phoebe Waller-Bridge).

Locating the Success of Caitlin Moran and *Raised by Wolves*

Though both Caitlin and Caroline wrote the script and created the series, the narrative structure of *Raised by Wolves* bears striking similarities to Caitlin Moran's earlier novels. Therefore, I begin this chapter by examining her semi-autobiographical books to understand her 'brand' of humour and feminism. Jennifer Ann McCue argues that, in *How to Be a Woman*, she 'provides a broader perspective into the lives of contemporary women – the experiences of whom have historically been silenced or Othered' (2014: 1). More specifically, McCue argues that 'the narrative voice belongs to the adult narrator who combines her earlier adolescent perspective with her current knowledge and hindsight, which allow her to reflect on her behaviour in this coming-of-age period using the conceptual framework of feminist and postfeminist discourse' (2014: 69). This is arguably the narrative skeleton of *Raised by Wolves*, which combines adolescent perspectives of the young, fictionalised versions of Caitlin and Caroline in a contemporary setting – thereby drawing attention to structures of the past and the present in a way that enables the coming-of-age narrative to cross borders as well as generate feminist discourse within the series.

The connection between the past and the present is particularly significant to the show and is intimately related to Caitlin Moran's persona and knownness. When she was a teenager, Caitlin began her career as a music journalist in a male-dominated industry where she experienced sexual harassment (Moran, 2018). Her feminist actions stem from these beginnings, as she championed and continues championing the tastes of pop-loving young women. Andi Zeisler argues that 'women's journalism has long been read and evaluated through the lens of what could be called the genocide fallacy, the belief that writing about fluffy, disposable subjects (movie stars, fashion, oneself) must mean the author has no interest in, or capacity to cover, More Serious Issues'. However, she believes that with women writers such as Caitlin Moran, the boundary between pop and politics is dissipating (2016). This can be seen in Caitlin's successful memoir *How to Be a Woman* (which has now been adapted into a feature-length Hollywood film) and her TV series *Raised by Wolves*, both of which can be considered extensions of Caitlin's personality and previous fame, as well as examples of how the popular and political intersect. This intersection is particularly evident in Caitlin's body of work, as her novel *How to be a Woman* documents her early life (from teens until mid-thirties), intending to make feminism more accessible for contemporary women in the 2010s, while *Raised by Wolves* is set in the present-day – also in the 2010s – but is loosely based around Caitlin and Caroline's upbringing in the 1990s.

We can see here how Caitlin's celebrity is shaped by enduring longevity. When I interviewed Caroline Moran, she asserted that people wanted to know about Caitlin's life and that the series was commissioned on the back of her status as an important media personality:

> Caitlin was such a big name that added to the desire for people to have autobiographical material, I guess because they were curious about her. So that helped us enormously, and I think maybe that was part of the bubble we were in was that kind of her notoriety meant that the story could be told as we wanted to tell it.

The semi-autobiographical format of the TV series *Raised by Wolves* was essential to its conception – to understand more about Caitlin Moran as a persona and star, as well as for the sisters to create a sitcom about their lives.

Both *How to Be a Woman* and *Raised by Wolves* are also similar in their feminist content, which Diane Negra has criticised. Discussing Caitlin Moran and Tina Fey's memoirs, she argues that a feature of their books is that they are 'indifferent to or unknowledgeable about academic feminism, though they sometimes claim the opposite'. Moran's recurrent use of the outdated term 'The Patriarchy' belies her claim to having explored contemporary feminist work' (2014: 280). Caitlin Moran also uses this terminology in *Raised by Wolves*. In the episode 'Working Girl' (S02E04), for instance, Germaine (Helen Monks) – a younger, fictionalised version of Caitlin – is recruited at the pharmacy where her mother works. When one of the male shop assistants tells her to clear up a spillage in Feminine Hygiene, he tells her to wear gloves because 'that Vagulon is corrosive'. She retorts: 'No, dude. Your patriarchal attitude is corrosive'. The term is comically used here as a sarcastic reproach to authority and to mock men's fears of women's bodily functions. For critics such as Negra, this is an archaic approach, but 'the patriarchy' is a phrase no longer outdated in the popular imagination. Charlotte Higgins argues that 'patriarchy' has, in the 2010s, 'bloomed in common parlance and popular culture. Once you tune into it, you cannot escape it: it is emblazoned on banners and T-shirts; it is an unexpected recent addition to the vocabulary of the red-carpet interview; it is there in newspaper headlines' (2018). The intersection between academic and popular feminism is slippery, then, and it also brings into question what women are allowed to get 'wrong' regarding their own feminist politics. When discussing how 'anger changes the world', Ellie Mae O'Hagan similarly implies that Moran's brand of feminism and her lack of anger cannot inspire change. As she suggests, 'contemporary feminism is at a crossroads: for every feminist summer school, we have Caitlin Moran's swashbuckling, blokey feminism, which seems to be about making lots of witty observations about sexism, without ever putting them in the context of social oppression' (2013).

Criticism of Caitlin Moran in feminist academic circles is aplenty, but the terminology used to frame Moran negatively is noteworthy because it correlates with masculinity. 'Swashbuckling' and 'blokey' have clear links with the term 'ladette', verbiage Caitlin has criticised in the past (Moran, 2019a). Angela Smith contends that the term 'ladette' originated in the 1990s, with the press generating and fuelling a moral panic around 'excessive' behaviours such as:

> binge drinking, alcohol-induced violence, and increasing levels of sexually transmitted diseases in the young [. . .] Much of this attention has been aimed at young women, young women who are commonly referred to as 'ladettes' because of their perceived adoption of behaviours more usually associated with young British men. (2011: 153)

Indeed, Moran was a teenager in the 1990s and has argued that she was/is subject to this moral panic (which she outlines in her memoir *How to Be a Woman*). In an article for *Stylist*, she argues:

> a measure of cheerful, sweet girl-dollness was fundamental to your likeability. If you had any actual human urges – if you liked telling jokes, or having sexual intercourse, or you'd once smoked a fag whilst saying, 'Fuck off' – you were not a woman any more, but a 'ladette' instead [. . .]

> Oh, the word ladette was enraging. As if men had invented fucking, and telling jokes, and The Wife of Bath, Elizabeth Taylor, Janis Joplin, Grace Jones, Dorothy Parker, Virginia Woolf, Bananarama, Nancy Mitford and every friend, sister, aunt and grandmother you'd ever known hadn't existed. (Moran, 2019a)

Evidently, gendered expectations placed upon women have extended far beyond the 1990s – given that Ellie Mae O'Hagan describes Caitlin Moran's feminism as 'swashbuckling' and 'blokey' in the 2010s. Moran believes that contemporary women comedians would have also been defined in similar terms if they were around in the 1990s: 'if Amy Schumer, the *Broad City* girls, Tina Fey, Amy Poehler, Rebel Wilson, Phoebe Waller-Bridge, Jennifer Lawrence, Adele, Rihanna, Katy Perry, Awkwafina, Lizzo or Katherine Ryan existed then, they would have been accused of being "blokey"' (Moran, 2019a). In the 1990s, these women may have been considered excessive for adopting the model of the 'unruly' woman, characterised as rule-breakers, joke-makers, and public spectacles (Rowe, 1995: 12). However, even in the 2010s, they continue to be labeled in this way, without being seen as masculine, unlike Caitlin Moran. This is because 'blokey' and 'ladette' are closely related and synonyms for British working-class masculinity. Significantly, the writers Caitlin outlines here are predominantly American/Canadian, and while 'class has proved a vital identity marker in both British society and British television studies', in America, 'more common have been studies of gender, sexuality, and race' (Gray and Lotz, 2019: 50) – particularly in comedy. Given this disparity, it is significant to note that Phoebe Waller-Bridge is the only British writer and performer Caitlin lists. As a distinctly middle-class writer, her persona is wholly different from Caitlin's and has been articulated as such by the press. This is particularly notable in terms of the writer's respective fashion styles and performances.

Jess Cartner-Morley has described Phoebe Waller-Bridge as 'one of those people who is glamorous in a way that transcends clothes. She is bewitching and beguiling. That unmistakable Mitford bob. The wide mouth made for lipstick. The supermodel height (5ft 11in)' (2019). This description sets Waller-Bridge apart from Caitlin, who is well known for her bold eyeliner, messy hairstyle and tomboy aesthetic. In an interview with British clothes company *Topshop*, she was questioned on her 'rock 'n' roll' taste:

> That's just not washing and brushing my hair! The hair should be big, I think that's the working class thing [. . .] If you can't afford delicious handbags and jewellery, then the best accessory is your hair. You can

> grow it and embolden it and if you get drunk you're not going to lose it in the back of a cab or in the club because its stuck to your head, so it's the perfect accessory. Black eyeliner, big hair, shoes I can dance in, keys in my pocket and I'm ready to go. (*Topshop Blog*, 2018)

While Waller-Bridge is described as 'glamorous', 'bewitching', 'beguiling' and other positive signifiers based on her middle-class appearance, Caitlin instead focuses on the 'messy' and disorderly – dancing and drinking as opposed to the composed and classed portrait of Waller-Bridge, despite both partaking in these behaviours. If ladettes 'represent women as a threat to themselves (on account of the fact that their drinking leaves them more exposed to the risks of assault and ill-health) and to patriarchy (through the challenges they pose to established norms of female passivity)' (Smith, 2011: 153), then Moran situates herself in this space as doubly threatening to the status quo. In fact, this is only magnified through her admission and reclamation of these behaviours. Here we can see links with ladettes and Kathleen Rowe's conception of the 'unruly' woman who has the potential to radically invert the traditional masks of femininity, 'breaking physical and social boundaries of femininity with her size, behavior, and appropriations of male prerogatives such as being drunk' (Mizejewski, 2014: 22). Caitlin Moran not only breaks physical and social boundaries of femininity via her personality and style but through her political views, commenting on class, feminism and other social issues.

In some ways, though she does not perform on-screen, Caitlin can be perceived as a performer in the way that she is portrayed and portrays herself in the media. Caroline, however, sees herself in different terms. In our interview, she described herself as 'dyspraxic', 'hypermobile' and 'physically awkward':

> I didn't go to school so I was absolutely socially depleted and disabled, and then I went to an adult education college, so I was immediately around people that were older than me, and so with the adaptability, what the working-classes so often have, I thought I need to pretend to be a good girl. I need to fit in, I need to do it right and to not raise my voice, you know, things that you just learn, those social rules, and I think the older you get the more used to that you get. It's just that kind of persona thing and again something that, if you come from a different background, has been trained in you from the very beginning.

In thinking about classed and gendered bodies, as well as bodies of work, it is significant to note how Caroline has viewed her own. While the 'unruly' woman is deemed too excessive, and in television, the working-class woman is often portrayed as such to stigmatise, sensationalise, and demonise her, Caroline taught herself to adapt and assimilate in specific situations. This is a controlled and measured persona that works in opposition to the 'unruly' woman who presents herself as rebellious, disorderly and uncontrollable (Rowe, 1995). The pair use their disparate personalities and images to transform the representation of their characters on-screen. If, as Stephen Gundle argues, we should read stars as 'cultural symbols and conduits for ideas about gender, values and national identity' (2008: 263), then we need to examine how these women perform class and gender differently.

Representing the Midlands and Working-Class Wulfrunians

Caitlin Moran's comedy has been negatively framed by Diane Negra and Ellie Mae O'Hagan, with O'Hagan implying that her brand of feminism/ humour cannot produce astute insights through its 'swashbuckling', 'blokey' qualities. However, I argue that Caitlin Moran and her sister Caroline have made astute insights through the creation of working-class characters in *Raised by Wolves* – a TV series which has been a powerful tool in representing the lives of women/girls in Wolverhampton.

In the British media, Caitlin and Caroline Moran's voices are important as those from the Midlands are side-lined in TV narratives, with a North/ South dichotomy typically prevailing. Speaking of his experience as a writer from Birmingham focusing on Birmingham, the creator of BBC Three sitcom *Man like Mobeen* (BBC Three, 2017–), Guz Khan, has questioned the region's lack of representation:

> The West Midlands is my home and I bloody love it. So why do I barely see it on the big old telly? [. . .] I know everyone from the Spaghetti Junction to Bolivia loves *Peaky Blinders* – it's a great show – but it hardly feels like it's created here. (2019)

While series such as *Peaky Blinders* (BBC Two/BBC One, 2013–22) have captured the UK's imagination, the post-World War 1 setting, for Khan, means that it cannot accurately represent the West Midlands as it is today – its contemporary architecture or as a recognisable space/place for modern audiences. Instead, *Peaky Blinders* prides itself on visual excess and a distinctly masculine approach to TV. Caitlin and Caroline Moran are two writers who have showcased the diversity of the West Midlands as it is today from a female perspective, and part of the praise for *Raised by Wolves* comes from its representation of a Black Country council estate. As Stuart Jeffries contends, it 'pleasingly' subverts 'Channel 4's prole porn factual commissioning parameters. *Benefits Street* might have been shot a few miles down the road in Birmingham, but the same channel's *Raised by Wolves* is a million miles from its philosophy' (2015). He further contends that Caitlin and Caroline 'have plundered their Wulfrunian childhoods for a sitcom set in the broken Britain that *Benefits Street* and *Shameless* were too chicken to imagine, one in which the leads not only have vocabularies and library cards but know how to use them' (2015). *Raised by Wolves* is often compared to *Benefits Street* (Channel 4, 2014–15) because both shows aired on Channel 4 and are set in similar locations in the Midlands. However, unlike the reality TV series *Benefits Street*, which documents the lives of several residents on a Birmingham street and has been seen as negatively framing council estate residents, *Raised by Wolves* has not been perceived as 'poverty porn'.

Conceptualised by Tracey Jensen (2013, 2014), the term 'poverty porn' has been attributed to TV series in the UK, such as *Benefits Street*, *Benefits Britain: Life on the Dole* (Channel 5, 2014–16) and *Can't Pay? We'll Take It Away!* (Channel 5, 2014–18), which blame and shame people with low incomes through specific televisual techniques. For instance, Beverley Skeggs argues that reality TV uses different psychological techniques such as the 'judgement shot', an intense close-up on working-class people that incites 'shame and guilt' (2009: 635). This can be seen as an intensified continuation of some social realist films that depicted the working classes from the perspective of middle-class outsiders, framed as objects 'in a rather passive role–either as a victim or as a self-sacrificing heroic figure' (Creeber, 2009: 424). Some contemporary TV series have been fighting such stereotypes. The characters in *Raised by Wolves* are not presented as passive objects but active subjects. Its privileging of female perspectives and the matriarchal family unit in a working-class setting is not typically represented on television, and even in series where women do have agency (such as *Shameless*), there remains a patriarch at the centre of the family dynamic. Caitlin Moran told Broadcast's *Talking TV* podcast, '[w]e were very aware it was the only sitcom about and written by working class women in Britain, which is pretty shameful given that the working classes are the funniest of all of the classes' (Moran, quoted in White, 2016). The legacy of working-class women in British TV comedy – from Carla Lane to Victoria Wood, Kay Mellor to

Caroline Aherne – has extended to the contemporary televisual landscape. In its focus on comedic women who belong to the working class, there are apparent similarities between *Raised by Wolves*, Michaela Coel's *Chewing Gum* and Lisa McGee's *Derry Girls*. Though set in distinctly different areas (Wolverhampton/London/Derry), they share similar strategies in their regional representations, targeting youth audiences with their colourful and vivid aesthetics (Woods, 2017).

The opening of *Raised by Wolves* makes this clear – it begins with shots of Wolverhampton as upbeat, 80s rock music plays alongside images of the city, establishing the tone of the series. This is not a dark, depressing and drab take on the Midlands; it is bright, bold and anything but boring. For instance, at the beginning of the first episode, 'Hand Jam' (S01E01), the scene is filmed in slow motion and from Germaine's subjective point-of-view as she gazes lovingly at a trio of teenage boys acting childishly. She kisses the window, her nose pressed against the class as American glam metal band Poison's 'Talk Dirty to Me' plays comically in the background. Germaine soon snaps from this 'romantic' fantasy when she knocks her sister's Sea Monkeys to the floor, with the audience also being pulled back to reality through the sudden and humorous shift in mood. Such aesthetics are significant in that they set the tone of the series. Though Caitlin and Caroline Moran's labour is related chiefly to narrative, the screenplays and writing, this does not necessarily extend to the visual grammar of *Raised by Wolves*. However, it is worth noting that the excessive stylistics of the series bear similarities to Caitlin Moran's own ostentatious appearance, with the branding of Channel 4 and Caitlin Moran being framed in analogous terms. Indeed, when Channel 4 rebranded itself in 2015, the broadcaster argued that its new identity 'demonstrate[d] our remit; to be irreverent, innovative, alternative and challenging' (Tucker, 2015), while the company has more broadly asserted that it aims to 'deliver high quality, innovative, experimental and distinctive content across a range of platforms' (*Channel 4*, 2019a). Given that Caitlin Moran has a distinctive look, it makes sense that Caitlin Moran and *Raised by Wolves* have become part of an extension of Channel 4 and its brand (Johnson, 2012).

This is also evident in the broadcaster's decision to champion outspoken and outlandish women, such as Caitlin Moran and Michaela Coel, with their focus on 'British youth' television. In deciding to cast teenage versions of themselves, Helen Monks as Caitlin Moran and Alexa Davies as Caroline Moran, of *Raised by Wolves* make a conscious decision to cater to a younger audience, much like in creating, writing and performing as 20-something-year-old

Tracey in *Chewing Gum*, Michaela Coel appeals to this demographic. Faye Woods believes that 'British youth drama can be situated loosely within televisual traditions of social realism [. . .] In particular [. . .] "heightened realism" or "social surrealism"' (2019, 429). More specifically, in this genre, she argues that there is a specific tonal address 'built on a comic bluntness and pleasure in excess, which plays off a desire for "authenticity", whether this be through forms of speech, a focus on mundanity or humiliation, the desire for rebellion or an intensity of emotion' (2014). What Woods describes as 'comic bluntness' can be seen in *Raised by Wolves* and its 'forms of speech' or, as I argue, its verbal excess. While *Shameless*, for instance, focuses on the protagonist and patriarch Frank's pontifications, *Raised by Wolves* ascribes such intellectual discourse to multiple female characters within the show.

This excess associated with the 'unruly' woman can be seen at the very beginning of the series. 'There's nothing more internationally recognised than telly', Germaine exclaims in the pilot episode, almost as if Caitlin Moran, through the representation of her younger self, is proudly proclaiming to the audience that she has now made a series after years of writing television reviews for *The Times*. This self-referential take on both the past and the present is particularly poignant and can also be seen in the quick, fast-paced dialogue of the characters within the show. Pop culture references are peppered throughout, with the pilot episode including nods to Gok Wan, *The A-Team*, *Star Wars*, Mama Cass, Sylvia Plath, Ted Hughes and Harry Potter, to name a few. Drawing attention to the character's knowledge of what is deemed stereotypically 'high' culture (Sylvia Plath and Ted Hughes) and 'low' culture (Gok Wan), this 'self-consciously clever dialogue' has been perceived as 'clunky and inauthentic' by a critic from *The Herald* (2015), a moment of posturing for Caitlin and Caroline Moran.

Yet Caitlin has noted that this seemingly out-of-place intellectualism and attention to detail is deliberate. As she argues in an article for *The Guardian*, '[t]elly never has any smart, amusing intellectuals living on a council estate. That's why we wrote the sitcom. Well, that and the chance to make a load of jokes about vaginas' (2013). This is linked more broadly to the lack of working-class representation in the Midlands, particularly positive representations, with Caitlin Moran contending elsewhere that:

> [t]he lack of working-class people in culture at the moment is notable [. . .] And when they are represented . . . Take [Channel 4 documentary series] *Benefits Street*. It's the only time I've seen people on benefits on television, but you didn't get to hear them talking about their ideas on

> philosophy or politics, you didn't get to see them being joyful – it was simply about surviving, and that made them look like animals. It didn't show them as human beings, so that's what we wanted to do with *Raised by Wolves*. (Moran, quoted in Jackson, 2016)

In the show, characters discuss philosophy, politics and pop culture in a self-aware manner, typically alluding to gender and the broader televisual landscape. When Aretha and Germaine are tasked with mowing the lawn, for instance, Aretha pushes her sister into the spider-ridden shed, leaving her terrified in its dingy depths. Panicking, Germaine chants, 'I'm Kirstie Allsopp, I'm thinking about bunting, I'm thinking about bunting'. Here, she references the lifestyle television presenter of TV series such as *Kirstie's Homemade Home* (Channel 4, 2009–) and *Kirstie's Handmade Britain* (Channel 4, 2011–), series that reiterate traditional gendered values through the 'use of austerity discourse' (Yates, 2015). These shows draw on images of the Second World War to, as Candida Yates (2015) argues, affect contemporary notions of motherhood from a neoliberal standpoint. This tongue-in-cheek remark, then, has further implications. It draws attention to other series that Channel 4 has commissioned, with *Raised by Wolves* providing a stark contrast to both 'poverty porn' and the middle-class sensibilities seen in other Channel 4 programming.[1] Through this, Caitlin and Caroline Moran have comedically highlighted the differences between *Raised by Wolves* and Channel 4's middle-class offerings while more explicitly commenting on how '*Benefits Street* made working-class people look like animals' (Jackson, 2016). The meticulously crafted indictment of other shows broadcast by the channel showcases Caitlin and Caroline Moran's thoughtful consideration of classed and gendered identities.

This 'fastidious' attention to detail can be seen elsewhere in the show. In the episode 'Yoko's Got Talent' (S01E02), for instance, all the series female characters – Della and her five daughters Germaine, Aretha, Yoko, Mariah and baby Cher – are shopping for clothes in Wolverhampton's town centre, with a P. Diddy song playing in the background as the camera pans to each character's faces in slow-motion as they strut across town. Decelerating film shots are traditionally utilised to showcase the action hero's detachment, coolness and self-assuredness (Sconce, 2014). *Raised by Wolves* repurposes this technique to comedically highlight dichotomies between the inherent masculinity of these films and the female-focused nature of the TV series, which is particularly significant given that Caroline Moran has asserted that Della's character was based on Linda Hamilton from

The Terminator (Cameron, 1984) franchise. In my interview with Caroline, she further argues that Della's characterisation responds to the typical depiction of female characters in sitcoms – as nagging, sensible 'fun-killers'. Despite seeming outdated, according to Jack Simmons and Leigh E. Rich,

> the notion of women/wives/mothers as fun-killers has thoroughly infiltrated the collective sitcom consciousness in the twenty-first century. Shows such as *Everybody Loves Raymond*, *'til Death*, *How I Met Your Mother*, *Gary Unmarried*, and *Two and a Half Men* play upon this new trope—woman as man's worst enemy. (2013: 10)

Through Della's character, Caitlin and Caroline undercut this trope, with Caroline positing the question: 'what if the dynamic is that it's the children who are doing that [something crazy] and [...] [she] comes in and wants to do something more mental or she's got an incredible speech to give, or she wants to draw focus because *she* is the boss?'. In *Raised by Wolves*, Della is simultaneously in charge of her children and a part of their schemes.

Caitlin and Caroline do not simply reverse the archetypical 'fun-killer' trope – Della is a woman in control of her children because she is their mother; however, she is also involved in comical adventures typically played out by male characters in sitcoms. For Caroline, in showcasing Della as both mother and 'unruly' woman, she states that:

> once I've switched from my own perspective to that of other characters, I find it much easier to be abrasive, so Della in *Raised by Wolves*, she is an actual joy to write because she didn't give a shit. It's like it's okay, it's fine, I can say what I wanna say through these characters, and so then you're almost smuggling things that you wouldn't dare say into your writing.

Though Caroline does not perform 'unruliness' as Roseanne, Miss Piggy, or Caitlin do, she *is* 'unruly' in her writing. Like Roseanne, '[p]erhaps her greatest unruliness lies in the presentation of herself as author rather than actor' (1995: 65), to create and control not her own image but the images of numerous women and mothers across the Midlands who are being marginalised and misunderstood. As Caroline further suggests, Della, as a mother and 'unruly' woman, is:

> General Patton in the war. She's got shit to do, she hasn't got time – which is based on Caitlin's experience of being a parent, she hasn't got

> time for this shit, and to have that being a riding principle. She's got a household to run, she's got money to bring in, she's got a car to sort out, she's got a dad to sort out, so she just doesn't have time for it. There's so many of those archetypes and you start looking at them and you're just like we'll have a bit of this – there's the drill sergeant, you know basically someone in uniform shouting, then you put that in, and that feels like a great shortcut there.

The drill sergeant can be seen in multiple British and American sitcoms that have combined comedy and war to create a new sub-genre on television. In Britain, *'Allo 'Allo* (BBC1, 1982–92), *Dad's Army* (BBC1, 1968–77) and *Blackadder Goes Forth* (BBC1, 1989) were all incredibly popular TV series that focused on how men navigated war. However, in *Raised by Wolves*, Caitlin and Caroline have appropriated masculinity to comment on working-class families in the Midlands. Jack Simmons and Leigh E. Rich view this negatively, contending that 'role reversal demonstrates only a superficial transformation in the communal notions of femininity and motherhood and, ironically, maintains the long-standing form of masculine visual pleasure' (2013: 9). While there is some weight to this argument, as such representational strategies uphold conventional methods of storytelling associated with masculinity, when I asked Caroline whether she sees her work as different from the male output in comedy, she responds with the argument that 'flipping' the gender of characters 'can be quite useful, especially in comedy'. This is because 'it still looks like the comedy that everyone is used to but there's ladies in it instead, and people start to go "Oh yeah, okay, women are funny" because we're still having *that* debate'.

While Simmons and Rich argue that this may not appear revolutionary on the surface, I argue that it is an important technique in showcasing women's performative talents on-screen and women's writing off-screen. Caroline states that she wanted to develop 'more female archetypes' because:

> there's so many male archetypes in comedy – from Charlie Chaplin to David Brent – you can say they're a 'such and such type', and immediately, there's a shorthand for it. With female characters, there's very little, and now we've got some new ones, you know we have *Fleabag*, *Miranda*, notably all upper-class, the new female comedy characters we're seeing, you know, even French and Saunders were from quite well-to-do backgrounds.

For Caroline, then, frequently taking up space in the UK's cultural imagination is an important method in producing new archetypes, inspiring empathy in TV audiences and creating an intimate sense of familiarity with working-class female characters. This approach from the invisible hand of the screenwriter to create a fresh narrative experience reflects Caroline's teaching of the subject at Sheffield Hallam University. She uses Maureen Murdock's *The Heroine's Journey: Woman's Quest for Wholeness* (1990) as a reference to make the point that 'there's nowhere near as much scholarly stuff' around the 'feminine point of view' because of historical focus with masculine narratives 'steeped in myth'. As such, Caroline contends that we have got 'millennia of catching up to do, to get our own version of that' because 'audiences have been trained' to want male-led stories, and '[i]f you're a working screenwriter, you have to kind of present the industry with something it at least recognises because a 30-minute jazz odyssey of dance and noise probably isn't gonna get commissioned in the comedy stream on BBC'. Offering a recognisable sitcom while reconstructing what we have seen in the media of working-class women, Caroline's knowledge of television and screenwriting is significant in slowly changing the contemporary mediascape. This stems from Caroline's concern with accuracy and detail, as well as her painstaking diligence and 'fastidiousness'. 'Fastidious' women navigate the (political) landscape to produce spaces in which women's humour can thrive – and Caroline Moran has demonstrated this in her sensitivity to the changing nature of television and what broadcasters want from comedy in the second decade of the twenty-first century.

Problematising Caitlin Moran and Understanding the New 'Fastidious' Funny Woman

While Caitlin and Caroline Moran have been praised for their depiction of the Midlands, as has been argued, Caitlin has been criticised elsewhere for her brand of feminism. Diane Negra argues that Caitlin Moran's previous works are 'often unapologetically and crassly self-interested' (2014: 279), promoting a 'relentless idealisation of motherhood [which] stunt the feminism of these books' (ibid). Consequently, they 'raise trenchant questions about who is currently authorised to make claims to feminism' (ibid: 279–84). Yet laying claim to what is 'good' feminism and what is 'bad' feminism is thorny and knotty, and it may be more pertinent to ask: what are the main areas that need to be addressed in order to strive for this equality in television? Caroline believes that 'it comes down to the commissioners', arguing that '[t]hey need to be out there looking for interesting new stuff" (Moran, quoted in Alexander, 2016). In our interview, she similarly states that the 'onus is on the production companies' and on the broadcasters to represent those who are typically 'othered': 'you have to go and look for them, they're not in the places you normally look, they're not just all on stage at Footlights, they're not just all on stage in Edinburgh, people are going to have to get out of London and go and look for things'.

The commissioning editor for *Raised by Wolves*, Fiona McDermott, is also the commissioning editor for other female-led and female-created comedies outside of London, such as *Derry Girls* and *Hullraisers*. She was not the only woman in an important role – in fact, *Raised by Wolves'* crew was predominantly female, with producers Kate Crowther and Caroline Norris taking the helm. In my interview with Caroline Moran, she stated that:

> In a way, I've actually had more experience of being made aware of my gender since *Raised by Wolves*. I think [in] *Raised by Wolves* [. . .] we were almost in a bit of a bubble because it was so female-heavy, and we had a female commissioner and a female executive, so we were slightly insulated from that.

Both Caitlin and Caroline have a vested interest in women's agency, which materialised when an open letter from 76 writers accused UK TV drama commissioners of short-changing female voices. According to Robin Parker, 'Caitlin Moran added her name to the campaign to get more scripted shows from women on air' (2018). Although she has registered her interest and investment in television's equality measures, Caitlin has been heavily criticised for speaking from a financially secure, white and heterosexual perspective. Feminist media outlet *Bitch* has refused to publish an interview with Moran after one Twitter user chastised her for failing to bring up issues of race when interviewing Lena Dunham about her hit American TV comedy/drama series *Girls*. They argued that the show's overwhelmingly white cast did not adequately or accurately represent the people of New York. In retaliation to these tweets, Moran simply stated that she 'couldn't give a shit'.

Consequently, *Bitch* editor Kjerstin Johnson no longer wanted to run the interview, finding troubling similarities in Caitlin Moran's tweets and her book *How to Be a Woman*. She states that 'jokes about devastating wars in non-Western countries, flippant use of the word "tranny," burlesque is cool/burqas are bad—confirmed a nonintersectional feminism I don't want to support. Moran's lack of public accountability didn't help either' (2012).

Caitlin Moran's refusal to discuss and disseminate her brand of feminism has drawn criticism – particularly because she can be perceived as a 'celebrity feminist' who has, according to Nicola Rivers, 'been successful in popularizing the concept of feminism' and therefore has an important role to play in its image (2017: 66). When discussing Caitlin Moran and other celebrity feminists, Rivers also argues that their 'adoption of the label "feminist" seems to have enhanced their status as contemporary cultural icons, rather than detracted from their success'. Feminism has thus become central to Caitlin's 'brand' (2017: 61).

From scholars and the media, then, Caitlin Moran has been criticised for exercising her privilege and feminist credentials in situations where they believe she could have been more critical. For instance, Diane Negra also believes that 'the autobiographies of Tina Fey and Caitlin Moran produce much trenchant commentary and should be credited for extending feminist ideas to broad readerships, yet they are in some ways compromised by their failure to acknowledge the culturally privileged position the authors write from' (2014: 283). Caitlin, however, sees her experiences differently. When *Raised by Wolves* was axed by Channel 4, she was unsurprised by the decision, arguing that her working-class background ultimately led to the series' demise:

> if you come from a working class background you always presume something bad is going to happen at some point. They're gonna close your pit down, they're gonna elect Margaret Thatcher, they're not gonna recommission your award-winning sitcom, you're just ready for bad things to happen [. . .] But, when bad things happen you just gather your communities together and try and carry on, which is the spirit that we've started the crowdfunder with. We have literally no idea what we're doing, no-one's ever done this before. (Moran, quoted in Eames, 2016)

While the underrepresentation of working-class Wulfrunians is indeed an issue that needs to be examined, particularly because the Midlands is a region largely ignored in film and television, cancelling 'an award-winning sitcom' cannot be compared with the closure of coal pits and the loss of jobs for thousands of miners. Though this comparison appears intentionally hyperbolic for comedic effect, the rhetoric Moran uses may alienate those she wishes to connect with via her TV series – and further the argument of critics and scholars that she is woefully out of touch with intersectional feminist politics. I argue that the complexities surrounding this make

Caitlin Moran more than 'unruly'. After all, what is it to be 'unruly'? If it were once being too loud, aggressive and fat, as Kathleen Rowe (1995) contends, can it now, in the contemporary climate, mean she is not feminist enough, not intersectional enough, not loud enough when and where it 'counts'? Increasingly, women with feminist concerns are held to impossible standards by the media (namely, that they should be able to speak on behalf of all women everywhere all the time), particularly because of the movement's growing popularity. In many ways, this situates her as what I define as the new 'unruly' woman and 'fastidious' in that she is treated ambivalently by critics – either not feminist enough by left-leaning critics or too leftist by right-wing journalists. For instance, right-wing paper *The Sun* frequently notes Caitlin Moran's economic position by describing her as a 'millionaire leftie luvvie' who lives in 'a swish £2million North London pad' (Walker, 2016).

Caitlin Moran's politics are messy and have been called into question because of the popularity of fourth-wave feminism in the 2010s. This has enabled and promoted 'call out culture'. Ealasaid Munro argues that this is an integral part of the shift from 'third-wave' to 'fourth-wave' feminism, with the internet creating a 'call-out' culture 'in which sexism or misogyny can be "called out" and challenged' (2013). Moran has been 'called out' on more than one occasion. Her flippant use of the word 'tranny' has been heavily criticised (significantly, her character's namesake in *Raised by Wolves*, Germaine Greer, has also been 'called-out' for her transphobic comments, see: Wahlquist, 2016; Edwards and Nagouse, 2018), with her response to this backlash emphasising her original intentions of its usage:

> I've learned a lot about language over the past couple of years [. . .] I've got some grief referring to 'trannies'—I spent all of my teenage years in drag clubs, where trannies called each other trannies. I had no idea that was a derogatory term; I issued a big apology for that (Moran, quoted in Oyler, 2015).

As previously argued, Caitlin Moran is performative with her look and language, and this performativity can be perceived as another form of 'drag'. As such, it is interesting that there is a disconnect here between Moran, drag queens and feminists – but this disconnect forms part of Caitlin's celebrity and, in part, stems from her focus on the 1990s *and* the 2010s in her work, a detachment between past forms of acceptability and present forms of acceptability.

Her lack of concern around issues of race, as pointed out, has also been criticised, and *Raised by Wolves* has an all-white cast. Significantly, though she does not stand by her use of the slur 'trannies', she stands by her tweet commenting on race in Lena Dunham's *Girls*:

> If you're writing stories, you can't always be political [...] If Lena Dunham wants to write a show about spoiled white girls in New York because that's her experience, that's what she knows about, [and] those are the jokes that she feels comfortable making, then [she] can do that. We can't say that you're not allowed to simply talk about your personal experience. If she's going around saying racist things or being horrible to people, that's another conversation, but to say that every single piece of art must be representative of everybody is illogical. We've never made art like that; we never can. (quoted in Oyler, 2015)

Caitlin Moran's argument here echoes Hannah McCann's assertion that in *Girls* 'we may find that to insert Black characters into Dunham's story of white success despite the odds would merely compound the cruel optimism already circulating in the show' (2017: 99). In the current cultural climate where intersectionality is increasingly important to popular feminist concerns, where do comedy writers like Caitlin Moran and Lena Dunham fit? The issue seems to be where women are allowed to be political. Caitlin Moran and Lena Dunham are too focused on whiteness, too focused on comedy and are not political enough in some areas as opposed to being 'too much' (in Kathleen Rowe's terms).

In my interview with Caroline Moran, she also discussed the politics and personas of writer/performers who have specific expectations placed upon them, stating, 'I think there's more of a costume if you're a performer and a writer you know, because you have to become well-known and that is a burden in itself and can be off-putting to a lot of people'. The cultural dynamics of being a female writer/performer suggests that there is 'interest and pleasure in the misfortunes of female celebrities', as Su Holmes and Diane Negra argue (2008), and so 'we are invited to play a "waiting game" to see when their hard-won achievements will collapse under the simultaneous weight of relationships, family, and career' (2008). It is thus clear why being a writer *and* performer is 'off-putting' for Caroline Moran. As Lauren Christiansen contends, for the celebrity white woman, at first she is a 'media darling – and then we start to sour. Even though she may remain popular or successful, she becomes hateable. This cycle happens particularly to white women, while their white male colleagues seem to skate by unscathed' (2020). Christiansen cites Phoebe Waller-Bridge as an example of this phenomenon, and Caitlin Moran has told us to 'prepare for the inevitable Phoebe Waller-Bridge backlash' (Moran, 2019b), even as she herself is receiving backlash from media critics and academics. This is not a defence or indictment of Caitlin Moran; instead, it provides a starting point to consider contemporary female comedians' ambivalence, or 'fastidiousness', and their place within the current cultural landscape.

In this chapter, examining Caitlin and Caroline through the lens of 'fastidiousness' has been central in understanding how this comic duo have used their respective personalities, creativity and craft to demonstrate 'unruliness' on-screen. In our interview, Caroline Moran outlined how she has been 'unruly' in her writing rather than her image or persona like Caitlin Moran. Kathleen Rowe argues that 'women are constructed as gendered subjects in the language of spectacle and the visual' (1995: 11), and she analyses the radical potential of women to disrupt the masculine visual power of space. However, this chapter has showcased how the quiet moments behind the screen and women's invisible labour – the roles of female producers, commissioners and writers who are not necessarily in the limelight – are essential in making the 'unruly' woman on television visible, much like with Julia Davis. Interviewing Caroline Moran has been instrumental in exploring the dynamics and differences between her and her sister, allowing us to see and hear women in/on television.

As I have also argued throughout this chapter, 'fastidiousness' has also been a significant concept in examining how Caitlin Moran is treated ambivalently in the contemporary feminist landscape. Like Phoebe Waller-Bridge, she has been heavily condemned by critics and audiences.

When I have discussed the writers being explored in this book – Phoebe Waller-Bridge, Michaela Coel, Julia Davis, Caitlin and Caroline Moran and Sharon Horgan – I am frequently asked: 'Why Caitlin Moran? Why *Raised by Wolves*?'. I suspect there are three reasons for this: (1) *Raised by Wolves* is Caitlin and Caroline Moran's first and only TV series to date (as a duo), (2) there are other female comedians who have garnered mainstream attention for their series who have arguably made more of an impression on the comedy circuit and (3) perhaps the most pertinent point is that people find Caitlin 'problematic', as the critics cited throughout have critiqued her personal politics.

In some ways, then, Caitlin Moran and her work are significant in that they engender debate about who gets to speak and for what group(s). A political tool that can be complex and contradictory, to be 'unruly', then, is not always to be perceived as a 'good' feminist or to be easily defined even – she is above all a 'fastidious' and 'ambivalent' figure, much like how the 'unruly' woman's fatness, for instance, 'is ambivalent, carrying positive associations of abundance on the one hand and negative ones of loss of control on the other' (Rowe, 1995: 37). This ambivalence is reflected in Caroline and Caitlin's relationship, as the combination of their disparate personalities makes them a forceful and evocative comedy duo.

Note

1. It is worth noting here that Channel 4 do not create their own programming and would argue that they do not have a political perspective or one-sided slant: 'Channel 4 is a strong supporter of the independent production sector. Unlike the BBC and ITV, Channel 4 does not have any in-house production resources and is dependent on independent producers for its programming output' (House of Lords Committee, 2006).

4

Michaela Coel, Colourful Comedy and Challenging the Status Quo: New Representations of Race in TV

In the same vein as Caitlin and Caroline Moran, Michaela Coel is also a writer/performer concerned with comedy and class. Her TV series, however, are intersectionally informed and explicitly focus on race, which stems from her background. Coel is the daughter of Ghanaian immigrants. She grew up in the dividing line between Hackney and Tower Hamlets with her sister and mother. Like Phoebe Waller-Bridge, Michaela Coel began in theatre with her one-woman play – *Chewing Gum Dreams* (2013) – which is semi-autobiographical. Unlike Waller-Bridge, however, Coel enrolled in the Guildhall School of Music and Drama in 2009, the first Black woman to be accepted in five years. She was surrounded by an overwhelming number of white and upper-middle class students, an experience exemplified during a class exercise in which 'students whose families owned their houses went to one end of the room; those whose families didn't went to the other. Coel was the only one who went to the latter side' (Jung, 2020). She mixes cultural forms in straddling these disparate spaces: Ghana/Britain, Hackney/Tower Hamlets and upper middle-class/working-class cultures.

Michaela Coel's early experiences significantly influenced her debut series and the adaptation of her first play, *Chewing Gum*, which premiered on the broadcaster E4 in 2015. This channel is, according to Faye Woods, 'imbued with youthful irreverence' (2016: 38), targeting 16–34 year olds by presenting itself as a 'bizarre, ironic or anarchic presence within British landscapes or mundane spaces' (ibid: 43). *Chewing Gum* embodies E4's ethos through its playful and comedic focus on 24-year-old Tracey Gordon (played by Coel), a naïve and sheltered shop assistant who sets out to lose her virginity. Complicating matters, Tracey lives with her strict religious mother (Shola Adewusi) and her highly strung sister, Cynthia (Susie Wokoma). Repressed by her religious upbringing, she only finds solace at the home of her sexually experienced best friend Candice (Danielle Walters). *Chewing Gum* exuberantly explores themes of sex, relationships, friendship and religion in London's East End, a place in which Michaela Coel has articulated resistant narratives. She argues that the TV series is set on a council estate that isn't 'sad or morbid like a lot of shows portray working class life to be' (Coel, cited in Gajanan, 2017). I, in turn, argue that East London has been positioned as a site of difference in Coel's *Chewing Gum*, which is complemented by the ways in which she creates a colourful and complex depiction of working-class life for a young Black woman in Tower Hamlets.

Through this, I contend that Coel has transformed what it means to be 'unruly' in her deconstruction of pejorative stereotypes that have plagued the portrayal of Black women, who are often denoted as sexually aggressive or angry Jezebels (see West, 2012 and Cheers, 2017). Instead, Coel shows the potential for Black women to define themselves as innocent, sexually naïve and affable. If Kathleen Rowe argues that the 'unruly' woman is 'associated with looseness and occasionally whoreish-ness' (1995: 35), then she has not taken into account how Black women have historically been represented on-screen: as unrestrained in their sexuality. This chapter thus examines how Coel has dismantled such stereotypes in her depiction of the new 'unruly' woman.

As this chapter further suggests, *Chewing Gum* has served as a soft springboard for Coel to explore race and gender in relation to consent, trauma and contemporary relationships. Her comedy-drama *I May Destroy You* revolves around Arabella, played by Coel, a millennial writer who is dealing with the aftermath of a traumatic sexual assault. I explore the production contexts around this series and how she exercises power in the TV industry. Coel remains funny, loud and over the top but conscientious of other issues facing underrepresented women. Through an analysis of her original TV sitcom *Chewing Gum* and hit series *I May Destroy You*, I argue that she is 'fastidious', diligent, and hardworking – both textually and extratextually – in order to overcome institutional obstacles.

Locating Race in the Anglo-American TV Industries

Since race is an important part of this chapter, I will examine how Blackness[1] has been constructed and contested in the Anglo-American TV industries. According to Angelica Jade Bastién,

> 2016 was a banner year for black people in front of and behind the camera. The growth hasn't come out of nowhere; instead it is built on

the success that showrunners like the powerhouses Shonda Rhimes and Mara Brock Akil have worked for in recent years. When *Scandal*'s Olivia Pope sauntered onto television screens in 2012, she was the first black female TV lead in almost 40 years. Now, she and her creator, Rhimes, are no longer anomalies at a time when TV is bursting with new and returning black-led series, many of which are also helmed by black showrunners. Last year alone saw the arrival of new shows including *Atlanta*, *Insecure*, *Queen Sugar*, *Chewing Gum*, and *Luke Cage*, and the return of others, such *as Being Mary Jane*, *Black-ish*, *Scandal*, *How to Get Away With Murder*, *Empire*, and *Power*.

Whether this positive change can be sustained has yet to be determined. It is worth noting, though, that representations of race have tended to operate differently in comedy television. As Sarita Malik argues, 'comedy tends to home in on current preoccupations and particularities in present climates, it relies heavily on "the situation" and on the effects of repetition and familiarity, making the history of "race sitcoms" and Black comedy a useful barometer of popular opinion on race at specific moments and over time' (2002: 91). The critical acclaim surrounding these shows, and comedies such as *Chewing Gum*, demonstrate that TV is more inclusive at this particular moment in time (the 2010s) and that Black stories are not only for a small, specific and niche audience.

The majority of the series named by Bastién are American, with the only British programme on this list being Coel's *Chewing Gum*. At the Women and Comedy Symposium held at Salford University in 2017, Black British stand-up comedian Eva Vidal bemoaned this lack of diversity in comedy TV. She stated that Michaela Coel is 'the exception rather than the rule' in Britain and that she was 'really lucky' because Black women making it in comedy 'hardly ever happens'. As she went on to argue, there are 'so many Black female comedians out there' who are not recognised. Vidal felt further marginalised in public school; she was not accepted because people could not comprehend that she was middle class rather than working class, stereotyping her as poor because of her skin colour. This 'in-between' space, she felt, was difficult – but not as difficult as being typecast as the 'Angry Black Woman', a trope that characterises Black women as strong, opinionated and ill-tempered. Coel has commented on this trope and the use of lazy language that stereotypes and simplifies, stating: 'We're sexual vixens or we're angry, we're feisty. I get that a lot whenever I get a casting notice. It's got the word feisty a lot and it's tiring. Which is why I made Trac[e]y a vulnerable naive character' (Coel, quoted in Matthews, 2017).

Black women on film/TV are not only seen as 'angry' or one-dimensional, but they are rarely seen at all. Riz Ahmed gave a scathing speech about the lack of inclusivity in/on TV when he delivered Channel 4's annual diversity lecture in 2017. Accusing British broadcasters of failing to represent all ethnicities in their programming, he stated that: 'It takes American remakes of British shows to cast someone like me [. . .] We end up going to America to find work. I meet with producers and directors here and they say, "We don't have anything for you, all our stories are set in Cornwall in the 1600s"' (Ahmed, quoted in Stolworthy, 2017). Transatlantic ties, for underrepresented actors, are perceived as important in securing work that does not typecast or stereotype. In his speech, he mentioned Coel as being an 'exception that proves the rule' in the same terms as Vidal and argued that such 'prominent successes can mask structural problems' (Ahmed, quoted in Stolworthy, 2017).

Indeed, there has been an exodus of Black British actors to the US due to the lack of opportunities in the UK, both in film and television. With a lack of roles, acclaimed Black British actors such as Thandiwe Newton have said that they cannot work in the UK. Speaking to the *Sunday Times Magazine*, she said: 'I love being here, but I can't work, because I can't do *Downton Abbey*, can't be in *Victoria*, can't be in *Call the Midwife* – well, I could, but I don't want to play someone who's being racially abused' (Newton, quoted in Glass, 2017). In Britain, the costume drama is still perceived as superior in 'quality', with the BFI finding that 'the genre least likely to feature Black actors is the historical/period drama, with around 80 percent of the films in this period failing to feature a single black actor with a named character' (Hoyes, 2016). With Black actors in period pieces waning – a significant national genre because it represents British literary 'culture' (Chapman, 2014: 132) – it is no surprise that these British expatriates have migrated across the Atlantic to find roles where they are not portrayed in stereotypical roles such as slaves or gangsters.

Other Black American actors have pointed out that Black British actors have migrated to the States for good reason. Morgan Freeman has argued that 'the British film industry [. . .] needs to catch up with the times; it has much more progress to make' (Freeman, quoted in Walker, 2012), while Samuel L. Jackson criticised Black British actors being cast in American roles, specifically Daniel Kaluuya in Jordan Peele's *Get Out* (2017), an American horror which centres around an interracial relationship. Jackson asserts that 'Daniel grew up in a country where they've been interracial dating for a hundred years', so 'what would a brother from America have made of that role? Some things are universal, but [not everything]' (Jackson, quoted in Mumford, 2017). Responding to Jackson's comments that an African-American actor would have been more authentic, *Homeland* (Showtime, 2011–20) actor David Harwood writes that he and other Black British performers are able 'to unshackle ourselves from the burden of racial realities – and simply play what's on the page' (Harwood, quoted in Addley, 2017).

With wider discussion in the British media industries about Black actors and their lack of voice, the BFI is one organisation that has been paying attention. In July 2016 they unveiled Black Star, described as 'the UK's biggest ever season of film and television dedicated to celebrating the range, versatility, and power of Black actors. Black Star celebrates the relationship between stars and the audiences who love them, spotlighting great performances by black actors on screen'. This event also focused on the LGBTQ community by screening films such as *The Watermelon Woman* (Dunye, 1996) and *Paris is Burning* (Livingston, 1990) while reissuing key films in areas such as Blaxploitation and hip-hop cinema. Filled with interactive moments such as seminars, concerts and interviews, the BFI paid homage to contemporary and classic films involving actors such as David Oyelowo and Sidney Poitier.

Though the BFI's initiative is indicative of a positive change in the UK TV industry, as previously identified, Black British actors have travelled to America because it is impossible to get work in the UK. According to Anamik Saha, British public service broadcasting has 'a particularly critical role to play in determining the extent to which racialised minorities are recognised, represented and catered for within the national [British] imaginary' (2017: 50). With questionable representation on public service broadcasters each year, Saha further argues that 'it is widely understood – by academics and the industry itself – that television has a problem with race' (2017: 50). Though *Chewing Gum* is on E4 and owned by Channel 4, a broadcaster that has a remit to cater to 'the tastes and interests of a culturally diverse society' (Communications Act, 2003), there are still diversity issues in the UK TV industry. Coel has explained that her experiences in the industry remain disheartening:

> My God, it is bleak, mate. It is bleak. Having diversity behind the screen affects so much [. . .] So many times on jobs, I have had to say, 'Do you see that that's how you've done it? You're not thinking.' I can watch a TV show, and I can tell you: The exec, the producers, the directors. . .. No one in there is BAME. There might not even be any women involved in that. (Coel, quoted in Myers, 2017)

To balance this inequality in the TV industry, Coel has thought carefully about who she hires. The executive producer, the continuity woman, as well as the production coordinator for *Chewing Gum* are Black, with Coel saying that 'there was just a difference' in hiring them (ibid).

Though she had some control over who to hire, in an interview with *Vulture*, Coel revealed that the executives from the production company Retort, then a subsidiary of Fremantle Media, refused to make her an executive producer: 'The production office felt like the place I had no access to [. . .] the curtain rod behind where Jesus is dwelling. You come to my trailer whenever you need something, but I can't access *you*' (Coel, quoted in Jung, 2020, original emphasis). As well as experiencing isolation herself, Coel has said that five Black actors were confined to a single trailer while another white cast member had her own to use, stating that it looked like 'a fucking slave ship'. She subsequently complained to the production company: 'In that moment, I was like, "This is disgraceful. While the mess is going on outside, you sat here, clueless"' (Coel, quoted in Jung, 2020). Though Immani M. Cheers argues that '[u]ntil the 1980s, television shows with predominantly Black casts that focused on Black themes were under the creative control of White studio and network executives' (2017: 2), the marginalisation of Coel and other actors behind the screen demonstrates that this is still occurring. Talkback Thames' four separate production companies, Boundless, Retort, Talkback and Thames, have commissioned cult classics such as *The IT Crowd* (Channel 4, 2006–13), *Brass Eye* and *I'm Alan Partridge* (BBC Two, 1997–2002), specialising in sitcoms and sketch shows that are heavily focused around white and/or male comedians.

While creatives in the TV industry have insinuated that Coel has been lucky in her endeavours, professional challenges she has had to endure demonstrate that, as a Black woman, she faces unique issues in the TV industry. Coel demonstrates traits of the 'unruly' woman, for instance, being headstrong in the way she interacts with production companies, but she must also carefully navigate a predominantly white industry. It is in this way, I argue, she demonstrates 'fastidiousness', as she 'talks back' to the industry and exercises control in the way she discusses it via the press. The 'fastidious' work that has gone into creating *Chewing Gum*, as well as hiring and defending Black creatives, is reflected in the series' wider themes of community. As Michaela Coel has stated, 'On my estate everyone's different racially but economic circumstances give people a particular culture. I know Tower Hamlets is one of the poorest boroughs in the UK but I'd rather write about all the great stuff than the misery [...] I loved my estate!' (Coel, quoted in Tate, 2015a). The decision to write about 'great stuff' and use the sitcom as a generic mode to explore religion, sex, class and race demonstrates how the format functions as a form of visual communication – whether obliquely or overtly – to confront the racial, political, economic and social issues gripping different regions in the UK.

Situating *Chewing Gum's* Generic Roots

Chewing Gum, however, did not begin as a sitcom. Michaela Coel has used her experiences to shape the show which initially began on stage as her one-woman, 45-minute play *Chewing Gum Dreams* (before it was picked up by Channel 4). For her final project at Guildhall in 2012, according to Abby Bien, Coel 'either had to perform a classic text or write something new for herself. She went with her own words [...] In a perfect full-circle moment, the solo script *Chewing Gum Dreams* grew from a piece of poetry about her own school experiences, into her senior project', and then finally to the theatre stage (2020). It tells the story of Tracey Gordon, a 14-year-old Black girl growing up in a working-class area in Hackney. A loud, foul-mouthed teenager, Tracey is a poor student who is scraping by at school, much like her best friend Candice who is in an abusive relationship. Tracey herself has fallen for Aaron, a white classmate who dreams of being a writer. The TV series shares similarities with the play in that it revolves around these characters, but it has been subject to certain changes. In the play, the protagonist is ten years younger than her televisual counterpart. This naturally shapes our perception of the character. At 14 years old, her naivety and limited life experience are justifiable. However, in the TV series, Tracey is depicted as a 24-year-old working at a corner shop. Given her age, we anticipate that she would possess more maturity than she had in her adolescence. There have also been generic changes to the play. Harriet Baker describes *Chewing Gum Dreams* as a 'sharp, unsentimental snapshot of inner-city teenage life' (2014), and while the TV translation is not overly sentimental, it is certainly not 'sharp' in its depiction of working-class life. Although *Chewing Gum* can be uncomfortably cringe-worthy at times, its edges have been sanded and smoothed down through conventions of the TV sitcom.

Sitcom is a genre that has often been subject to judgements of quality and taste. More often than not, it is perceived as 'low art'. As Brett Mills points out (2009: 1–2), critics have argued that 'there's something inherently small-time about sitcoms', and, in response, Mills contends that 'small-time' can be perceived and understood in a number of ways: '[f]irstly, it could refer to the nature of the industry which produces it' in that the sitcom is created 'by small groups of people and without investment and returns seen in other areas of television'. Secondly, the term 'small-time' in this context may refer to the domestic scale and typical social scenarios commonly depicted in sitcoms. Mills also argues that the genre's 'social value might be seen as "small-time" [. . .] its social role is more difficult to delineate than might be the case for other television genres. Finally, the term "small-time" could be seen to refer to the lack of artistry in the genre, a sense that sitcom is rarely groundbreaking'. Clearly, from these characteristics, series such as Coel's *Chewing Gum* are traditionally seen as less culturally worthy than other genres, but – like Brett Mills – this book sees the sitcom as 'anything but small-time' (2009: 2).

In fact, Coel points out three reasons why *Chewing Gum* initially received a quiet reception – all institutionally, culturally and socially influenced:

> I think people saw a show that a) was on E4, which is quite a small channel; then b) you've got a black female protagonist; and c) it's on a council estate and everyone's poor. Then people can assume that it's not for them. What the Baftas did, which I'm really grateful for, is that it made people go, 'Oh, what's that?' But it's a shame people need that. (Coel, quoted in Lewis, 2017)

The use of the word 'small' here by Coel is interesting for various reasons – E4 is 'quite a small channel' to Coel because it initially launched as an entertainment companion to Channel 4. Faye Woods is one scholar who has examined the significance of E4 and its obligations when examining teen TV: '[f]rom the outset, its channel brand offered an oppositional identity, one built around entertainment, with a core audience of 16–34 year olds' (2016: 38). It comes as no surprise, then, that Coel's *Chewing Gum* aired on E4, as it targeted a specific audience with its fresh take on being a young Black woman in contemporary Britain. Since *Chewing Gum* was added to Netflix Worldwide in 2016, it has soared in popularity with American audiences, so much so that the company bought the worldwide rights to a romantic musical starring Michaela Coel in a multi-million-dollar deal. According to Zeba Blay, this 'reportedly makes it the largest single acquisition of a U.K. film ever by the company' (2017).

The sitcom, then, needs to be estimated in the contemporary televisual landscape, and what interests me here is its 'social value' and how 'value' is constructed and ascribed. While Tania Modleski (1979) and many other feminist TV scholars have legitimated the study of soap operas by examining the pleasures they elicit, sitcoms have typically not been viewed in similar terms because, as Mills states, 'the sitcom is often presented as a problem, whose humour contributes (unwittingly?) to stereotyped representations of underprivileged groups, turning such social issues into nothing more than something worthy of laughter' (2009: 10). Coel's series has not been presented as a 'problem' in this respect, however. *Chewing Gum* has been praised for its sensitive yet silly portrayals of race, gender and sexuality, often being described as sex-positive and body-positive in the media.

Chewing Gum, 'Cringe Comedy' and (Re)constructing Black Femininities

The popularity of Coel's series has been exacerbated by the popularity of intersectionality in TV criticism. As has been discussed, it is now commonplace internet vernacular. The term intersectionality signals a change in feminist activism and indicates why Michaela Coel's series, and the writer/performer herself, have been celebrated by critics and audiences in recent years (see, for instance, Bloodworth, 2020 and Dowell, 2020). One of Kathleen Rowe's key figures of 'unruliness', Roseanne Barr, has not embraced these changes in the second decade of the twenty-first century. Though, in the 1980s and 1990s, her comedy series *Roseanne* (ABC, 1988–97 and 2018) was lauded for its realistic portrayal of a working-class American family, after Barr rebooted the sitcom in 2018 it was swiftly cancelled by ABC after the comedy star left a slew of racist tweets likening former President Barack Obama's aide to an ape. According to Jessica Ford: 'Barr's tweet and the cancellation of *Roseanne*, highlight the limits of nostalgia and Roseanne/Barr's particular brand of white feminism [. . .] the political landscape has shifted since the 1990s, with the rise of third and fourth-wave feminisms and intersectional activism' (2018). Suzanne Leonard similarly suggests that 'Barr's scandal has much to teach about the long and complex history of oppression in the United States, the television industry and feminist television studies as a discipline, which has for years celebrated Barr's brash, unapologetic unruliness' (2020: 597).

The complex relationship between 'unruliness' and American society also came to the fore when Donald Trump called Roseanne Barr to congratulate her personally on the comeback of her TV series (BBC News, 2018). As Leonard further suggests, there are striking similarities between the two stars:

> Barr and Trump's […] personas are quite similarly dependent on the idea that they have defied conventions and challenged establishments. We might do well to interrogate this celebration of rulebreaking, especially at a moment when the United States appear to be experiencing a complete breakdown in the social contract precisely thanks to having elected a present who promised—and is delivering—unruliness at every turn. (2020: 599)

With both Barr and Trump 'breaking the rules', there are inevitable limitations to 'unruliness' in feminist media studies when considering its recent use for political conservatism. Coel, however, embodies a new shift taking place, with her focus on Black British femininity and an intersectional approach to televisual storytelling differing greatly from Rowe's focus on the white female body in 1980s/90s America. This begs the question: where do these changes leave Rowe's model of 'unruliness' and Barr's embodiment of said 'unruliness'? In popular film and television, the female body does not have to be transgressive and challenge the status quo to be subversive. As such, an updated model of 'unruliness' needs to account for changes in popular culture, focus on deeper textual/authorial analysis and explore social/cultural changes in comedy representation that, as of late, have showcased an interest in overlapping social issues.

In *Chewing Gum*, intersectionality is conveyed through Tracey's relationships with other characters. For instance, Coel highlights the similarities and differences between Tracey, a working-class Black woman, and Connor, a working-class white man, who both live in the same block of flats and later become boyfriend and girlfriend. In the second episode of *Chewing Gum's* first series, Tracey decides to lose her virginity to Connor at Candice's party. Dressed in her conservative pastel pink and white striped pyjamas, she joins him in the bedroom and straddles him, kissing him passionately. This sounds intense and romantic, but Tracey begins stressing out when her nose starts bleeding. She reassures Connor that she has a nosebleed because she 'really likes' him and then proceeds to dry hump him while licking his eyelids, sucking on his nose and sticking her tongue in his ear. Pushing him down to sit on his face, Tracey turns to the camera and clearly wants to ask us a question we all know the answer to: 'I don't remember if I was supposed to wear clothes for this bit or not. Was it. . .? No, it's too late'. In this scene, Tracey awkwardly tries to navigate Connor's form in a surreal and exaggerated manner via her comically grotesque actions.

Michaela Coel's decision to dress Tracey in pink and white pastel, long-sleeved pyjamas – refusing to show her body – is a visual display of sexual innocence that negates the imagery of Black women as (sexually) aggressive. Black women are often, as Charisse Jones and Kumea Shorter-Gooden argue, 'routinely defined by a specific set of grotesque caricatures that are reductive, inaccurate, and unfair' (2003: 3), but Coel transgresses social respectability – licking, sucking and mounting Connor – to instead exacerbate Tracey's naivety. This subversion of traditional and stereotypical notions of the grotesque is further complicated by the racial dynamics at play here as Tracey, a Black woman, straddles Connor's white, alien body. At the beginning of the episode, she explains how she initially feared kissing a white man, stating:

> I always thought white people were bad kissers and it's not their fault; it's just that they've got really small lips . . . and then they try to compensate for the lack of lips with the tongue, and then the tongue just ends up everywhere just flapping about, you get my drift? (S01E02).

As Kathleen Rowe suggests, the grotesque may be used to interrogate and ultimately subvert patriarchal notions of masculinity and authority, but here it is distinctly white notions of masculinity that are questioned by Tracey's description of white men's tongues as 'flapping about'. In her eyes *they* are grotesque, and this Black female point-of-view that has historically been absent in cultural discourse is presented as both legitimate and logical in this popular comedy's representations.

Similar representational strategies are utilised in the second series when Tracey begins dating an affluent white man – Ash (Jonathan Bailey) – after she breaks up with Connor. While there are racial differences between Tracey and Connor, there are glaring racial *and* class differences between Tracey and Ash. To make matters worse, Ash fetishises Black women. He exoticises Tracey's skin, and because she has been kicked out of the family home and needs somewhere to stay, Tracey attempts to appeal to Ash's sexual fantasies. Dressing in traditional garb, she channels 'tribal Africa' and performs a ritualistic dance in his living room while he masturbates. Filipa Jodelka (2015) argues that Coel's 'incredible timing, warmth and gift for physical comedy basically make her [...] the second coming of Lucille Ball', star of American 1950s sitcom *I Love Lucy* (CBS, 1951–7). When Tracey dances for Ash, it is hilariously exaggerated and absurd, while also overtly desexualised. While the audience laugh at Tracey and her get up here, her actions are so over the top they instead points to the preposterousness of Ash's fantasies instead. Through this, Coel reconfigures how Black women are perceived: they can be awkward as opposed to being stereotyped or typecast as the 'Angry Black Woman' – a trope that characterises Black women as ill-tempered, illogical and ill-mannered.

Coel's decision to display Tracey's sexual innocence in both scenes is important in that she intervenes in the pervasive ideology surrounding hypersexual Black womanhood. Historically, as April D. Lundy argues, '[i]n the 1700s and 1800s, in books and other forms of literature, Europeans habitually depicted African men and women naked and as possessing unusually large sexual organs. Belief in their unrestrained sexuality can be seen in depictions of art as well' (2018). The 'unruly' woman has been defined in similar terms. Using Mikhail Bakhtin's terminology, Kathleen Rowe suggests that she is associated with the grotesque, arguing that '[w]here the classical body privileges its "upper stratum" (the head, the eyes, the faculties of reason), the grotesque body is the body in its "lower stratum" (the eating, drinking, defecating, copulating body)' (1995: 33). This notion of the grotesque body, Rowe further argues, 'bears most relevance to the unruly woman, who so often makes a spectacle of herself with her fatness, pregnancy, age, or loose behavior' (ibid). Yet Rowe fails to recognise how this has functioned across sexual as well as racial lines, given that Black women have often been fetishised, exoticised and demonised through their 'sexual organs' and lower body parts. Coel, however, eschews the typical embrace of grotesque stereotypes. She asserts autonomy over the Black female form by altering its perception, opting to portray herself as innocent and inexperienced. Ironically, she does so while donning a 'tribal' outfit, a nod to racial clichés. In doing so, Coel exposes and undermines the complex, stratified relationships between racial groups through her comedic act.

This awkward characterisation is not to suggest that Tracey has relinquished control in *Chewing Gum* – she remains visually dominant throughout – but Coel's new approach to televisual storytelling has shifted depictions of working-class Black women and what it means to be 'unruly'. In turning to the camera and speaking to the audience directly in these moments, *Chewing Gum* is concerned with what Tracey both sees and does not see via the use of direct address. This technique intensifies 'comic abjection and affective intensity' (Woods, 2019), but it also allows women to take back some degree of control of how their bodies are presented, playing with our expectations as both voyeur and confidante. The audience are heard, their presence felt by the female protagonist. Though this can be seen in other contemporary British comedies by women – such as *Fleabag* and *Miranda* – these are told from distinctly white, middle-class viewpoints. Direct address in *Chewing Gum* fuels empathy for Tracey who has typically been seen as a British cultural 'other' inspiring both fascination and fear. In fact, she is triply demarcated as 'other' through her race, gender *and* class. Discussing race in terms of the 'unruly' woman, Linda Mizejewski argues that:

> [f]or the traditionally attractive white woman in white culture, unruliness can be a liberating quality of female individualism. For the black woman in white culture—someone who is already under suspicion as part of an "unruly" subculture—the opposite occurs: her subjectivity diminishes as she slides into racial stereotype. (2007)

Michaela Coel is subversive because she demonstrates female 'unruliness' by undermining such stereotypes. Tracey is extremely awkward, quirky and unburdened by shame. Her subjectivity is enhanced by direct address, visual control and her loud but endearing characterisation. Coel plays with Black stereotypes and her character lets us in on this, articulating counter-hegemonic perspectives through her comedic display to the audience. It is this delicate balance – and Michaela Coel's 'fastidious' attention to detail in her writing/performance – that has enabled a new version of 'unruliness' to be present in contemporary television.

Indeed, in *Chewing Gum*, it is Ash who is demarcated as different, a rich man located outside of the council estate who attempts to take advantage of Tracey as a working-class Black woman from an East London borough. Michaela Coel does not only showcase an awareness of intersectional thought by contrasting Tracey with white, male characters in the show, however. When Ash's ex-wife Judith (Ayesha Antoine) walks through the door and catches Tracey with her former husband, the audience, seeing that both women are Black, immediately recognise that Ash fetishises *all* Black women. Yet there are significant differences in costume between Judith and Tracey. Judith is dressed in a professional, navy pencil dress – starkly contrasting with the indigenous outfit and colourful ensembles Tracey typically wears – which highlights class differences between the two as well as Ash's absurd homogenisation of Black women's cultural identities.

To overcome this homogenisation, Tracey and Judith join forces against Ash. After rummaging through his kitchen, Tracey angrily pours red wine and smothers marmite on his white sofa, exclaiming 'Would you like some wine with that sir? Yes, black and white, just like you want'. Calmly handing the marmite over to Judith, Tracey utters a thank you before leaving. Judith, smirking, then squeezes more marmite on Ash's sofa in quiet yet exultant glee. The two women's 'unruly' comedic excess here is used as a grotesque form of communication to achieve agency. Kathleen Rowe argues that '[t]he grotesque body is above all the female body, the maternal body, which, through menstruation, pregnancy, childbirth, and lactation, participates uniquely in the process of "becoming"' (1995: 33). This grotesque female body is overflowing, leaking, and although the fluids Tracey and Judith use are not bodily – they nevertheless stand in for the body because, as Tracey asserts, these fluids are 'Black' like their skin. By refusing to use fluids from the body, Michaela Coel again refuses to adhere to traditional notions of the grotesque. Wine and marmite are instead used as emancipatory symbols to repudiate and rebuke, from white males like Ash, attempts to possess ownership over their figures. The grotesque here – that is, the hyperbolic, liberating spray of fluids over the white symbol of patriarchy, capitalism and toxic masculinity (Ash's sofa) – gives these women the opportunity to harness a comedic and chaotic energy.

Though Tracey and Judith share similar life experiences and racial fetishisation from Ash, *Chewing Gum* focuses on class in conjunction with race and gender. Class differences between the pair are alluded to when Judith refers to Candice (who is waiting downstairs) as a 'Peckham princess', to which Tracey replies: 'Judith, my best friend is not a Peckham princess, we are from Tower Hamlets'. The differentiation between these two areas is important for Tracey – with Tower Hamlets being in East London and Peckham in South London. From the 1960s onwards, with mass immigration into London from Black and Asian people, Gillian Evans argues that '[t]he lack of a strong collective vision governing the integration of immigrants into white working-class neighbourhoods led, in some cases, to the forming of racial and ethnic enclaves [. . .] Peckham become known as a "black peoples' manor"' (2010: 123–4).

Images of South London have been depicted in comedies such as *Only Fools and Horses* (BBC One, 1981–2003) and *Desmond's* (Channel 4, 1989–94), the latter being one of the few Black 'shows to successfully reach a mainstream comedy audience in Britain', according to Sarita Malik (2002: 101).

Though Peckham shares similarities with Tower Hamlets because it is also a space where Black working-class families have settled and put down their roots, Tracey is offended that they have been homogenised and conflated by Judith. In her eyes, they cannot be compared. Places perform a crucial function in anchoring people's lives and identities, and for Michaela Coel, working-class communities are separate and distinct. The classed differences between Tracey/Judith and the gendered and racialised differences between Tracey/Ash thus highlight Michaela Coel's concerns with multiple social issues and the ways in which they intersect in *Chewing Gum's* East End, complicating 'unruliness' in the process.

Michaela Coel thus demonstrates that the 'unruly' female body is not only associated with whiteness, and the Black female body disrupts and demonstrates flaws inherent in the concept. Though this form of resistance is not typically afforded to underrepresented groups and is no longer perceived as viable if solely based on visibility, Coel embodies significant changes in feminism from the 1990s to the 2010s. She highlights the importance of liberating Black bodies both from and within the structures of 'unruliness'.

Comedy and Power: From *Chewing Gum* to *I May Destroy You*

Though a sitcom at heart, Coel believes that it is *Chewing Gum's* dramatic elements that are most significant to the show: 'if you look beneath the laughter [...] there is a drama there. I don't believe in comedy as a TV genre – I think there's drama that is funny. Because beyond the laughs there has to be cost and there has to be heart' (Coel, quoted in Yates, 2017). This tendency to favour the dramatic is significant in the contemporary television landscape, particularly since TV drama has seen a resurgence in recent years (see Newman and Levine, 2012), with comedy/dramas, or 'dramedies', being seen as superior to other forms of comedy (Horton, 2016). Coel's interest in drama led to her creating the critically acclaimed British comedy-drama *I May Destroy You* – written, co-directed and executive produced by Coel for BBC One and HBO. As I argue now, the creation of this TV series exemplifies her growing agency in the TV industry.

Coel's gravitation towards drama and her increasing influence in the television industry culminated in the creation of *I May Destroy You*, a series that draws from her own experiences shared at the Edinburgh International Television Festival in 2018. In the prestigious closing MacTaggart Lecture, Coel revealed that she had been sexually assaulted while writing *Chewing Gum* and that this experience inspired the series. Of the forty-two people who have given the speech, Coel is the fifth woman, first person of colour and youngest to deliver the lecture so far. This demonstrates a conscious effort on behalf of the industry to diversify, contemporise and move television forward by providing a platform to somebody new. An annual media event in the UK that brings together those in the industry to discuss problems facing TV, Coel used the Edinburgh TV Festival as an opportunity to speak about how she had been treated by production companies and peers in the wake of her sexual assault, as well as what it is like to be a 'misfit' in TV. In the lecture, Coel recalled her own attack: 'I had an episode due at 7am. I took a break and had a drink with a good friend who was nearby. I emerged into consciousness typing season two, many hours later. I was lucky. I had a flashback. It turned out I'd been sexually assaulted by strangers'. Demonstrating the importance of a relationship between the writer and TV executives, she stated that: 'The first people I called after the police, before my own family, were the producers. How do we operate in this family of television when there is an emergency?'.

Coel's ambivalent relationship with the TV industry did not end here. When she wrote *I May Destroy You*, her initial decision was to go to Netflix because of their history and relationship. *Chewing Gum* was picked up by Netflix, where Michaela Coel gained a broader audience, and in 2018, she starred in the TV series *Black Earth Rising* (BBC Two/Netflix, 2018) and the musical-drama film *Been So Long* (Krishnan, 2018), both (co)produced by the company. Much to Coel's dismay, though Netflix offered her $1 million to create and produce *I May Destroy You*, as Josh Wilson states, 'the sum had strings attached, including full rights ownership away from the creator, something Coel pushed back against' (2020). Unable to even own 0.5% of the show's copyright, she decided to work with British broadcaster BBC One, with financial help from HBO, to maintain artistic and creative control (ibid). According to Coel, the BBC responded to her with an email 'saying she would have everything she wanted: a seat at the table on the production side, full creative control, and the rights to the work' (Coel, quoted in Scott, 2020). Working with the BBC thus gave her creative freedom. To regulate TV, the Communications Act of 2003 in the UK deems that 'qualifying producers—producers whose companies aren't owned by more than

25% by a larger broadcasting entity—retain underlying intellectual property in programmes that are successfully commissioned by U.K. public service broadcasters' (Wilson, 2020). Coel's decision to partner with BBC One and HBO, ensuring her creative ownership, contrasts sharply with Netflix's approach. Though the company has curated new content categories such as 'Representation Matters' and 'Black Lives Matter', a demonstration of inclusivity and solidarity that the company was praised for, Coel's experience underscores the complex negotiation of control in television. These contexts serve to remind us that companies are fuelled by economic logic and the desire to appeal to consumers as opposed to a purely altruistic display of allyship that puts the control firmly in the hands of TV creators.

Talking further about her experiences in the industry, Coel believes she would not be with the BBC right now if she did not start asking Netflix questions. In an interview with *Variety*, she asserts that:

> I think that's the difficult bit — daring to ask questions. That wasn't easy. But then the minute you begin to ask, and you realize that the answers aren't clear, for me then it was very easy [. . .] Keep asking questions and watch people stutter. I began to enjoy it. I began to enjoy realizing that they thought I was just going to take it, then being like 'Surprise bitches, I'm not taking it.' And then actually I was really empowered. (Coel, quoted in Ramachandran, 2020)

It is useful to think about 'empowerment' here, specifically what this term means for Coel and how the 'unruly' woman has often been configured in terms of power dynamics. Kathleen Rowe argues that '[t]he unruly woman points to new ways of thinking about visibility as power. Masquerade concerns itself not only with a woman's ability to look, after all, but also with her ability to affect the terms on which she is seen' (1995: 11). Power creates possibilities, but it has different discursive meanings depending on who is wielding it. Black women are a structurally oppressed group, positioned as subordinate in a hierarchy, and must exercise agency via multiple means. Shardé M. Davis argues that it is words that have 'the capacity to inflict more pain, damage, and humiliation than physical acts—a point illustrated in [bell] hooks's "Tongues of Fire"' (2018: 304). Other Black feminist literature similarly asserts that 'groups lacking social power can "talk back" to external hostilities as a way to resist domination and transform society' (Davis, 2019: 302), with Black women 'self-constructing their own style of speech that is forthright and assertive to dispel stereotypes and display competence in environments rendering them the minority' (ibid: 304, see also Collins, 2015).

These power relations are significant in examining how marginalised women – particularly Black women who are often decentred in TV narratives – are 'unruly' in writing new stories, undermining stereotypes and including those who are typically excluded. Michaela Coel's beginnings in comedy and the subsequent hurdles she has had to overcome demonstrate how contemporary 'unruliness' is rooted in perseverance and asking questions. The term 'fastidious' often implies a meticulous or demanding attitude, which, although sometimes viewed negatively when attributed to women, is in fact a vital characteristic for Black, working-class women striving for excellence in the television industry. Coel's power, that is, her decision to ask questions and persist with her own vision, has been integral in regaining and retaining authorial control. This is entrenched in gendered and racial discourses, as it is not only Coel's 'visible' disruption of social boundaries on-screen that render her 'unruly', but acts that have historically empowered Black women: language, speech and talking back. Perhaps this is why Coel's voice – the way she talks to the camera in *Chewing Gum*, her keynote address at the Edinburgh TV Festival, her negotiation skills with producers and the powerful monologues she gives in *I May Destroy You* – are so impactful.

Indeed, Coel embodies a new kind of 'unruliness', and in many ways, she strays further from Kathleen Rowe's definition than the other women examined in this book – particularly when considering Phoebe Waller-Bridge and Caitlin Moran's lack of intersectional foresight. This is arguably because Coel, and her work, exemplify concerns of fourth-wave feminism at its core, with the movement's focus on intersectionality, rape culture, humour and social media reflected in *Chewing Gum* and *I May Destroy You* (Cochrane, 2013 and 2014; Munro; 2014). This differs heavily from second-wave feminist politics associated with the 'unruly' woman and comedy writer/performer Roseanne Barr, a problematic star whose concerns rest with the white female body and working women. By contrast, Coel's focus on Black British femininity has undermined notions of the 'grotesque' and the body's difficult history with racial discourse. The argument established initially by Kathleen Rowe (1995) – that female comic performance is a social/cultural unruliness as well as grotesque in nature – is ultimately inadequate in exploring Coel's Black, female comic performance in *Chewing Gum*, which I argue requires a new analytical conception to interpret the text.

Note

1. The word 'Black' is capitalised throughout this chapter and in this book to denote someone's race. This is a widely accepted practice by the *New York Times*, *Associated Press* and *Columbia Journalism Review*, who have changed their style guidelines to describe people, culture, art and communities. As Catherine MacKinnon argued in 1982: 'Black is conventionally (I am told) regarded as a color rather than a racial or national designation, hence is not usually capitalized. I do not regard Black as merely a color of skin pigmentation, but as a heritage, an experience, a cultural and personal identity'. Following MacKinnon's reasoning, the renaming and reclaiming of language is used throughout to combat anti-Blackness.

5

Sharon Horgan, Comedy Screenwriting and Starting Merman: Recognising Authorship and Entrepreneurship in TV Comedy

So far, this book has examined British writer/performers in relation to class, gender, race and regionality. This chapter will therefore acknowledge the importance of Irish authors to the current comedy landscape. Shilpa Ganatra argues that there is a 'a new wave of Irish women playing a central role in TV comedy' (2018), and Sharon Horgan in particular has gained significant attention from critics and audiences for her televisual output. However, she shares more in common with comics such as Phoebe Waller-Bridge and Julia Davis for her caustic and wry humour. As Horgan herself puts it, she has made a career of portraying woman who are a 'bit messy' (Horgan, quoted in Harrison, 2019). Examining her body of work from the 2010s – *Pulling, Motherland, Catastrophe, Shining Vale* and *Bad Sisters* – I specifically look at how she has used comedy as a vehicle to explore the stages of life: from 'messy' young women in their twenties; to mothers in their thirties and forties 'behaving badly'; and women in their forties or older who are filing for divorce or are otherwise in failed marriages. These characters are 'unruly' in their funny and filthy behaviour.

While this chapter looks at the textual depiction of these women, it also explores Horgan's roles as an Irish showrunner, writer, (executive) producer and performer – exploring in detail why she has been coined 'the busiest woman in British television' (Harrison, 2019). It examines Horgan as a transnational writer and comedian, specifically the relationship between her Irish roots, London-centric series and recent American comedy, to analyse how women in TV comedy navigate the broader televisual landscape. Though both writing and portraying 'unruly' women who struggle with modern womanhood and motherhood, Horgan's multiple roles showcase how women's television work functions as a form of intense labour. This chapter will, therefore, also study Horgan's entrepreneurship as the co-owner of production company Merman. By examining Horgan's work on-screen via textual analysis, her identity as an Irish emigrant and ageing star, as well as interviews which convey the ideologies of her entrepreneurship and relationship with industry, this chapter takes a holistic approach to analyse Horgan as a complex, skilled and 'fastidious' comedian.

First, however, it is important to provide a brief history of Horgan's personal life and professional career thus far. Horgan was born in Hackney but grew up on a turkey farm in Bellewstown, County Meath. She returned to London in her twenties to be 'discovered', attending drama courses as a struggling actor. Here, she worked at a Jobcentre in Kilburn for six years, quitting at age twenty-seven to study English and American Studies at Brunel University (Bromwich, 2015). After graduating in 2000, she worked with her writing partner Dennis Kelly, winning the 2001 BBC New Comedy award for Sketch Writing and Performance (Murphy, 2013). There followed several TV appearances before the pair came to prominence with the BBC Three sitcom *Pulling*, which ran for two series from 2006–8. The TV series that arguably catapulted Sharon Horgan to international fame was her transatlantic TV series *Catastrophe*, which she co-wrote and starred in with American comedian, actor and writer Rob Delaney. After watching her TV series *Pulling*, Delaney had admired Horgan from afar, and the pair connected on Twitter before meeting in person and deciding to write the series together (Blake, 2015). *Catastrophe* aired on British terrestrial television in 2015 before reaching American audiences via Amazon Prime's streaming service in 2017. This import/export relationship between UK and US TV production is reflected in the series plot. *Catastrophe* follows an Irish primary school teacher, Sharon, who unexpectedly becomes pregnant following a fling with Rob, an American advertising executive, while visiting London on a business trip. Sharon decides to keep the baby, and the sitcom follows the domestic interpersonal dynamics between the pair, that is, their blossoming relationship and the complexities of having a baby with a relative stranger.

Comedy, *Catastrophe* and Conventional Depictions of 'Unruliness'

This first section will explore Horgan's characters on-screen, specifically how they display conventions of 'unruliness' dictated by Rowe (1995). Unlike Phoebe Waller-Bridge and her dramatic personas in *Fleabag* and *Crashing*,

I argue that Horgan's 'unruliness' is shaped by her disavowal of middle-class values and that, because of this, she escapes criticism from cultural critics. This highlights how an understanding of class is integral to understanding the politics of women's comedy television.

As noted throughout this book, Kathleen Rowe characterises the 'unruly' woman by her excessive corporeality and unmanageable desires or behaviours (1995), traits that are evident in the opening sequence of *Catastrophe*. In the series' first episode, Sharon Horgan's character is having sex with Rob Delaney after meeting at a busy bar. For Kathleen Rowe, the 'unruly' woman 'has sex voraciously' (ibid: 36), and this is depicted as open, 'messy' and humorous, with Caroline Bainbridge similarly arguing that 'Horgan's work puts "difficult" female experience and feelings centre screen, avoiding the use of pedestrian gendered stereotypes once so predominantly associated with the television sitcom' (2020: 72). For instance, when Sharon goes back to Rob's hotel room, they passionately kiss as she expresses her surprise over his lack of hairiness. Rob tells her that he does, in fact, have 'hairy balls' while unknowingly lowering Sharon onto the leftover pizza he had abandoned on his bed the night before. Apologising, he throws the plate of pizza at the wall, and Sharon laughs when the plate smashes into pieces. As the opening montage of *Catastrophe* demonstrates, Horgan and Delaney have used comedy to articulate the active sexuality of middle-aged women via 'sexual realism', that is, a deglamourised and 'cringe-worthy' spectacle (Wheatley, 2016). Helen Wheatley has noted that, in several key dramas, 'the spectacle of sex is tied to the portrayal of recognisable experience' (2016: 204). In her 'Television Desire Survey', she discovered that a considerable number of women find that realism is key to their appreciation of sex on television, whether it's in portraying the often clumsy or challenging aspects of sex, or in showing sex as it realistically happens within an unfolding story (ibid). This engagement with female desires, identities and stories that challenge social conventions is evident in *Catastrophe*. Though it privileges the heterosexual couple – and is certainly not radical in its sexual politics – comedy as a genre offers the potential for liberatory and transformative constructions of femininity, with the hedonistic behaviour of Sharon evident in her carefree attitude and Cheshire cat grin.

The portrayal of the 'unruly' woman in television is often designed to appeal to female viewers who seek solace and identification with characters that challenge dominant norms of femininity. This is evident in *Catastrophe*, where the main character, Sharon, experiences an unexpected pregnancy. The concept of motherhood is further explored in *Motherland*, a series that draws on stories from the female writers of the show – Sharon Horgan, Holly Walsh (*Dead Boss, The Other One*) and Helen Serafinowicz – to portray the politics of PTA meetings, school-gate drop-offs, playdates and forced interaction with other mothers. In both *Catastrophe* and *Motherland*, as Jo Littler argues, this chaotic comedy is a critical representational strategy in foregrounding the 'mother behaving badly', a figure who is 'not castigated, but rather presented as simultaneously fun, risqué and as justified in adopting these moments of carnivalesque excess' (2020: 500). Littler reiterates this when discussing how '*Motherland* satirizes the chaos and the temporary, carnivalesque behaviour that not only gets them through the day but indicates women on the edge' (ibid: 506). Women 'on the edge' in *Motherland* include the perpetually flustered and uptight Julia (Anna Maxwell Martin); blunt, quick-witted and single mother Liz (Diane Morgan); as well as smug, alpha-mum Amanda (Lucy Punch).

Carnivalesque pleasures and excess are often connected to the 'unruly' woman's appearance and behaviours, as she subverts the dominant culture through humour, chaos, hyperbole and anarchy. The 'unruly' woman also offers a model of women's carnival collective action. Despite this, in *Motherland*, there are instances where this supposed collectivity deteriorates and 'unruliness' loses its political power. For instance, Liz is the clear outlier of the show's mothers (and father): Julia, Liz, Meg, Anne, Amanda and Kevin. Morgan's distinctive regional (Bolton) accent demarcates her as 'other' because she is a working-class mother amongst a sea of competitive middle-class women. Littler suggests that she problematically plays 'a pedagogic role from which the middle-classes learn. This is the case [. . .] with Liz in *Motherland*, who helps the character through which the series is "focalized", Julia, to be less uptight and "cut loose"' (2020: 512). The juxtaposition of Liz's working-classness with her middle-class peers not only highlights the social divisions within the group but also sets the stage for Horgan's self-reflective critique of the show's limited representation.

Unlike Phoebe Waller-Bridge, Horgan has not been criticised by the public or the press for her 'unruly' depictions of middle-class womanhood, in part because Horgan has admitted to oversights in her work. For instance, *Motherland* was initially comprised solely of white women's experiences. Sharon Horgan has said she belatedly realised that this was an oversight: '"We thought it was really fucking white," [. . .] "By the time we came to watch it, we thought, "shame on us"' (Horgan, quoted in *Chortle*, 2019). Unlike comedians such as Caitlin Moran, Horgan has navigated contemporary politics through an understanding that 'intersectionality has become an ideal benchmark for feminism' (Kanai, 2021: 519). To remedy this, in series 2, the creators of *Motherland* added a new Black character to the roster of mums: Tanya Moodie as Meg, the raucous socialite. She, too, is typically 'unruly' in her behaviour, excessively drinking and laughing from the off, at one point being held up by the police for urinating in the street. However, it is clear that *Motherland* differs from other comedies, such as Michaela Coel's *Chewing Gum* and *I May Destroy You*, as it reinforces comedic stereotypes of Black women. For instance, Meg fits into the stereotype of the 'strong Black woman' (SBW). After drinking, she wakes up hangover-free wakes up hangover-free, ready to start the day with her five children and job as a high-flying executive. In series 3, when she is diagnosed with cancer, she is shown to be naturally resilient, independent and emotionally controlled (see Wallace, 1978 and Woods-Giscombé, 2010), handling her diagnosis with quiet calmness and with almost no side effects other than hair loss. As Roxanne A. Donovan and Lindsey M. West argue, these '[c]hallenges that would break others just make SBW stronger' (2015: 385). This complicated representation of race demonstrates how women in British and Irish TV comedy predominantly focus on the politics of whiteness, as well as how intersectionality as a concept has benefitted white women's work.

Horgan has also evaded criticism often aimed at women comedy writers because she writes working-class characters with particular reverence. In an interview with the *Financial Times*, Horgan maintains that she identifies with embattled Julia's frenzied energy but that she would love to be more like the laidback and droll Liz, who is based on a friend of hers (Horgan, quoted in Jacobs, 2017). These characters actively disavow middle-class tastes and values, much like Horgan's 'unlikeable' women in *Pulling*. This series draws on her experiences as a twenty-something year old living in 'low-level shared accommodation for years' as well as being 'in rubbish relationships' and 'shit jobs' (Horgan, quoted in Raphael, 2009). It follows Donna (played by Horgan), who moves in with her two friends, Karen (Tanya Franks) and Louise (Rebekah Staton), after breaking up with her fiancé in the series' first episode. Navigating their thirties in Penge, south London, *Pulling* focuses on the romantic and professional misadventures of these three dysfunctional women, and as Horgan argues, the show has 'no moral centre' (ibid).

In *Pulling's* first series, the rejection of a middle-class identity becomes evident when Donna dates Sam (Tom Ellis), who has 'highbrow' tastes and wants her to attend an art gallery to meet his friends (S01E06). Her ex-boyfriend Karl (Cavan Clerkin), who she frequently visits to watch the

British cookery programme *Saturday Kitchen* (BBC One, 2002–), tells her that she'll hate it because she cried at the Tate Modern when her feet were sore. As Karl notes, she also prefers reading celebrity gossip in *Heat* magazine. Donna, however, maintains that reading *Heat* is 'ironic' and she enjoys watching movies like *Miss Congeniality 2* (Pasquin, 2005) with Karl because 'you can't believe how bad it is, but you have to keep watching'. Her lack of middle-class decorum becomes further apparent when she attends the art gallery with Sam and tells the exhibition curator, Sam's friend Alice (played by Alice Lowe), that the art is 'shit' without realising it is her work.

On the one hand, Donna's so-called 'ironic' consumption of 'lowbrow' products is a way to position herself above perceived working-class tastes and those who consume 'bad' cultural objects. Yet, on the other hand, the audience laughs *at* Donna because her enjoyment of these 'bad' cultural objects is still palpable. Broadly speaking, Donna's tastes and values reject the aspirational model of femininity almost impossible to achieve. This differentiates Sharon Horgan from other 'unruly' and 'fastidious' comedians such as Phoebe Waller-Bridge, who critics and audiences regard ambivalently for producing a common-sense 'truth' of middle/upper-classness.

It can be questioned whether some depictions of 'unruliness' have lost their socio-political force in a postfeminist milieu that heavily focuses on privilege being maintained within a discourse of individualism, specifically in TV series such as *Pulling*, *Catastrophe* and *Fleabag*. Yet, as Meg Tully cogently argues, *Catastrophe* applies 'postfeminist pressures to marriage and parenthood, eviscerating the stereotype of the woman who "has it all", using irony and spectacle to offer a 'feminist antidote to postfeminist culture' (2018). Tully's reference to irony here is significant in that this is a comedic mode often used for incongruity or, as Rowe puts it, to 'evoke ambivalence through delight on the one hand, and unease, derision, or fear on the other' (1995: 30). Female protagonists in series by Sharon Horgan often enact deviant behaviours and subvert what is deemed socially acceptable for women. As Nancy A. Walker and Zita Dresner argue, incongruity decodes the patriarchy's myths by 'exposing the discrepancies between the realities of women's lives and the images of women promoted by the culture' (1998: 174). Horgan creates such characters in *Catastrophe*, *Motherland* and *Pulling* who, according to Caroline Bainbridge are 'crudely and boldly enunciating sometimes shocking or distasteful opinions and thoughts' (2020: 73). Bainbridge further suggests that '[t]hese moments reveal the importance of incongruity in the conventions of comedy, such that the apparent disparity between what is expected of women and what women actually say and do produces laughter' (ibid). This is evident in *Pulling* from the offset. When Donna wakes up one day and realises that she no longer loves her fiancé, Karl, she tells her friends that she was 'looking at him snoring, with a bit of saliva falling out of his mouth – and [. . .] wondered what it would be like to cut his head off' (S01E01). Despite this, Donna plans her hen night, and Karen tells the group that she has organised strippers for the occasion. Donna informs Karen that her other friend Tanya is actually the maid of honour and has planned an evening at the bingo hall. Incredulously, Karen retorts, 'I thought you just gave her that cause she's fat? You can't be serious, Donna, little fat Tanya?'. With Donna dreaming of her fiancé's death and Karen's cruel jokes, Horgan and Kelly create comedy through incongruity, that is, from the perceived violation of norms and social order of what is expected from women. Textually, a rich river of cruel comedy runs through Horgan's work, much like in the works of Julia Davis and Phoebe Waller-Bridge, via the ambivalent and abject. On-screen, their characters are noisy, joke-making and excessively vulgar rebels.

Sharon Horgan's Relationship with Nationality and Ageing

So far, this chapter has detailed how Sharon Horgan creates 'unruly' characters on-screen. This section will explore how Horgan's role as an Irish showrunner, writer, (executive) producer and actor has affected her work. The social and cultural analysis of Horgan's identity will reveal how her nationality and age have affected the ways in which her image is produced, distributed and shown. Such an analysis will create a divergence between the author and their 'unruly' characters, frequently conflated in cultural discourse, to explore the nuances of Horgan's identity as a woman in comedy.

In the twenty-first century, according to Ciara Barrett, 'Irishness as cultural currency, or as a potential star attribute, has been effectively incompatible with "femininity" in popular media' (2014: 62). Instead, 'Irishness' as an 'ethnic and cultural marker has, for the most part, been understood and made appreciable as a star attribute (and thus commodifiable and consumable for a mass market) when it is gendered male' (ibid: 63). During the 2010s, the entertainment industry saw a surge of talented Irish women, such as comedians, writers and performers. Notable figures include Lisa McGee, Yasmine Akram, Catherine Bohart and Joanne McNally. Among them, Sharon Horgan and Aisling Bea stand out for their deep bond, which they describe as 'sisterly.'

This connection is vividly portrayed in Bea's series *This Way Up*, where they act as on-screen sisters, with Horgan also serving as the show's producer. The collaboration of these two women exemplifies the growing presence and impact of Irish women in comedy. Their success is intimately intertwined with their 'fluid transnational mobility', as Anthony P. McIntyre contends (2022: 156). Twenty-first century cultural expressions of Irishness take this for granted, with McIntyre arguing that their stardom is configured through three elements (ibid): corporeal movement (living, working and visiting Ireland, Britain and America), textual content (with their TV series or other creative content being set in these nations as well as referencing them implicitly or explicitly) and their status as entrepreneurs within an industry that now has the infrastructure to support mobility (with the development of subscription video on demand, for instance).

Sharon Horgan's Irish identity is integral to understanding her creative output, then, particularly textually. For instance, *Catastrophe* draws on her experiences meeting her then-husband Jeremy Rainbird, who, like protagonist Rob, works in advertising. It also documents her surprise when she found out she was pregnant six months into their relationship; only in *Catastrophe*, Sharon becomes pregnant after a brief fling. Horgan's character Sharon gives her baby the Irish name Muireann, a name Rob cannot pronounce, but Sharon and her Irish family can. This storyline is based in reality: Sharon's then real-life husband Rainbird cried at the prospect of naming their eldest daughter Muireann, and the pair compromised by calling her Sadhbh instead (Monaghan, 2016). Significantly, Irish names are referred to throughout the series, despite Sharon Horgan's star power and Irishness not being contained in her own. Pat Fitzpatrick's tongue-in-cheek book *101 Reasons Why Ireland Is Better Than England* (2020: 57) states that Sharon Horgan is successful because 'you can pronounce her name phonetically. This last bit matters a lot if you're going to make it in the UK. It would have been more of a struggle if she was called Caoimhe'. Her name is relatively common amongst English speakers, allowing her to traverse Ireland, Britain and America with greater ease. Elsewhere in *Catastrophe*, Horgan frequently incorporates Irish references that she argues only Irish citizens can understand, for instance, when her characters discuss having a post office bank account with no money (O'Connor, 2017). This semi-autobiographical mining of collective and national memories differs from other offerings by women that exclusively focus on the individual and the personal, thereby drawing attention to the importance of Horgan's roots as well as the material, social and cultural realities of what it means to be a flourishing emigrant traversing Ireland, Britain and America in the twenty-first century.

Examining Horgan's work through the prism of nationality, her hybridity has affected relations and exchanges in the Anglo-American TV broadcasting ecology (with its shared language and cultural heritage). Horgan has spoken of this relationship in multiple interviews, arguing that two significant changes have increased the visibility of her work. First, she contends that television networks are driven by economic factors and have recognised that Irish sitcoms have the potential to achieve remarkable international success (Horgan, quoted in Harrison, 2021). Second, Horgan notes that the 'special relationship' between Britain and North America has been strengthened in comedy, and a broader 'world connection' has been established through the popularity of series such as the French comedy-drama *Call My Agent!* (France Télévisions and Netflix, 2015–) (ibid). As well as creating series set in Ireland (*Women on the Verge*), Britain (*Dead Boss, Motherland, Pulling*) and America (*Divorce, Shining Vale*), Horgan has teamed up with Paul Feig (*Bridesmaids*) and Lionsgate to remake *Motherland* for an American audience (Kanter, 2021), demonstrating how transatlanticism has shifted into a new normalised cultural space on English-language television.

Alongside Horgan's Irishness, her age has been a topic of interest in the press. Horgan frequently writes from her own experiences and has created TV series that, as of late, tell the stories of women who are typically in their forties and older. For instance, horror-comedy *Shining Vale* stars Courtney Cox as Pat Phelps, who, after cheating on her husband with the handyman, moves to Shining Vale to navigate mid-life, marriage problems and raising terrible teens. In *Shining Vale*, Pat Phelps is convinced that she is either depressed or possessed because she dreams about a woman named Rosemary (Mira Sorvino), who is a ghost, demon or a part of Pat's psyche. In many ways, the series evokes the unease older women experience when going through menopause, and Horgan has discussed the difficulties of this period when writing Cox's character:

> It's hard to always diagnose when you're losing your marbles just through life in general at this stage of your life. Because I just think it's the hardest possible period. You're in a situation where chemically, you're all over the place. Your children are reaching an age where, usually, they're teenagers going through terrible times themselves, and you're at the least emotionally equipped to deal with it, because you're also off your nut. Your parents are getting older. You're losing

> people. It's a really emotionally draining tough time. And so I think with Pat, we just gave her all of that. (Horgan, quoted in McFarland, 2022)

Here, Horgan discusses both the physical and emotional changes women face during this time. However, Pat Phelps is still depicted as a 'sexed' being rather than a 'sexless' body commonly associated with ageing women because she displays deep corporeal desires. Rather than objectifying Cox's character, Horgan contributes to a realist sensibility in televisual fiction by depicting the complexities of women's wants and needs.

Horgan has been treated ambivalently in the press, however, and she has been subject to myths circulating around traditional gender roles and expectations of ageing. For one, Horgan has frequently been described as 'making up for lost time' because she did not find fame until she was in her 30s (see *You Magazine*, 2021). Management of the ageing self is thus articulated within the neoliberal context of personal responsibility. Decca Aitkenhead, when interviewing Horgan for *The Times*, similarly frames ageing in this way when she states that '[m]ost sensible young actors set themselves a target: if they haven't made a success of their career by 30, it will be time to do something else. [...] But every now and then someone blows a hole through the theory — and top of that list would be Sharon Horgan' (2019).

Much like Julia Davis, Horgan's ageing and creative process are connected to her characters on-screen, with interviewer Eva Wiseman for *Stylist* stating that '[t]o meet 45-year-old Horgan is to be confused, because the characters she plays feel so close to real life it's hard to know where Sharon Horgan ends and Sharon *Catastrophe* begins. They look very similar' (2016). This, of course, is a tongue-in-cheek reference to Horgan using her real name in the series, but a focus on where the fictional begins and the real ends has affected expectations of her performance and craft. Female comic creativity often defaults to an assumption of autobiography, and in an interview with Brian Moylan for *The Guardian*, Horgan and Delaney say that they 'settled on the fact that everything is about 49% autobiographical' in *Catastrophe* (Moylan, 2015). Forty-nine per cent is a significant figure to use. It suggests that, though the author and their characters are often conflated for women comedians in particular, Horgan has been careful to note that the autobiographical does not form the majority of her work.

When interviewing Horgan, critic Hadley Freeman notes that she lacks the qualities of her on-screen characters. Freeman expects her 'to be prickly like Julia in Motherland, self-confident like Sharon in Catastrophe, maybe even a little cruel, like Donna in Pulling' (2022). Nevertheless, Horgan seems 'mainly anxious, peppering her conversation with self-deprecation and hesitant "um, y'knows". She has the nervy energy of someone who has 17 things left on her to-do list and it's five minutes to midnight' (ibid). Journalists often conflate both character and creator when discussing women in comedy. In some ways, this is intimately connected to the policing of ageing female bodies in terms of how they display normative markers of traditional femininity. Eva Wiseman notes that '[t]here's an initial softness to Horgan that she doesn't write into her characters' (2016). As argued in the chapter on Julia Davis, there is an expectation on the comedy writer/performer to act and behave as their on-screen personas because of the breakdown between stardom and celebrity (Mills, 2010). This is also clear in articles on Sharon Horgan. Though the description of her 'softness' can be seen as celebratory, she was expected to be like her characters – 'prickly' and 'cruel'. The media often portrays older women as bitter, mean and complaintive, highlighting the intense scrutiny ageing women face (Lemish & Muhlbauer, 2012). Sharon Horgan's public perception and success are thus significantly influenced by gender roles, expectations surrounding age and the conflation of her characters with her real-life personality. These factors mirror broader issues in the media's treatment of women in comedy and the cultural privileging of youth over age. Her experiences highlight the challenges faced by women in the entertainment industry as they navigate societal expectations and stereotypes while pursuing their creative endeavours.

Moving to Merman: Female Comedians and Entrepreneurship

The following section examines Horgan's role as an author and entrepreneur to foreground the labour needed for women to succeed in the contemporary Anglo-American mediascape. This approach underlines the significance of Horgan's craft and hence her comic creativity. Here, I will examine Horgan and her production company Merman, which she co-founded with Clelia Mountford. This will reveal how Horgan's labour is constructed in the media, specifically how her transnational mobility is intimately intertwined with her 'fastidiousness' and status as 'the busiest woman in British television' (Harrison, 2019).

In 2014, Merman was created by Horgan and Mountford. As a company, it has (co)produced many shows, including Horgan's own series *Divorce*, *Catastrophe*, *Motherland*, *Women on the Verge* (W, 2018) and *Bad Sisters*, as well as other TV series created by and/or centring women, including *There She Goes* (BBC, 2018–20), *This Way Up*, *Frayed* (ABC and Sky, 2019–) and a collection of Halloween-themed comedy shorts curated by the company, directed by new and established female directors. In 2020, the company released their first feature film, *Herself*, a drama directed by Phyllida Lloyd which tells the story of a single mother in Ireland who escapes her abusive partner with her two young children. Merman's work extends past the televisual landscape – with the company also producing commercials and branded content. Before founding Merman, Clelia held roles as Head of Comedy at RDF and Head of Radio and TV Script Associate at TalkbackThames. She has developed and produced many other projects in the UK and US including, *Mr. Sloane* (Sky Atlantic, 2014), *Cockroaches* (ITV2, 2015) and *A Young Doctor's Notebook* (Sky Arts, 2012–13). Like other comedy auteures in this book, Sharon Horgan collaborates with women frequently, and her working relationship with Mountford has been imperative to the creation of Merman. They met on the set of *The Increasingly Poor Decisions of Todd Margaret* (IFC and More4, 2010–16), with Horgan as actor and Mountford as producer. Mountford also produced Horgan's directorial debut, *The Week Before Christmas* (2012), for Sky's *Little Crackers* strand. After working together, the pair decided to team up to take creative and financial control over their own work (McLean, 2016). Since then, the company has worked on multiple large-scale projects, and it has signed a two-year deal with Comcast in the US and Sky television in the UK (White, 2019).

This partnership demonstrates the impact of a female presence within the industry. From the 1990s, as Julia Hallam argues, women were successfully challenging the male-dominated hierarchies of Britain's broadcast institutions (2007), and, since then, production companies like Merman, Red Production Company (for more on Red see Johnson, 2019), Monumental Pictures, Wildgaze Films and the aptly named Sister Pictures are showcasing women's representation in senior positions. The increasing presence of women in media and cultural production industries has challenged the previous male dominance in these fields. This shift has led to more diverse on-screen representations and has compelled companies to cater to previously underserved audiences. The change is driven by heightened competition in a saturated market, where companies must differentiate themselves and appeal to a broader range of viewers to remain competitive.

When discussing their collaborative efforts, both Horgan and Mountford have stressed that they work with many female talents and creatives. In an apt interview with *CherryPicks*, a 100% female force of film critics, Mountford has said that the 'managing director, finance director, and head of production all have a great productive energy and shorthand together [...] I think the relationships between the women in our team are similar to a sisterly dynamic' (2021). The term 'sister' holds significant weight and is a familial bond often referred to by women in the cultural and creative industries. This is exemplified by Horgan's series *Bad Sisters*, in which she describes sisterhood on the show as 'an intimate thing' and a 'passionate kind of love' (Horgan, quoted in Webley Adler, 2022). These relationships are emulated off-screen, too, as Horgan hired, for the most part, all female editors and all female directors of photography (Ebejer, 2022).

Collaborators of Horgan have also emphasised their strong connection with her. In an interview with Channel 4, Aisling Bea discussed her relationship with Sharon Horgan, stating, 'I look up to her in a big sisterly way. I'm a massive fan of hers. I have an absolute desire to make her laugh' (Channel 4, 2019b). The term embodies deeper significance for the female-led production company Sister. When one of the founders, Elisabeth Murdoch, is asked about the name and its principles, she argues that it is 'more about values than the gender. The values of sisterhood like friendship, honesty, [and] loyalty [...] it's the idea of having a safe place where you'll find support' (Murdoch, quoted in Fleming Jr, 2019). While female producers and companies tend to note that their workforce is primarily (though not entirely) women-centric, their programming, on the other hand, consists of both male and female-driven content, and the desire to move away from focusing exclusively on gender is clear in Sister's statement about its values. It also points to the struggle female producers have in categorising their work by gender/sex, as this ultimately compartmentalises and constrains their work.

In their examination of creative professionals in comedy and the British television industry, Brett Mills and Sarah Ralph highlight the inherent uncertainties surrounding the concept of 'feminine humour'. As they suggest, 'denying that there is something we call "feminine humour", but then arguing that more women should be involved in production because they are likely to bring different creative ideas to the table, is evidence of the recurring contradictions of binary gender models' (2015: 105). This tension is evident in the responses of both Merman and Sister, who are eager to reclaim female voices and female experiences but do not want to create boundaries and borders around their work – with Mountford reassuring the interviewer for *CherryPicks* that there are *some* men on the team (2021). This tension is also evident within this book, which strives not to create a mode of 'feminine' or 'female' humour but nevertheless notices important similarities between the women who generate comedy in Britain and Ireland. Horgan evidently does not approve of this terminology either, arguing that '"[w]omen's comedy" has never felt like a thing for me in terms of what I watch, read or write. Something's either funny or it's not' (Horgan, quoted in Tate, 2015b). This is reflected in Horgan's creative work in that she collaborates with both men and women frequently (for instance, with Dennis Kelly on her hit breakthrough series *Pulling*, Rob Delaney on *Catastrophe* and Holly Walsh on *Dead Boss* and *Motherland*).

However, Horgan notes that she is determined to employ female creatives and fights back against those who deny women access:

> Women looking out for other women is part of what we're trying to do at Merman. If we're suggesting directors for something, we put together a very female-heavy list – I think you have to do that at the moment to force change. You have to vouch for people. If they don't have the experience – which they won't have because it's been a male-dominated industry for so many years – then you have to say, 'Well look, *we* have the experience and *we've* made TV, so I suggest you trust this person'. The big thing is people have to keep pushing forward with it. It can't be an idea that's in vogue now, it has to be something that's continued and the push for change has to be relentless. (Horgan, quoted in Goddard, 2020)

Key words here, such as 'force' and 'push', emphasise how strength, willpower and vigour are needed when employing women in the media industry – to navigate the social, political and cultural landscape in ways that emphasise and endorse women's success. As discussed in the chapter examining Michaela Coel, her perseverance and being hard to please, of being 'fastidious' in her exactitude, are central to her contemporary 'unruliness'. Coel's identity as a Black, working-class woman, however, has added barriers to the success that Horgan has achieved.

The ways in which Horgan has created her own company with Clelia Mountford through these specific industrial practices positions her as an 'auteur-entrepreneur' (McIntyre, 2020), that is, a business owner and televisual creator who straddles two seemingly opposite concepts: creativity and industry. Helene Ahl and Susan Marlow argue that '[s]uccessful liberated independent working women are celebrated as those who have effectively used their agency to negotiate the complexities of contemporary society to take advantage of the opportunities offered'. Since women's entrepreneurship is centred upon the agentic potential of the self, it has been heavily discussed in debates around postfeminism (see Lewis, 2014 and Gill, 2014, for instance). These discussions often revolve around themes of individualism, autonomy and self-governance. On a professional and personal level, entrepreneurship offers a stable production context for women's careers while also enhancing their institutional reputation. By navigating the contemporary televisual landscape – creating new ventures as their independent and enterprising selves – women in comedy carve out new spaces in a distinctly neoliberal context that stresses personal agency, responsibility and freedom of choice. Horgan's enterprise and hard work are often discussed in news/magazine articles and interviews, where she is described as rarely taking breaks and, if at all, procrastinating. Rob Delaney, for instance, talks admiringly of Horgan, stating that she has a 'work ethic that is superhuman', with both comics being 'workaholics to the point of self-harm' (Delaney, quoted in Day, 2015). Horgan herself has admitted that her habits are unhealthy in interviews (see Elmhirst, 2019). Contemporary cultural work is, as Jennifer Whitson, Bart Simon and Felan Parker argue, 'rooted both in individualizing discourses of creative genius and wider neoliberal pressures to individualize responsibility and risk' (2021: 620), which is evident in discussions of Horgan's workload(s). In other words, the discussion of Horgan's 'creative genius' undermines the structural issues in the television industry, thereby contributing to inequalities in the field.

In considering Horgan's status as an entrepreneur dictated by societal discourses and identity politics, it is useful to consider Patricia Lewis's (2014) framework: that women occupy one of four entrepreneurial femininities, each characterised by varying degrees of masculinity and femininity. These are as follows: individualised, maternal, relational and excessive. 'Individualised entrepreneurial femininity', she argues, emphasises 'the gender neutrality and meritocracy of the world of entrepreneurship' (ibid: 118). More specifically, Lewis contends that in this mode of entrepreneurship, success is perceived as performing 'gender-neutral methods, routines and rituals, allied to a strong belief that individuals have an equal chance to succeed if they are ambitious and hard-working' (ibid). This conforms to the postfeminist perspective that women are now active, dynamic and autonomous individuals who establish a 'strict separation between home and work' (ibid). By contrast, the second category is based around the maternal and connects to the long-standing idea that women launch businesses to secure flexibility around childcare responsibilities and domestic work.

Third, women who participate in 'relational entrepreneurial femininity' draw on the discourse of difference, in which it is suggested that women 'lead through participation, power-sharing, and information exchange [...] rejecting hierarchical relationships in favour of a team-based approach characterized by understanding and sympathy for others; [...] and putting an emphasis on cooperation and networking over competition and growth' (ibid: 121). This highlights the contribution that women's unique viewpoints can bring to organisational structures, in which the conventional masculine idea of entrepreneurship heavily differs. Finally, 'excessive entrepreneurial femininity' refers to women who are perceived as displaying too much femininity or the wrong kind of femininity within a business context. The value of femininity in organisations is often seen as dependent on two factors. First, women are expected to be 'properly' feminine, meaning they should exhibit enough feminine qualities to benefit the business without engaging in overt or unwarranted displays of femininity. Second, when women do display stereotypically feminine behaviours, there is often an expectation that they must compensate for this by also conforming to traditionally masculine norms of professionalism. In other words, women in business are often expected to strike a delicate balance between being feminine enough to be seen as valuable, but not so feminine as to be seen as unprofessional or inappropriate in a business setting.

These four entrepreneurial femininities can be complementary and overlapping, with Horgan embodying both the 'relational' model and the 'individualised' model. She represents the former in that Merman, as a company, clearly values cooperation. This can be said of television more broadly, given that it is a fundamentally collaborative medium involving numerous personnel, but for Horgan, '[t]here's something about helping someone bring their vision together' (Horgan, quoted in Ingle, 2021). Clelia Mountford has specifically emphasised how important this work style is to the company. For instance, when discussing the creation of *Motherland*, she affirms how the series was a distillation of many ideas:

> It was everyone's experience. I've got kids, and we all threw in experiences of our own and we created this document of stories. In the early days, we had a writer's room of stand-ups, who were parents, and who also came up with ideas and stories. Helen Linehan, whose idea it originally was, has got amazing stories from being a mother [...] With the second series, Holly Walsh and Sharon Horgan wrote together, and Helen and Barunka O'Shaughnessy wrote together. They each wrote

three scripts and then swapped over and made notes on each other's scripts. (2021: 134)

This example showcases how women-owned production companies operate: with teamwork inciting greater diversity in what ideas get expressed and exchanged in the creative process of writing. Off-screen, Horgan is using her influence to foster new opportunities for women across Ireland, Britain and America, which Anthony P. McIntyre argues 'bears similarity to the diasporic networking for employment opportunities that has been a mainstay of Irish emigration for generations' (2022: 164). She also has great impact on ageing female workers in the industry, employing women in their forties and older. In 2018, Ofcom found that on British television 'the ratio of people on screen who appear to be younger than 45 was broadly equal, but for people aged 45 and over was skewed so that there were two to three times more men than women' (2018: 20). Similarly, on prime-time American television, Martha M. Lauzen found '39% of male characters were 40 and older but only 24% of female characters were 40 and older' (2018: 8). With this in mind, it is significant that Horgan works with many ageing women in lead roles and supporting roles, from Britain and America, including Courtney Cox, Sarah Jessica Parker, Anna Maxwell-Martin, Tanya Moodie, Molly Shannon, Talia Balsam, Ashley Jensen and Carrie Fisher, to name a few.

Alongside this, Horgan also symbolises an 'individualised entrepreneurial femininity' in that she emphasises how important it is to be an autonomous, freely choosing subject when considering herself as a business and in aiding other women's success. In an interview with the women's lifestyle magazine *Elle*, for instance, she argues that confidence is incredibly important, stating, 'I had to wait for my confidence to catch up [...] I had to work for success like a dog' (Horgan, quoted in Craik, 2019). In other interviews, she has stressed that it is essential to address a lack of confidence in women working within the media industries (see Kiefer, 2017 and Freeman, 2022). The idea that women are lacking in confidence when compared to men (the 'confidence gap') – and that this is the reason for avoiding self-promotion, leadership roles and pay rises – forces women to internalise their 'failures' and therefore partake in labour to combat the 'problems' a lack of confidence engenders. To understand this phenomenon, Shani Orgad and Rosalind Gill interrogate how 'confidence culture' has permeated contemporary culture via the neoliberalisation of feminism. Orgad and Gill depart from the idea that neoliberalism is 'purely rational and calculating' (2022: 16) but create a new understanding at an 'affective or emotional level, the extent to which neoliberalism incites particular qualities, dispositions, and feelings—among them confidence' (ibid: 16). They conclude that 'confidence is mobilized as a device to manage the intensifying precarity and flexibility in the labor market and is a response to the increasing disinvestment in social welfare and the privatization and individualization of social risks' (ibid: 144). While Horgan has supported women in her role as the co-founder of a successful production company, she still tends to portray individual, psychological, and social problems as the responsibility of women to solve. As Orgad and Gill argue, this framing suggests that women need to change themselves, rather than focusing on changing the broader societal structures and norms that contribute to these issues.

This straightforward idea of neoliberal subjectification positions Horgan as a competitive economic subject regulated by a postfeminist rationale. Yet individual endeavours can be complex, transgressive and inherently 'messy', much like configurations of the 'unruly' woman on-screen. Indeed, there is an apparent tension between treating oneself as a business and treating oneself as a creative being. David Lee has found that, when analysing the changing attitudes towards craft and creativity within the field of factual television production in the British independent television sector, there is a set of discursive attitudes favouring 'enterprise, commercialism, competition, flexibility and individualism', as well as another set of competing discourses 'promoting values of craft, cooperation and public service' (2014: 157). Though Lee refers explicitly to the labour of television workers from documentary to reality genres, these tensions are evident in Horgan's entrepreneurship through the 'relational' and 'individualised' modes of entrepreneurship she embodies. This ambivalence, I suggest, is a key characteristic of the 'fastidious' woman. Sharon Horgan, as a writer, performer and entrepreneur, embodies the complexities of women in comedy. She emphasises the importance of individualism and confidence while collaborating and working with teams of women. Despite her ability to portray harsh and rebellious characters on screen, she is seen as soft-spoken and anxious during interviews. As this analysis has demonstrated, it is not enough to examine women who make spectacles of themselves, we must also examine the ways in which comedians operate beyond the text.

In examining Horgan's comedic persona, the 'fastidious' attention to detail and skill that remains central to women's authorship has been made visible.

At the same time, the contradictions of Horgan's stardom has been highlighted and may be defined by oppositions. The characters she creates are by no means aspirational, but they are nevertheless middle-class. Disavowing their class position, Horgan's characters comment on contemporary postfeminisms and, as Caroline Bainbridge argues, give 'voice to the Anglo-American postfeminist experience of women who identify with her protagonists, as well as to those who take pleasure in viewing the depiction of women's rage and discontent with neoliberal, white, middle-class strictures' (2020: 84). This 'heterodoxical style' (ibid) is reflected in her working patterns off-screen. She works collectively and collaboratively with others while simultaneously displaying the individual sensibilities and self-regulating spirit embodied by postfeminism's set of ideologies. Textually and extratextually, Horgan straddles oppositional spaces with great skill, avoiding the criticism women in comedy often face. This is arguably tied to issues of mobility in which her identity is intimately bound. After all, she is an Irish showrunner who consistently moves between Ireland, Britain and America and can thus traverse spaces and transcend the boundaries of comfortability.

This is also intertwined with her identity as a white, middle-class woman, as Horgan has greater access to choice because of her social positioning. Postfeminism consists of narratives about feminism's 'success' in achieving gender equity, something which is often remarked upon in the interviews analysed. In this way, it has been seen as devoid of political power and deprived of its radical and activist history. However, this is rather simplistic and does not account for a model of feminist power, solidarity and collectivity that is prevalent in contemporary televisual politics – particularly in women's comedy. Horgan's series acknowledges the collective national identity of Ireland and the collective need for women's creative comic spaces. Though postfeminism remains a current force in our culture, it is important to examine emerging areas in which feminist solidarity champions mutual support between women, a key aspect of fourth-wave feminism. As with Phoebe Waller-Bridge, however, it has to be questioned whether this is built across the boundaries of class, nation, ethnicity and religion. Though Tanya Moodie was hired to play Meg in *Motherland*, this was an 'afterthought' that speaks to the current cultural climate in which it is acknowledged that broadcasters need to employ approaches to measure and evaluate intersectionality, addressing inequalities in the television industry. As one successful woman in the TV industry, is clear that the battle for gender equity cannot remain the burden on Horgan's shoulders alone.

Conclusion: Rethinking Women's Place in Contemporary UK Television Comedy

As this book has illustrated, the contemporary 'unruly' woman in Britain and Ireland, whom I describe as 'fastidious,' expresses her rebellion not only through her physical representation. I have analysed the importance of female writers and/or performers, including Julia Davis, Phoebe Waller-Bridge, Caitlin and Caroline Moran, Michaela Coel and Sharon Horgan. Though their characters on-screen may be 'messy' and transgressive – 'unruly' in Rowe's terms - they have also been carefully crafted off-screen. Rowe's concept of 'unruliness' has thus served as an important foundation in creating this new theoretical model, and I have specifically argued that the 'fastidious' women:

- frequently engages in collaboration with other women, be it within familial, friendly, or professional circles;
- is met with mixed reactions from critics and audiences alike, and is frequently analysed through the lens of social class – a British comedic tradition that continues to hold relevance in the 2010s;
- can embody traditional 'unruliness' – being 'too loud', 'excessive' and 'over the top' in her texts – while also displaying 'fastidiousness' in 'talking back' to the industry, crafting intricate TV series and navigating the political landscape where her actions are frequently judged;
- can no longer be defined as simply 'unruly' in the shift from second/third-wave to fourth-wave feminism. Her 'unruliness' is dependent on the relationship between craft, creator and context. A blanket application of 'unruliness' is no longer fruitful in the contemporary media landscape concerned with intersectionality.

There are inevitable complications in examining a wide array of women in comedy who are informed by a multiplicity of feminisms. They can be disruptive, resistant and joyous but also exclusionary, harmful and oppressive depending on and in relation to their lived experiences. For instance, though I argue that the 'fastidious' woman collaborates with women often, this may be exclusionary and keep a small circle of creative workers in power, but it may also be inclusionary by incorporating and championing new voices in the industry. This is related to 'the rise of popular feminism,' the idea that just because these women are visible, they are feminist figures (Banet-Weiser, 2018 and Perkins and Schreiber, 2019). Given the adaptability and transformability of feminisms, then, the new 'unruly' woman is difficult to define in the second decade of the twenty-first century. Nonetheless, given that both academic and media discussions of feminism have been significantly shaped by the rise of intersectionality during the 2010s and the emergence of fourth-wave feminism, my analysis has focused on how this dialogue has influenced the portrayal of women in television comedy, as well as the interplay between gender and other categories of social difference. This is doubly important to consider because comedy is a useful barometer in outlining and inspiring cultural change in any given society. Indeed, the surge in interest surrounding identity politics, catalysed by political events such as Brexit and the influence of conservative governments in the UK and the US, has spurred the emergence of coalitions and organisations advocating for their respective group's interests (i.e., the Me Too and Black Lives Matter movements). This divide has, significantly, found expression through humour. Like Maggie Hennefeld, I see 'parallels between the feminist protest culture of the early 1900s and our present-day moment [...] when satirical laughter and new media experimentation are again such vibrant parts of our collective imagination and activist resistance' because comedy, though jubilant and joyous, is often 'extremely violent and vividly obscene [...] particularly during moments of escalating social and political activism' (2018). As such, comedy is an important force for women to incite social change. The 'vividly obscene' or 'unruly' woman must adopt a meticulous approach to wield this power – her precision, exacting standards and unwavering commitment to the revolutionary potential of laughter are paramount.

In this book, I have also formed a new methodological approach to analyse 'fastidious' female comedy writer/performers in the complicated landscape of contemporary television, which began with Kathleen Rowe opening new spaces for feminist investigations of film and TV. Rowe's methodologies are diverse – ranging from semiotic analysis, narrative analysis and historical analysis. The first part of her book examines the semiotics of female 'unruliness' from the social and literary traditions of the carnivalesque, while the second part undertakes a historical account, examining a handful of films from the 1930s through the classical period to the postclassical period. While Rowe's framework is foundational, it requires updating to effectively analyse modern female-driven comedy. This includes exploring the blurring lines between public and private realms, the democratisation of fame, the rise of semi-autobiographical narratives in comedy and the emphasis on intersectional identity politics throughout the second decade of the twenty-first century. This book has thus outlined how comedy writer/performers have had to navigate a new and expanded stage that encompasses multiple media, with the 'messiness' and tensions of a star's visibility affecting their work.

To capture the complexities of this space for contemporary female writer/performers, I have argued that the relationship between creator, craft and context is central in foregrounding the comedy writer/performer's labour of production. Creator refers to the women who are the driving force behind the comedy shows. They are the writers, performers, directors and producers who bring their unique perspectives and voices to the television industry. Craft involves the meticulous process of creating television content, from the scriptwriting of Caroline Moran to the performances from Michaela Coel. It's about the attention to detail that goes into producing a comedy series. Context encompasses the broader environment in which these comedies are produced, including the political, social and cultural shifts of the 2010s. It also refers to the institutional logics of television that shape how feminine-gendered fiction is created and received. These three lines of inquiry cannot be examined in isolation, nor can 'fastidiousness', which I have argued examines both the visible power of women in comedy (on-screen) as well as their seemingly invisible power (off-screen). While Rowe moves from one form of analysis to another between her book's first and second parts, the methodological approach taken throughout this book has not been so consistent or straightforward because women's identities are coloured by (and colour) their experiences in/on television. Such analysis is inevitably disorderly as the analysis of creator, craft and context intersect and overlap. However, this approach reflects the complex nature of contemporary women in UK TV comedy and the many facets of 'fastidiousness': women who carefully navigate the media landscape, women who are treated ambivalently, and above all, women who create tightly woven televisual texts and demonstrate authorial authority.

Textually, it is clear that the women analysed throughout this book establish meaning through specific subgenres, modes and styles of comedy, including semi-autobiographical/confessional comedy, sitcom, 'cringe' comedy and dramedy. The series that have been analysed are a complex amalgamation of these, mixing codes and conventions to re-evaluate what is deemed 'masculine'/'feminine' and 'high art'/'low art' on television. The combination of British, Irish and American generic modes utilised by women writer/performers, in particular, give their texts cross-cultural and transnational appeal, contributing to their success worldwide. Many of the comedians under analysis have also started their careers in the theatre. Historically, anthology series dedicated to drama, such as *The Wednesday Play* from the BBC (1964–70) and ITV's *Armchair Theatre* (1956–74), often included adaptations of plays alongside original works, and they brought together prominent playwrights, directors and actors to collaborate. This sphere of TV drama has often been male-dominated, and, writing in the 1980s, Jill Hyem argued that 'the single play market is becoming increasingly inaccessible to any but top established writers (mostly men)' (1987: 152). Now, many female comedians, including the likes of Phoebe Waller-Bridge and Michaela Coel, are making the shift from theatre to television. They are demonstrating their multifaceted talents by working across different mediums, notably employing the technique of direct address to engage audiences.

Comedies that employ direct address have typically been semi-autobiographical. This form of comedy has emerged as a particularly popular genre among female writer/performers throughout the 2010s. According to Peter Dickinson et al., one of 'the long-standing criticisms of *women's comedy* is that it is too *autobiographical*, and thus less appealing to a broad general (read: male) audience' (2014: xxxiii, italics original). Despite this, female creators have not been discouraged from producing such works in today's television landscape. On the contrary, showrunners like Phoebe Waller-Bridge, Michaela Coel, Sharon Horgan and Caitlin and Caroline Moran have adopted this narrative approach. Their rise in popularity can be attributed to their candid and introspective style of storytelling. These semi-autobiographical tales are typically told through the sitcom, a genre which has occupied a new space in 'quality' TV offerings. Taylor Nygaard and Jorie Lagerway argue that this has 'also shifted its [the sitcom's] characters firmly into the middle and upper-middle classes', which is seen as 'a departure from British sitcoms' often working-class norms and aligns the British-produced programs [...] with US sitcom's middle-class norms' (2020: 60).

However, this is an over-generalisation that does not account for British comedies such as *Chewing Gum* and *Raised by Wolves*, sitcoms that stray from this new model. Notably, while middle/upper-class comedies like *Fleabag* have gained immense popularity, other creations like Sophie Willan's *Alma's Not Normal* (see Minor, 2023) have also gained traction. This trend is particularly noticeable in the use of sitcom tropes that have transformed representations, ranging from *Chewing Gum*'s fresh take on Black female sexuality to Caitlin and Caroline Moran's depiction of life in Wolverhampton and the Midlands. The emergence of these new narratives aligns with the changing paradigms surrounding social class and gender dynamics in the 2010s. While ensemble shows like *Shameless* once stood out for their vivid portrayal of the working-class, multiple female-led and female-created comedies have been made since then, including *My Mad Fat Diary* (E4, 2013–15), *Hullraisers*, *This Country* and *Mandy* (BBC Two, 2019–). These series are instrumental in redefining class-based representations, offering humorous yet heartwarming accounts of individuals who emphasise the importance of both the personal and collective. This transformation is particularly impactful given the backdrop of persistent inequalities faced by women during this decade, a period marked by economic disparities, austerity measures and attacks on the working-class, compounded by distinct feminist concerns surrounding housing and social class (Reis, 2019). These popular comedy TV series function as potent instruments of resistance within this broader socio-political context. Comedy, as Sam Friedman contends, has historically served to marginalise and pathologise those with limited cultural capital (2014). However, through the groundbreaking work of figures like Michaela Coel and Caitlin and Caroline Moran, new avenues for discourse emerge. This shift reveals the potential of comedy to expand the narratives surrounding class and regionality, giving voice to previously underrepresented segments of society such as Black working-class women and teenagers from the Midlands.

Class politics continues to be a central theme in UK TV comedy. The comedies I have examined have drawn attention to class, reflecting the UK's longstanding tradition of exploring sociopolitical issues through humour. In the 2010s, there has been 'a decade of austerity, acrimony and growing frustration at a lack of democratic accountability' (Bailey, 2020). For the 'fastidious' woman who is treated ambivalently by critics, such politics have been central to these discussions. For instance, Phoebe Waller-Bridge's white, upper-class sensibilities have deeply affected how she is perceived. Her replication of conventional class discourses generated negative press after *Fleabag* aired, and her appearance on *Saturday Night Live* cemented this perception. Simultaneously, however, her tightly woven and skilfully constructed series have attracted glowing reviews from critics. It is this ambivalence and assiduousness that render Waller-Bridge a 'fastidious' woman in the contemporary televisual landscape. Significantly, Sharon Horgan has not received the same backlash as Waller-Bridge, arguably because she disavows the behaviours of her middle-class characters. Julia Davis, though also appearing middle-class, has also consistently critiqued the banality of this social class in her textual 'unruliness' – making those around her uncomfortable via her excessive performance of femininity and showcasing how postfeminism has become adaptable through her roles from the late 1990s and early 2000s to the present-day. Michaela Coel and Caitlin and Caroline Moran differ in that they have focused on the working-class subjectivities of women in underrepresented groups and areas – and have been praised for doing so. The reception of these women showcases how, in UK class and culture, there remains a 'terrain of struggle' in popular culture – an 'arena of consent and resistance', as Stuart Hall argues (1998). The political meaning of popular production or consumption is never wholly influenced by the writer/performer, but the culture onto which their work is inscribed. UK TV comedy's rich and nuanced history has influenced its current role in the cultural imagination, with its emphasis on gender and class shaping how female comedians are perceived.

This transformation reflects the significant shifts that women have encountered, not just in terms of social class, but generational dynamics. As has been demonstrated, women in their twenties and thirties from the UK have used comedy in similar ways to their American counterparts, offering a window into how young people navigate conservatism amidst pervasive inequality. However, not all experiences have proven to be homogeneous. For instance, Michaela Coel has celebrated Black British culture, which has coincided with a rise of white, postfeminist TV series and feelings of precarity affecting the white middle-classes. Owen Jones suggests that '[t]he children of affluent and working-class parents alike can no longer expect home ownership, job security or a decent salary' (2020), and this shift has ultimately affected the 'dark' and 'edgy' themes of guilt in Waller-Bridge's work that focuses on grief. 'Having it all' (an idea in line with postfeminism) is now replaced with the uneasy feeling of losing it all. Similarly, Caitlin and Caroline Moran and Julia Davis have demonstrated how middle-aged British women have responded to the current climate in divergent ways because of the specific historical conditions in which their gendered sensibilities were formed. Julia Davis continues her examination and deconstruction of postfeminism through the characters she plays on-screen, examining the ignorance and pettiness of the middle-classes. Her desire to play characters who refuse to act their age, alongside Caitlin and Caroline Moran's decision to focus on their teenage selves, demonstrate that there remains a focus on younger women in television – particularly when considering how popular Waller-Bridge and Coel have become. Contemporary life, and its everyday representation on-screen, remains fixated on women in their twenties and thirties, with Hannah J. Swift and Ben Steeden's 'research suggest[ing] that media portrayals of older people have become increasingly negative, tending to represent older people as frail, dependent and in decline' (2020: 3). Writing in 1999, Kathleen M. Woodward argued that 'ageism is entrenched within feminism itself' (xi), noting that the preoccupations of second-wave feminism tended towards 'issues that are associated with the earlier years in the life course' (ibid). Though authors such as Sharon Horgan are providing significant spaces for ageing women's representation on television, it appears that not much has changed in contemporary comedy television – particularly with the hyper scrutiny of female celebrities and comedy authors who are now expected to look and behave younger.

On an extratextual level, structural, institutional and national changes have affected (re)presentations of women in comedy and vice versa. As has been identified in this book, the 2010s are defined by a perpetual state of crises in the Western world ('crises of democracy and the economy; of the climate and poverty; of international relations and national identity; of privacy and technology' [Beckett, 2019]). This decade of calamity and complexity has, according to Andy Beckett, 'opened up space for new political movements' as a result of the 'difficulties since 2010 of so many previously dominant value systems – capitalism, centrism, traditional conservatism, [and] white male supremacy' (2019). Though it may seem strange to discuss the bleak and alarming changes that have come to shape UK culture, given that this book is based around laughter, humour and the pleasures of women-authored comedy, the ambiguities and uncertainties of our modern times are reflected in the 'fastidious' woman who inspires extreme and polarising reactions from her appearances both in and out of comedy. She causes division from being 'too much' for some (overly loud, abrasive and dominant in the media) to 'not enough' for others (lacking in overtly feminist themes, ideologically hollow and unable to inspire social change). These gendered expectations are intimately related to postfeminist culture. For Angela McRobbie, in the contemporary media landscape, 'we find all ideas of gender justice and collective solidarity thrown overboard in favour of "excellence" and with the aim of creating new forms (and restoring old forms) of gender hierarchies through competition and elitism' (2015: 17), with critiques of men being 'conspicuously absent' in this discourse (ibid). Whether 'too much' or 'not enough', I have argued that standards placed upon women have affected how the contemporary comedic woman is perceived and situated in the contemporary media landscape. Nevertheless, as noted in the introduction to this book, we must also focus on 'emergent feminisms' (Keller and Ryan, 2018). A response to institutions of women's oppression has been to create genres of pleasure and to negotiate not only representations of women, but the structural and institutional foundation upon which these representations are based. This is where the interests of fourth-wave feminism – and its focus on laughter – have been critical.

For the United Kingdom in particular, changes in the national broadcasting ecology have affected what has been shown on screen. In 2011, the nation had 'the highest penetration of digital television in any global market and the second highest use of online television on-demand services behind the United States [...] It also had the heaviest users of social media in the world' (Strange, 2011: 133). The UK also 'became a host for government-led policy discussion about "being digital"' (Grainge and Johnson, 2015: 11). This has resulted in the televisual landscape becoming increasingly fragmented, thereby diversifying the kinds of stories that are told. For instance, in the last few years, notable new voices have also emerged from other areas of the globe – such as New Zealand stand-up Rose Matafeo, who created the BBC sitcom *Starstruck* (BBC One, 2021–), and Canadian non-binary comedian Mae Martin, who created the Channel 4/Netflix comedy-drama *Feel Good* (2020–21). After moving to the UK, and subsequently entering the British comedy scene, they have created semi-autobiographical tales that revolve around their experiences of emigration.

The changes in information technology have created new viewing habits, with multiplatform video on-demand services competing with broadcast television (and increasing the amount of TV consumed). For female comedy writer/performers, this newfound visibility and digital democracy has seen networks such as the BBC and Channel 4 take women, and their work, seriously. This concept has been explored throughout this book, with critics desperately searching for new showrunners to replace the next and attempting to create competition between women in the process – a potentially harmful approach to searching for emerging talent. Despite this, female comics, more often than not, have collaborated frequently with other women: whether that be through acting, writing, directing or producing. Caterina Petroni and Lidia Rodak contend that a key feature of fourth-wave feminism is sisterhood, or more specifically, 'an honest mutual support based solely on empathy and understanding as an expression of free will, with a potential of converting this into common action' (85–6). Off-screen, the professional support, mentorship and networking opportunities shared between women have provided spaces for gender equality, fair representation and equitable working environments.

Overall, this book has detailed the various ways women in the UK have created comedy television throughout the 2010s. By examining the creative outputs of Caitlin and Caroline Moran, Julia Davis, Phoebe Waller-Bridge, Sharon Horgan and Michaela Coel, I have argued that these comedians should be viewed as both 'unruly' and 'fastidious' – their work marked by excessive speech and performances, yet also characterised by their meticulous, industrious approach to crafting new narratives and presenting diverse female perspectives. The women featured in this analysis have not just reclaimed but redefined comedic storytelling, ensuring that their voices – and the laughter they provoke – resonate with precision, power and permanence.

References

Teleography

2 Broke Girls. 2011–17. CBS. September 19.
30 Rock. 2006–13. NBC. 11 October.
Absolutely Fabulous. 1992–2012. BBC One and BBC Two. 2 November.
Armchair Theatre. 1956–74. ITV. 8 July.
'Allo 'Allo. 1982–92. BBC One. 30 December.
A Young Doctor's Notebook. 2012–13. Sky Arts. 6 December.
Bad Sisters. 2022. Apple TV+. 19 August.
Benefits Street. 2014–15. Channel 4. 6 January.
Benefits Britain: Life on the Dole. 2014–16. Channel 5. 16 June.
Blackadder Goes Forth. 1989. BBC One. 28 September.
Black Earth Rising. 2018. BBC Two and Netflix. 10 September.
Blue Jam. 1997–99. BBC Radio 1. 4 November.
Brass Eye. 1997. Channel 4. 29 January.
Bread. 1986–91. BBC1. 1 May.
Breaking Bad. 2008–13. AMC. January 20.
Broad City. 2014–19. Comedy Central. January 22.
Butterflies. 1978–83. BBC2. 10 November.
Camping. 2016. Sky Atlantic. 12 April.
Camping. 2018. HBO. October 14.
Can't Pay? We'll Take it Away! 2014–18. Channel 5. 24 February.
Call My Agent! 2015–. France Télévisions and Netflix. 20 December.
Catastrophe. 2015–19. Channel 4. 19 January.
Chewing Gum. 2015–17. E4. 6 October.
Cockroaches. 2015. ITV2. 5 January.
Comedy Lab. 1998–2011. Channel 4/E4. 9 November.
Coronation Street. 1960–. ITV. 9 December.
Cougar Town. 2009–15. ABC/TBS. September 23.
Crazy Ex-Girlfriend. 2015–19. The CW. October 12.
Dad's Army. 1968–77. BBC One. 31 July.
Damned. 2016–18. Channel 4, 27 September.
Dead Boss. 2012. BBC Three, 14 June.
Derry Girls. 2018–. Channel 4. 4 January.
Divorce. 2016–19. HBO, October 9.

Doll and Em. 2014–15. Sky Living. February 18.
Drifters. 2013–16. E4. 31 October.
Father Ted. 1995–98. Channel 4. 21 April.
Feel Good. 2020–21. Channel 4 and Netflix. 18 March.
Fleabag. 2016–19. BBC. 21 July.
Frayed. 2019–. ABC and Sky. 26 September.
French and Saunders Show. 1987–2007. BBC Two. 9 March.
Gavin and Stacey. 2007–19. BBC One. 13 May.
Getting On. 2009–12. BBC Four. 8 July.
Girls. 2012–17. HBO, 15 April.
GLOW. 2017–19. Netflix. June 23.
Happy Valley. 2014–. BBC One. 29 April.
Homeland. 2011–20. Showtime. 2 October.
How to Live with Your Parents (For the Rest of Your Life). 2013. ABC. June 26.
Hullraisers. 2022–. Channel 4. 12 April.
Human Remains. 2000. BBC Two. 13 November.
Hunderby. 2012–15. Sky Atlantic. 27 August.
I'm Alan Partridge. 1997–2002. BBC Two. 3 November.
Insecure. 2016–. HBO. October 9.
I Love Lucy. 1951–57. CBS. 15 October.
I May Destroy You. 2020. BBC and HBO. 7 June.
Jane the Virgin. 2014–18. The CW. 13 October.
Katy Brand's Big Ass Show. 2007–09. ITV2. 19 October.
Killing Eve. 2018–. BBC America. 8 April.
Last Tango in Halifax. 2012–16. BBC One. 20 November.
Little Britain. 2003–20. BBC. 9 February.
Lizzie and Sarah. 2010. BBC Two. 20 March.
Love Island. 2015–. ITV2. 7 June.
Mad Men. 2007–15. AMC. July 19.
Mandy. 2019–. BBC Two. 25 July.
Man Like Mobeen. 2017–. BBC Three. 17 December.
Miranda. 2009–15. BBC Two/BBC One. 9 November.
Motherland. 2016–. BBC Two. 6 September.
Mount Pleasant. 2011–17. Sky. 24 August.
Mrs Browns Boys. 2011–. BBC One. 21 February.
Mr. Sloane. 2014. Sky Atlantic. 23 May.
My Mad Fat Diary. 2013–15. E4. 14 January.
Nighty Night. 2004–05. BBC Two. 6 January.
Nurse Jackie. 2009–15. Showtime. June 8.
Orange Is the New Black. 2013–19. Netflix. 11 July.
Peaky Blinders. 2013–22. BBC Two/One, 12 September.
Psychobitches. 2012–14. Sky Arts. 21 June.
Pulling. 2006–09. BBC Three. 23 November.
Raised by Wolves. 2013–16. Channel 4. 23 December.
Roseanne. 1998–97 & 2018. ABC. 18 October.

Saturday Kitchen. 2002–. BBC One/BBC Two. 26 January.
Saturday Night Live. 1975–. NBC. 11 October.
School of Comedy. 2009–10. E4. 1 October.
Scott and Bailey. 2011–16. ITV. 29 May.
Sex and the City. 1998–2004. HBO. 6 June.
Shameless. 2004–13. Channel 4. 13 January.
Smack the Pony. Channel 4. 1999–2003. 19 March.
Some Girls. 2012–14. BBC Three. 6 November.
Spaced. 1999–2001. Channel 4. 24 September.
Starstruck. 2021–. BBC Three. 25 April.
Stella. 2012–17. Sky One. 6 January.
Thirteen. 2016. BBC Three. 28 February.
Transparent. 2014–19. Amazon Studios. 6 February.
There She Goes. 2018–20. BBC Four and BBC Two. 16 October.
The Andrew Marr Show. 2005–21. BBC One. 11 September.
The Catherine Tate Show. BBC Two/One. 2004–15. 16 February.
The Increasingly Poor Decisions of Todd Margaret. 2010–16. IFC and More4. 27 November.
The Liver Birds. 1969–79. BBC1. 14 April.
The Office. 2001–03. BBC Two/One. 9 July.
The Mindy Project. 2012–17. FOX and Hulu. 25 September.
The Sopranos. 1999–2007. HBO. 10 January.
The Vicar of Dibley. BBC One. 1994–2007. 10 November.
The Wednesday Play. 1964–70. BBC 1. 28 October.
'The Week Before Christmas'. *Little Crackers*. 2012. Sky 1. 20 December.
This Way Up. 2019. Channel 4. 8 August.
Up the Women. 2013–15. BBC. 30 May.
Walking and Talking. 2012. Sky Atlantic. 25 June.
Women on the Verge. 2018–. W. 11 October.

Filmography

Been So Long. 2018. Tinge Krishnan, dir. UK: BFI Film Fund, Film4, and Greenacre Film.
Four Lions. 2010. Chris Morris, dir. UK: Film4 Productions, Wild Bunch and Warp Films.
Get Out. 2017. Jordan Peele, dir. USA: Blumhouse Productions, QC Entertainment and Monkeypaw Productions.
Herself. 2020. Phyllida Lloyd, dir. UK/Ireland: Element Pictures, BBC Films, Merman Films, British Film Institute, Screen Ireland.
Indiana Jones and the Dial of Destiny. 2023. James Mangold, dir. USA: Walt Disney Pictures and Lucasfilm Ltd.
Joker. 2019. Todd Phillips, dir. USA: Warner Bros. Pictures, DC Films, Joint Effort, Bron Creative and Village Roadshow Pictures.
Juno. 2007. Diablo Cody, dir. USA: Mandate Picture and Mr. Mudd.
Knives Out. 2019. Rian Johnson, dir. USA: MRC and T-Street.
Miss Congeniality 2: Armed and Fabulous. 2005. John Pasquin, dir. USA: Fortis Films, Castle Rock Entertainment and Village Roadshow Pictures.

No Time to Die. 2021. Cary Joji Fukunaga, dir. UK/USA: Metro-Goldwyn-Mayer and Eon Productions.

Parasite. 2019. Bong Joon-ho, dir. South Korea: Barunson E&A.

Paris is Burning. 1990. Jennie Livingston, dir. USA: Academy Entertainment and Off White Productions.

The Acting Class. 2017. Michael Wayne and Deirdre O'Neill, dir. UK: Inside Film Network.

The Iron Lady. 2011. Phyllida Lloyd, dir. UK/France: Pathé, Film4 Productions, UK Film Council, Yuk Films, Canal+, CinéCinéma, BBC Films and DJ Films.

The Terminator. 1984. James Cameron, dir. USA: Hemdale, Pacific Western Productions, Euro Film Funding, and Cinema '84.

The Watermelon Woman. 1996. Cheryl Dunye, dir. USA: Dancing Girl Productions.

Young Adult. 2011. Diablo Cody, dir. USA: Mandate Pictures, Mr. Mudd, Right of Way Films, and Denver and Delilah Films.

Bibliography

Abbott, K., et al., 2019. 'The 100 best TV shows of the 21st century', *The Guardian.* Available at: https://www.theguardian.com/tv-and-radio/2019/sep/16/100-best-tv-shows-of-the-21st-century (accessed 24/02/2021).

Addley, E., 2017. 'David Harewood says black British actors may be better suited to American roles', *The Guardian.* Available at: https://www.theguardian.com/culture/2017/mar/13/david-harewood-says-black-british-actors-may-be-better-suited-to-american-roles (accessed 30/10/2023).

Ahl, H., and Marlow, S., 2021. 'Exploring the false promise of entrepreneurship through a postfeminist critique of the enterprise policy discourse in Sweden and the UK', *Human Relations*, 74(1), pp. 41–68.

Aitkenhead, D., 2019. 'The Interview: actress Sharon Horgan on *Catastrophe*, fame and the joy of outsourcing domestic chores', *The Times.* Available at: https://www.thetimes.co.uk/article/the-interview-actress-sharon-horgan-on-catastrophe-fame-and-the-joy-of-outsourcing-domestic-chores-zc77wjbvx (accessed 21/01/2023).

Akass, K. and McCabe, J., 2018. 'HBO and the aristocracy of contemporary TV culture: affiliations and legitimatising television culture, post-2007', *Mise au point* (online). Available at: http://journals.openedition.org/map/2472 (accessed 07/02/2019).

Alexander, E., 2016. 'Exclusive: Caitlin Moran's guide to sisterhood, politics and Tinder', *Glamour.* Available at: https://www.glamourmagazine.co.uk/article/caitlin-moran-raised-by-wolves-interview-feminism-and-working-classes (accessed 02/01/2024).

Aroesti, R., 2015. 'Caitlin Moran: "The funniest people in the world are all women"', *The Guardian.* Available at: https://www.theguardian.com/tv-and-radio/2015/mar/07/raised-by-wolves-caitlin-moran (accessed 18/12/2019).

Aston, E. and Harris, G., 2012. *A Good Night Out for the Girls: Popular Feminisms in Contemporary Theatre and Performance.* Basingstoke: Palgrave MacMillan.

Atakav, E., 2010. '"Let's Do It! Let's Do It!": Gender politics and Victoria Wood', *Feminist Media Studies*, 10(3), pp. 359–63.

BAFTA Guru, 2017. Phoebe Waller-Bridge's worst audition (video). *YouTube.* Available at: https://www.youtube.com/watch?v=thq-gnGpzJY (accessed 22/05/2019).

Bailey, D. J., 2020. 'Decade of dissent: how protest is shaking the UK and why it's likely to continue', *The Conversation*. Available at: https://theconversation.com/decade-of-dissent-how-protest-is-shaking-the-uk-and-why-its-likely-to-continue-125843 (accessed 07/02/2021).

Bainbridge, C., 2020. 'Sharon Horgan and the transatlantic psycho-politics of "womantic" comedy: postfeminism as catastrophe?', in: B. J. Brickman, D. Jermyn, and T. L. Trost, eds., *Love Across the Atlantic*. Edinburgh: Edinburgh University Press.

Baker, H., 2014. '*Chewing Gum Dreams*, National Theatre (Shed), London – review', *The Financial Times*. Available at: https://www.ft.com/content/6bc64ce0-af57-11e3-bea5-00144feab7de (accessed 09/12/2017).

Banet-Weiser, S., 2018. *Empowered: Popular Feminism and Popular Misogyny*. Durham, NC: Duke University Press.

Banet-Weiser, S. and Portwood-Stacer, L., 2017. 'The traffic in feminism: an introduction to the commentary and criticism on popular feminism', *Feminist Media Studies*, 17(5), pp. 884–906.

Barrett, C., 2014. 'Black and white and green all over? The emergence of Irish female stardom in contemporary mainstream cinemas', *Journal of Postgraduate Research*, 13, pp. 24–38.

Bastién, A. J., 2017. 'Claiming the future of Black TV', *The Atlantic*. Available at: https://www.theatlantic.com//entertainment/archive/2017/01/claiming-the-future-of-black-tv/514562/ (accessed 09/12/2017).

BBC News, 2018. 'President Trump calls to congratulate Roseanne Barr'. *BBC News*. Available at: https://www.bbc.co.uk/news/entertainment-arts-43583982 (accessed 02/01/2024).

Beale, S., 2020. *The Comedy and Legacy of Music-Hall Women 1880–1920: Brazen Impudence and Boisterous Vulgarity*. London: Palgrave Macmillan.

Beckett, A., 2019. 'The age of perpetual crisis: how the 2010s disrupted everything but resolved nothing', *The Guardian*. Available at: https://www.theguardian.com/society/2019/dec/17/decade-of-perpetual-crisis-2010s-disrupted-everything-but-resolved-nothing (accessed 07/02/2021).

Bennion, C., 2020. 'Please, put us all out of our misery and kill off *Killing Eve* immediately', *The Independent*. Available at: https://www.telegraph.co.uk/tv/0/please-put-us-misery-kill-killing-eve-immediately/ (accessed 28/08/2020).

Benshoff, H. M. and Griffin, S., 2005. *Queer Images: A History of Gay and Lesbian Film in America*. Lanham, MD: Rowman and Littlefield.

Bernstein, A., 2018. 'Mad women: how angry sisterhood is taking over the small screen', *The Guardian*. Available at: https://www.theguardian.com/tv-and-radio/2018/mar/07/mad-women-angry-sisterhood-taking-over-tv (accessed 07/02/2019).

Bernstein, R., 2012. 'How to be a woman', *Marie Clare*. Available at: https://www.marieclaire.com/celebrity/a7259/caitlin-moran-interview/ (accessed 08/10/2019).

Bien, A., 2020. 'How Theater Shaped Michaela Coel's Career', *Today Tix*. Available at: https://www.todaytix.com/insider/nyc/posts/how-theater-shaped-michaela-coels-career (accessed 14/01/2021).

Bilge, S., 2013. 'Intersectionality undone: saving intersectionality from feminist intersectionality studies'. *Du Bois Review: Social Science Research on Race*, 10(2), pp. 405–24.

Bilge, S., 2014. 'Whitening intersectionality', *Racism and Sociology*, 5, p. 175.

Blake, M., 2015. 'Q&A: Rob Delaney and Sharon Horgan on their "brutally honest" rom-com "Catastrophe"', *The LA Times*. Available at: https://www.latimes.com/

entertainment/tv/showtracker/la-et-st-rob-delaney-sharon-horgan-catastrophe-amazon-20150619-story.html (accessed 21/01/2023).

Blay, Z., 2017. 'Michaela Coel's musical lands multi-million dollar deal with netflix', *Huffington Post*. Available at: http://www.huffingtonpost.co.uk/entry/michaela-coels-musical-lands-multi-million-dollar-deal-with-netflix_us_59b15703e4b0354e440fe0bd (accessed 09/12/2017).

Bloodworth, A., 2020. '"A true artist": how the unstoppable Michaela Coel became the most exciting talent in TV - by those who know her', *HuffPost*. Available at: https://www.huffpost.com/archive/in/entry/michaela-coel-i-may-destroy-you_in_5f39eaef-c5b6959911e6458e (accessed 02/01/2024).

Brennan, C., 2021. 'RTE's Ryan Tubridy amazed by sisterly bond that Aisling Bea has with *This Way Up* co-star Sharon Horgan', *Irish Mirror*. Available at: https://www.irishmirror.ie/shobiz/irish-showbiz/rtes-ryan-tubridy-amazed-sisterly-24549993 (accessed 21/01/2023).

Bromwich, K., 2015. 'On my radar: Sharon Horgan's cultural highlights', *The Guardian*. Available at: https://www.theguardian.com/culture/2015/oct/25/on-my-radar-sharon-horgan-palio-metronomy-kate-bush-bridget-christie-sara-pascoe-lucky-chip-burgers (accessed 21/01/2023).

Brown, M., 2017. 'Class crisis in the arts must be cracked, says Labour report', *The Guardian*. Available at: https://www.theguardian.com/culture/2017/aug/10/class-crisis-arts-must-be-cracked-says-labour-report (accessed 19/10/2020).

Bucciferro, C., 2019. 'Women and Netflix: disrupting traditional boundaries between television and film', *Feminist Media Studies*, 19(7), pp. 1053–6.

Butler, N. and Russell, D. S., 2018. 'No funny business: precarious work and emotional labour in stand-up comedy', *Human Relations*, 71(12), pp. 1666–86.

CAMEo, 2018. 'Workforce diversity in the UK screen sector: evidence review', *CAMEo Research Institute*: Leicester.

Carr, F., 2019. 'Could Aisling Bea and Sharon Horgan's new Channel 4 comedy be the next *Fleabag*?', *The Radio Times*. Available at: https://www.radiotimes.com/news/tv/2019-07-30/this-way-up-channel-4-aisling-bea-sharon-horgan-next-fleabag/ (accessed 28/08/2020).

Carter, I. and Anthony, A., 2011. 'Is Sky Atlantic bad for British television?', *The Guardian*. Available at: https://www.theguardian.com/tv-and-radio/2011/feb/06/sky-atlantic-boardwalk-empire-mad-men (accessed 08/05/2019).

Cartner-Morley, J., 2019. '*Fleabag* dressing: how the Phoebe Waller-Bridge character became a style inspiration', *The Guardian*. Available at: https://www.theguardian.com/fashion/2019/mar/19/fleabag-dressing-how-the-phoebe-waller-bridge-character-became-a-style-inspiration (accessed 18/12/2019).

Cefai, S., 2020. 'Contemporary feminist media cultures' in: K. Ross, ed. *The International Encyclopedia of Gender, Media, and Communication*. Chichester: Wiley Blackwell.

Channel 4, 2019a. 'Our tax strategy', *4 Corporate*. Available at: https://www.channel4.com/corporate/our-tax-strategy (accessed 18/12/2019).

Channel 4, 2019b. '*This Way Up*: interview with writer and star Aisling Bea (Aine)'. Channel 4. Available at: https://www.channel4.com/press/news/way-interview-writer-and-star-aisling-bea-aine (accessed 21/01/2023).

Chapman, J., 2014. '*Downton Abbey*: reinventing the British costume drama' in: J. Bignell and S. Lacey, eds., *British Television Drama: Past, Present and Future (Second Edition)*. Basingstoke: Palgrave Macmillan, pp. 131–42.

Cheers, I. M., 2017. *The Evolution of Black Women in Television: Mammies, Matriarchs and Mistresses*. New York: Routledge.

Chemaly, S., 2018. *Rage Becomes Her: The Power of Women's Anger*. New York: Atria Books.

Chortle, 2015. 'How the BBC turned down *Hunderby*'. *Chortle*. Available at: https://www.chortle.co.uk/news/2015/12/04/23726/how_the_bbc_turned_down_hunderby (accessed 28/10/2023).

Chortle, 2019. 'Shame on us for making *Motherland* so white'. *Chortle*. Available at: https://www.chortle.co.uk/features/2019/10/01/44429/shame_on_us_for_making_motherland_so_white (accessed 21/01/2023).

Cliff, A., 2019. 'Is *Fleabag* the best we can do?', *Huck*. Available at: https://www.huckmag.com/perspectives/opinion-perspectives/phoebe-waller-bridge-fleabag-vogue-shoot-privilege/ (accessed 28/08/2020).

Cobb, S., and Horeck, T., 2018. 'Post Weinstein: gendered power and harassment in the media industries', *Feminist Media Studies*, 18(3), pp. 489–91.

Cobb, S., Newsinger, J., and Nwonka, C. J., 2020. 'Introduction: diversity in British film and television: policy, industry and representation', *Journal of British Cinema and Television*, 17(1), pp. 1–5.

Cochrane, K., 2013. *All the Rebel Women: The Rise of the Fourth Wave of Feminism (Guardian Shorts)*. London: Guardian Publishers.

Cochrane, K., 2014. *All the Rebel Women: The Rise of the Fourth Wave Feminist*. London: Simon and Schuster.

Collins, L., 2019. 'The world according to Phoebe Waller-Bridge', *Vogue*. Available at: https://www.vogue.com/article/phoebe-waller-bridge-cover-december-2019 (accessed 28/08/2020).

Collins, P. H., 2015. 'No guarantees: symposium on Black feminist thought', *Ethnic and Racial Studies*, 38(13), pp. 2349–54.

Columpar, C., 2002. 'The dancing body: Sally Potter as feminist auteure' in J. Levitin, J. Plessis, and V. Raoul, eds., *Women Filmmakers: Refocusing*. Vancouver: University of British Columbia Press, pp. 108–16.

Communications Act 2003. Available at: https://www.legislation.gov.uk/ukpga/2003/21/section/198A (accessed 02/01/2024).

Cosslett, R. L., 2019. 'Stop comparing all women's art to *Fleabag*', *New Statesman*. Available at: https://www.newstatesman.com/culture/tv-radio/2019/10/stop-comparing-all-womens-art-fleabag (accessed 28/08/2020).

Craik, L., 2019. '*Catastrophe's* Sharon Horgan talks us through the stages of womanhood', *Elle*. Available at: https://www.elle.com/uk/life-and-culture/culture/a25920648/catastrophes-sharon-horgan-womanhood/ (accessed 21/01/2023).

Creative Diversity Network, 2021. 'Diamond: the fourth cut', *Creative Diversity Network*. Available at: https://creativediversitynetwork.com/wp-content/uploads/2021/01/CDN-Diamond4-JANUARY-27-FINAL.pdf (accessed 30/03/2021).

Creeber, G., 2009. 'The truth is out there! Not!': *Shameless* and the moral structures of contemporary social realism', *New Review of Film and Television Studies*, 7, pp. 421–39.

Darling, O., 2020. '"The moment you realise someone wants your body": neoliberalism, mindfulness and female embodiment in *Fleabag*', *Feminist Media Studies*, 22(1), 132–47.

Davies, H. and Ilott, S., 2018. 'Mocking the weak? context, theories, politics', in: H. Davies and S. Ilott, eds., *Comedy and the Politics of Representation: Mocking the Weak*. London: Springer, pp. 1–24.

Davies, S., 2019. 'Why *Fleabag's* second series is a near-perfect work of art', *The Telegraph*. Available at: https://www.telegraph.co.uk/tv/0/fleabag-series-2-finale-review-near-perfect-work-art/ (accessed 23/11/2020).

Davis, K., 2008. 'Intersectionality as buzzword: a sociology of science perspective on what makes a feminist theory successful', *Feminist Theory*, 9(1), pp. 67–85.

Davis, K., 2020. 'Who owns intersectionality? Some reflections on feminist debates on how theories travel', *European Journal of Women's Studies*, 27(2), pp. 113–27.

Davis, S. M., 2018. 'Taking back the power: an analysis of Black women's communicative resistance', *Review of Communication*, 18(4), pp. 301–18.

Day, E., 2015. 'Sharon Horgan: comedian with a keen eye and a sharp tongue', *The Guardian*. Available at: https://www.theguardian.com/theobserver/2015/feb/01/profile-sharon-horgan-catastrophe-dead-boss-pulling-rob-delaney (accessed 21/01/2023).

de Casparis, L., 2020. 'Fleabag's Sian Clifford talks Phoebe Waller Bridge and her new TV show quiz', *Elle*. Available at: https://www.elle.com/uk/life-and-culture/culture/a32157206/sian-clifford-quiz-itv/ (accessed 28/08/2020).

Dickens, A., 2012. 'Interview: Julia Davis', *Stylist*. Available at: https://www.stylist.co.uk/people/interview-julia-davis/17129 (accessed 16/11/2018).

Dickinson, P., Higgins, A., Matthew St. Pierre, P., Solomon, P. and Zwagerman, S., 2013. 'Introduction: Dorothy Parker's headache', in P. Dickinson, A. Higgins, P. Matthew St. Pierre, D. Solomon and S. Zwagerman, eds., *Women and Comedy: History, Theory, Practice*. Lanham, MA and Plymouth: Fairleigh Dickinson University Press, pp. xix–xxxix.

Dolan, J., 2019. 'Aging, stardom, and "the economy of celebrity"', in: D. Gu and M. E. Dupre, eds., *Encyclopedia of Gerontology and Population Aging*. New York City: Springer International Publishing, pp. 1–10.

Dolan, J. and Tincknell, E., 2013. *Representing Older Women in The Media: The Key Issues*. House of Commons. Available from: http://eprints.uwe.ac.uk/21953 (accessed 08/05/2019).

Donovan, R. A. and West, L. M., 2015. 'Stress and Mental Health: Moderating Role of the Strong Black Woman Stereotype', *Journal of Black Psychology*, 41(4), pp. 384–96.

Dowell, B., 2020. 'The rise of Michaela Coel: the award-winning star behind a must-see drama', *The Times*. Available at: https://www.thetimes.co.uk/article/the-rise-of-michaela-coel-the-award-winning-star-behind-a-must-see-drama-v7nz6fsbf (accessed 02/01/2024).

Draper, T., 2018. 'UK film industry has "class divide at its very heart", say experts', *Screen Daily*. Available at: https://www.screendaily.com/news/uk-film-industry-has-class-divide-at-its-very-heart-say-experts/5133794.article (accessed 19/10/2020).

Dyer, R., 1988. 'White', *Screen*, 29(4), pp. 44–64.

Dyer, R., 1993. *The Matter of Images: Essays on Representations*. London: Routledge.

Eames, T., 2016. 'Caitlin Moran needs YOU to save *Raised by Wolves* series 3: "We have no idea what we're doing"', *Digital Spy*. Available at: https://www.digitalspy.com/tv/a813152/caitlin-moran-needs-you-to-save-raised-by-wolves-series-3-we-have-no-idea-what-were-doing/ (accessed 02/01/2024).

Ebejer, S., 2022. 'Sharon Horgan wants to give women a voice in "*Bad Sisters*"', *Shondaland*. Available at: https://www.shondaland.com/inspire/a41626874/sharon-horgan-wants-to-give-women-a-voice-in-bad-sisters/ (accessed 02/01/2024).

Edwards, K. and Nagouse, E., 2018. 'Germaine Greer: from feminist firebrand to professional troll', *The Conversation*. Available at: http://theconversation.com/germaine-greer-from-feminist-firebrand-to-professional-troll-97645 (accessed 8/11/2019).

Ellis, J., 2000. *Seeing Things: Television in the Age of Uncertainty*. London and New York: I. B. Taurus.

Elmhirst, S., 2019. 'Sharon Horgan: hands down the funniest writer-director-actor-producer-showrunner around – on a TV screen near you', *The Gentlewoman*. Available at: https://thegentlewoman.co.uk/library/sharon-horgan (accessed 21/01/2023).

Evans, G., 2010. '"What about white people's history?": class, race and culture wars in twenty-first-century Britain', in: D. James, E. Plaice and C. Toren, eds., *Culture Wars: Context, Models and Anthropologists' Accounts*. New York and Oxford: Berghahn Books, pp. 115–35.

Fallon, K., 2019. 'The Next "*Fleabag*": Inside Daisy Haggard's Sensational New Series "*Back to Life*"', *The Daily Beast*. Available at: https://www.thedailybeast.com/the-next-fleabag-inside-daisy-haggards-sensational-new-series-back-to-life (accessed 28/08/2020).

Favaro, L. and Gill, R., 2018. 'Feminism rebranded: women's magazines online and "the return of the F-word"', *Revista Digitos*, 4, pp. 37–66.

Fey, T., 2011. *Bossypants*. Boston, MA: Little, Brown and Company.

Fields, A., 2017. *The Girl in the Show: Three Generations of Comedy, Culture, and Feminism*. New York: Arcade Publishing.

Fitzpatrick, P., 2020. *101 Reasons Why Ireland Is Better Than England*. Cork: Mercier Press.

Fleming Jr, M., 2019. 'Stacey Snider joins Elisabeth Murdoch and 'Chernobyl' EP Jane Featherstone in Sister, Global Indie Film & TV Content Producer', *Deadline*. Available at: https://deadline.com/2019/10/stacey-snider-elisabeth-murdoch-jane-featherstone-form-sister-global-indie-content-producer-sister-1202748931/ (accessed 21/01/2023).

Ford, J., 2018. 'Rebooting Roseanne: feminist voice across decades', *M/C Journal*, 21(5), https://doi.org/10.5204/mcj.1472.

Ford, J., 2019. 'Women's indie television: the intimate feminism of women-centric dramedies', *Feminist Media Studies*, 19(7), pp. 928–43.

Franklin, P., 2019. 'Why *Miranda* is more daring than *Fleabag*', *UnHerd*. Available at: https://unherd.com/2019/11/why-miranda-is-more-daring-than-fleabag/ (accessed 28/08/2020).

Freeman, H., 2022. 'Sharon Horgan: "when you're in your 50s, a sort of madness descends"', *The Guardian*. Available at: https://www.theguardian.com/tv-and-radio/2022/apr/09/sharon-horgan-when-youre-in-your-50s-madness-descends (accessed 21/01/2023).

Friedman, S., 2011. 'The cultural currency of a "good" sense of humour: British comedy and new forms of distinction', *British Journal of Sociology*, 62(2), pp. 347–70.

Friedman, S., 2014. *Comedy and Distinction: The Cultural Currency of a 'Good' Sense of Humour*. Abingdon and Oxon: Routledge.

Friedman, S., O'Brien, D. and Laurison, D., 2017. '"Like skydiving without a parachute": how class origin shapes occupational trajectories in british acting', *Sociology*, 51(5), pp. 992–1010.

Furness, H., 2015. 'Acting luminaries return to their roots to save regional theatre', *The Telegraph*. Available at: https://www.telegraph.co.uk/news/bbc/11946246/Acting-luminaries-return-to-their-roots-to-save-regional-theatre.html (accessed 19/10/ 2020).

Gajanan, Mahita., 2017. '*Chewing Gum's* Michaela Coel doesn't think you should make yourself presentable for anyone', *Time*. Available at: https://time.com/4724864/michaela-coels-chewing-gum-netflix-season-2/ (accessed 25/11/2021).

Ganatra, S., 2018. '"Humour is ingrained into our DNA": meet the Irish women making TV's best comedies', *The Guardian*. Available at: https://www.theguardian.com/tv-and-radio/2018/jan/26/humour-is-ingrained-into-our-dna-meet-the-irish-women-making-tvs-best-comedies (accessed 21/01/2023).

Gehring, W. D., 2014. *Chaplin War Triology: An Evolving Lens in Three Dark Comedies, 1918-1947*. Jefferson, MC: McFarland.

Genz, S., 2009. *Postfemininities in Popular Culture*. Basingstoke and New York: Palgrave Macmillan.

Genz, S., 2014. 'My job is me: postfeminist celebrity culture and the gendering of authenticity', *Feminist Media Studies*, 15(4), pp. 545–61.

Gerodetti, N. and McNaught-Davis, M., 2017. 'Feminisation of success or successful femininities? Disentangling "new femininities" under neoliberal conditions', *European Journal of Women's Studies*, 24(4), pp. 351–65.

Gibsone, H., 2018. 'Julia Davis: "I'm worried there's going to be a backlash"', *The Guardian*. Available at: https://www.theguardian.com/tv-and-radio/2018/oct/22/julia-davis-im-worried-theres-going-to-be-a-backlashsally4ever (accessed 16/11/2018).

Gilbert, G., 2010. 'Broad comedy: A new wave of funny women', *The Independent*. Available at: http://www.independent.co.uk/arts-entertainment/comedy/features/broad-comedy-a-new-wave-of-funny-women-1948100.html (accessed 10/11/2017).

Gilbert, G., 2012. 'Julia Davis: "I don't want to offend anyone"', *Independent*. Available at: https://www.independent.co.uk/news/people/profiles/julia-davis-i-dont-want-to-offend-anyone-8073418.html (accessed 16/11/2018).

Gilbert, G., 2015. 'Julia Davis interview: *Hunderby* creator on giving her darkest comic impulses free rein in the Bafta-winning sitcom', *Independent*. Available at: https://www.independent.co.uk/arts-entertainment/tv/features/julia-davis-interview-hunderby-creator-on-giving-her-darkest-comic-impulses-free-reign-in-the-bafta-a6762481.html (accessed 16/11/2018).

Gilbert, J., 2017. '"My Mom's a Cunt": New Bawds Ride the Fourth Wave', in: S. F. Abrams, ed. *Transgressive Humor of American Women Writers*. London: Palgrave Macmillan, pp. 203–30.

Gill, R. 2007. 'Postfeminist media culture: elements of a sensibility', *European Journal of Cultural Studies*, 10(2), pp. 147–66.

Gill, R., 2017. 'The affective, cultural and psychic life of postfeminism: a postfeminist sensibility 10 years on', *European Journal of Cultural Studies*, 20(6), pp. 606-26.

Gill, R. and Scharff, C., 2011. 'Introduction', in R. Gill and C. Scharff, eds., *New Femininities: Postfeminism, Neoliberalism and Subjectivity*. Basingstoke: Palgrave Macmillan. pp. 1–20.

Glass, K., 2017. 'The interview: Thandie Newton, actor', *The Sunday Times Magazine*. Available at: https://www.thetimes.co.uk/magazine/the-sunday-times-magazine/the-interview-thandie-newton-actor-2pr3v0lgf (accessed 30/10/2023).

Goddard, S., 2020. 'Sharon Horgan: "None of our lives are perfect, it's the mess behind it people need to see"', *Marie Claire*. Available at: https://www.marieclaire.co.uk/entertainment/sharon-horgan-2-692168 (accessed 21/01/2023).

Grandberg, B., 2011. 'The new age of the comedy auteur?', *Vulture*. Available at: https://www.vulture.com/2011/07/the-new-age-of-the-comedy-auteur.html (accessed 01/06/2020).

Grainge, P. and Johnson, C., 2015. *Promotional Screen Industries*. London and New York: Routledge.

Gray, F., 1994. *Women and Laughter*. Virginia: University of Virginia Press.

Gray, J. and Lotz, A. D., 2019. *Television Studies* (2nd ed.). Malden MA: Polity Press.

Gundle, S., 2008. 'Stars and stardom in the study of Italian cinema', *Italian Studies*, 63(2), pp. 261–6.

Hall, S., 1998. 'Notes on deconstructing "the popular"', in J. Storey. eds., *Cultural Theory and Popular Culture: A Reader*. Athens, GA: The University of Georgia Press, pp. 442–53.

Hallam, J., 2007. 'Independent women: creating TV drama in the UK in the 1990s', *Critical Studies in Television*, 2(1), pp. 18–34.

Harris, J. C. and Patton, L. D., 2019., 'Un/doing intersectionality through higher education research', *The Journal of Higher Education*, 90(3), pp. 347–72.

Harrison, E., 2019. 'Sharon Horgan: "It's f***ing annoying it took a sexual assault apocalypse to make female stories sell"', *The Independent*. Available at: https://www.independent.co.uk/arts-entertainment/tv/features/sharon-horgan-modern-love-motherland-tina-fey-anne-hathaway-phoebe-waller-bridge-catastrophe-a9152456.html (accessed 21/01/2023).

Harrison, E., 2021. '"Appalling behaviour is outrageously funny": how the Irish sitcom took over telly', *The Independent*. Available at: https://www.independent.co.uk/arts-entertainment/tv/features/derry-girls-catastrophe-irish-sitcoms-b1828434.html (accessed 21/01/2023).

Hattenstone, S., 2015. 'Julie Walters: "People like me wouldn't get a chance today"', *The Guardian*. Available at: https://www.theguardian.com/culture/2015/jan/24/julie-walters-people-like-me-wouldnt-get-a-chance-today (accessed 19/10/2020).

Havas, J. and Sulimma., 2018. 'Through the Gaps of My Fingers: Genre, Femininity, and Cringe Aesthetics in Dramedy Television', *Television & New Media*, 21(1), pp. 75–94.

Hennefeld, M., 2018. 'Comedy is part of feminist history—and we need it more than ever', *openDemocracy*, Available at: https://www.opendemocracy.net/en/transformation/comedy-is-part-of-feminist-history-and-we-need-it-more-than-ever/ (accessed 01/06/2020).

Higgins, C., 2018 'The age of patriarchy: how an unfashionable idea became a rallying cry for feminism today', *The Guardian*. Available at: https://www.theguardian.com/news/2018/jun/22/the-age-of-patriarchy-how-an-unfashionable-idea-became-a-rallying-cry-for-feminism-today (accessed 8/11/2019).

Hilton, B. and Ferguson, E., 2011. 'Are TV sitcoms too middle-class?', *The Guardian*. Available at: https://www.theguardian.com/commentisfree/2011/jan/30/danny-cohen-middle-class-comedy#:~:text=Controller%20of%20BBC1%20Danny%20Cohen,point%20%E2%80%93%20and%20whether%20it%20matters%E2%80%A6 (accessed 02/01/2024).

Hogg, C., 2020. 'A class act: an interview with Julie Hesmondhalgh on casting, representation and inclusion in British television drama', *Critical Studies in Television*, 15(3), pp. 302–11.

Hohenstein, S. and Thalmann, K., 2019. 'Difficult women: changing representations of female characters in contemporary television series', *Zeitschrift für Anglistik und Amerikanistik; Leipzig*, 67(2), pp. 109–29.

Holmes, S. and Negra, D., 2011. 'Introduction', in: S. Holmes and D. Negra, eds., *In the Limelight and Under the Microscope: Forms and Functions of Female Celebrity*. New York: Continuum, pp. 1–16.

Horton, E., 2016. 'A very special relationship: mapping the transatlanticism of contemporary golden age quality comedy', *Critical Studies in Television (CST) Blog*. Available at: https://cstonline.net/a-very-special-relationship-mapping-the-transatlanticism-of-contemporary-golden-age-quality-comedy-by-erica-horton/ (accessed 14/01/2021).

House of Lords Committee, 2006. *The Review of the BBC's Royal Charter: 1st Report of Session 2005-06*. London: The Stationery Office.

Hoyes, M., 2016. 'Infographic: the true picture for black actors in the UK film industry', *BFI*. Available at: https://www.bfi.org.uk/features/black-actors-british-film-industry-statistics (accessed 30/10/2023).

Hughes, S., 2016. 'Julia Davis talks new show *Camping* and the future of comedy', *Independent*. Available at: https://www.independent.co.uk/arts-entertainment/tv/features/comedian-julia-davis-says-the-future-of-comedy-is-scary-a6939086.html (accessed 16/11/2018).

Hughes, S., 2018. 'This time it's personal: the new wave of British female TV writers', *The Guardian*. Available at: https://www.theguardian.com/tv-and-radio/2018/nov/03/women-tv-writers-new-wave-personal-experience (accessed 16/11/2018).

Hunt, E., 2019. 'Here's to "*Fleabag*" – a searing examination of grief and love, and the comedy show of this decade', *NME*. Available at: https://www.nme.com/blogs/tv-blogs/fleabag-grief-love-comedy-show-decade-final-2474388 (accessed 28/08/2020).

Hunt, G., 2017. 'Intersectionality: locating and critiquing internal structures of oppression within feminism', in: C. Hay, ed., *Philosophy: Feminism*. New York: Macmillan Reference USA, pp. 121–38.

Hunt, L., 2013. *Cult British TV Comedy: From Reeves and Mortimer to Psychoville*. Manchester: Manchester University Press.

Hyem, J., 1987. 'Entering the arena: writing for television', in H. Baehr and G. Dyer, eds., *Boxed In: Women and Television*. London: Pandora, pp. 151–63.

Ingle, R., 2021. 'Sharon Horgan: "I don't believe age is just a number. That's b****cks"', *The Irish Times*. Available at: https://www.irishtimes.com/life-and-style/people/sharon-horgan-i-don-t-believe-age-is-just-a-number-that-s-b-cks-1.4651968 (accessed 21/01/2023).

Ishkanian, A., 2019. 'Social movements, Brexit, and social policy', *Social Policy and Society*, 18(1), pp. 147–59.

Jackson, J., 2016. 'Caitlin Moran: benefits street made working-class people look like animals', *The Guardian*. Available at: https://www.theguardian.com/media/2016/feb/23/caitlin-moran-benefits-street-working-class (accessed 8/11/2019).

Jackson, S., 2018. 'Young feminists, feminism and digital media', *Feminism and Psychology*, 28(1), pp. 32–49.

Jacobs, E., 2016. 'Phoebe Waller-Bridge & Vicky Jones on creating hit series "*Fleabag*"'. *The Financial Times*. Available at: https://www.ft.com/content/febac644-bc05-11e6-8b45-b8b81dd5d080 (accessed 10/11/2017).

Jacobs, E., 2017. 'Sharon Horgan on marital catastrophes and her new show "*Motherland*"', *The Financial Times*. Available at: https://www.ft.com/content/0812b33a-c418-11e7-a1d2-6786f39ef675 (accessed 21/01/2023).

Jeffries, S., 2015. '*Raised by Wolves* review – a heartwarming tale of Black Country folk', *The Guardian*. Available at: https://www.theguardian.com/tv-and-radio/2015/mar/17/raised-by-wolves-funny-sitcom-black-country (accessed 8/11/2019).

Jenner, M., 2018. *Netflix and the Re-invention of Television*. Cham: Palgrave Macmillan.

Jodelka, F., 2015. 'Council estate of mind: Michaela Coel's *Chewing Gum* is smart, bawdy and brilliant', *The Guardian*. Available at: https://www.theguardian.com/tv-and-radio/2015/oct/06/chewing-gum-michaela-coel (accessed 19/12/2017).

Johnson, B., 2019. 'Leading, collaborating, championing: RED's arresting women', *Journal of British Cinema and Television*, 16(3), pp. 327–45.

Johnson B., and Peirse, A., 2021. 'Genre, gender and television screenwriting: the problem of pigeonholing', *European Journal of Cultural Studies*, 24(3), pp. 658–72.

Johnson, C., 2012. *Branding Television*. London: Routledge.

Johnson, K., 2012. 'Why I Didn't Run the Caitlin Moran Interview', *Bitch Media*. Available at: <https://www.bitchmedia.org/post/why-i-didnt-run-the-caitlin-moran-interview. (accessed 8/11/2019).

Jolles, M., 2012. 'Going rogue: postfeminism and the privilege of breaking rules', *Feminist Formations*, 24(3), pp. 43–61.

Jones, C. and Shorter-Gooden, K., 2003. *Shifting: The Double Lives of Black Women in America*. New York: HarperCollins.

Jones, E. E., 2019. '*Fleabag* is a work of undeniable genius. But it is for posh girls', *The Guardian*. Available at: https://www.theguardian.com/tv-and-radio/2019/apr/20/fleabag-posh-girl-television (accessed 02/01/2024).

Jones, O., 2020. 'The British middle class is in freefall, its young people pushed into precarity', *The Guardian*. Available at: https://www.theguardian.com/commentisfree/2020/dec/12/british-middle-class-young-people-class-home-ownership-job-security (accessed 10/02/2021).

Jouët, J., 2018. 'Digital feminism: questioning the renewal of activism', *Journal of Research in Gender Studies*, 8(1), pp. 133–57.

Jung, E. A., 2020. 'Michaela the destroyer: how a young talent from East London went from open-mic nights to making the most sublimely unsettling show of the year', *Vulture*. Available at: https://www.vulture.com/article/michaela-coel-i-may-destroy-you.html. (accessed 14/01/2021).

Kaklamanidou, B. and Tally, M., eds., 2014. *HBO's Girls: Questions of Gender, Politics, and Millennial Angst*. Newcastle Upon Tyne: Cambridge Scholars Publishing.

Kanai, A., 2021. 'Intersectionality in digital feminist knowledge cultures: the practices and politics of a travelling theory', *Feminist Theory*, 22(4), pp. 518–35.

Kanter, J., 2021. 'Sharon Horgan's Merman teams with Paul Feig, Lionsgate to remake BBC Comedy 'Motherland' in the U.S.', *Deadline*. Available at: https://deadline.com/2021/03/sharon-horgan-merman-team-with-paul-feig-to-remake-bbc-motherland-1234721570/ (accessed 21/01/2023).

Kantar Media, 2017. *Channel 4 Corporation Remit*. Available at: https://www.ofcom.org.uk/__data/assets/pdf_file/0018/104094/Channel-4-Corporation-Remit-Research-Report-2017.pdf (accessed 10/11/2017).

Kay, J. B., 2020. *Gender, Media and Voice: Communicative Injustice and Public Speech*. Basingstoke: Palgrave.

Keller, J. and Ringrose, J., 2015. '"But then feminism goes out the window!": exploring teenage girls' critical response to celebrity feminism', *Celebrity Studies*, 6(1), pp. 132–5.

Keller, J. and Ryan, M. E., 2018. 'Introduction: mapping emergent feminisms', in: J. Keller and M. E. Ryan, eds., *Emergent Feminisms: Complicating a Postfeminist Media Culture*. London and New York: Routledge, pp. 1–21.

Khan, G., 2019. 'Our friend in the Midlands: Guz Khan on regional representation', *Royal Television Society*. Available at: https://rts.org.uk/article/our-friend-midlands-guz-khan-regional-representation (accessed 8/11/2019).

Khomami, N., 2018. 'Outdated thinking "is still holding female TV writers back"', *The Guardian*. Available at: https://www.theguardian.com/media/2018/feb/28/female-tv-writers-protest-about-glass-ceiling-for-women (accessed 07/02/2019).

Kiefer, B., 2017. 'Sharon Horgan on confidence, creativity and closing the gender gap', *Campaign*. Available at: https://www.campaignlive.co.uk/article/sharon-horgan-confidence-creativity-closing-gender-gap/1440079 (accessed 21/01/2023).

Knappe, H. and Lang, S., 2014. 'Between whisper and voice: online women's movement outreach in the UK and Germany', *European Journal of Women's Studies*, 21(4), pp. 361–81.

Kohen, Y., 2012. *We Killed: The Rise of Women in American Comedy*. New York: Pan Macmillan.

Kosin, J., 2016. '"*Fleabag*" creator and star Phoebe Waller-Bridge is the voice of a new generation of women'. *Harper's Bazaar*. Available at: http://www.harpersbazaar.com/culture/film-tv/news/a17977/phoebe-waller-bridge-fleabag-interview/ (accessed 10/11/2017).

Kreager, A. and Follows, S., 2018. 'Gender inequality and screenwriters: a study of the impact of gender on equality of opportunity for screenwriters and key creatives in the UK film and television industries', *The Writers Guild of Great Britain*. Available at: https://writersguild.org.uk/wp-content/uploads/2018/05/Gender-Inequality-and-Screenwriters.pdf (accessed 30/03/2021).

Lamont, T., 2010. 'Julia Davis and Jessica Hynes: "We're curious about what goes on in strangers' heads"', *The Guardian*. Available at: https://www.theguardian.com/stage/2010/oct/24/julia-davis-jessica-hynes-interview (accessed 16/11/2018).

Lampen, C. and Arnold, A., 2020. 'Obama also loves *Fleabag*', *The Cut*. Available at: https://www.thecut.com/2020/01/barack-obama-names-fleabag-in-best-television-shows-of-2019.html (accessed 23/11/2020).

Landrum, G. N., 2007. *Paranoia and Power: Fear and Fame of Entertainment Icons*. Garden City, NY: Morgan James

Larson, S., 2017. 'The rise of the television-comedy auteur', *The New Yorker*. Available at: https://www.newyorker.com/magazine/2017/09/04/the-rise-of-the-television-comedy-auteur (accessed 01/06/2020).

Lauzen M. M., 2018. 'Boxed in 2017–18: women on screen and behind the scenes in television'. Center for the Study of Women in Television and Film, San Diego State University.

Lawrence, B., 2019. '*Fleabag* "just for posh girls"? That kind of inverse snobbery threatens creativity', *The Telegraph*. Available at: https://www.telegraph.co.uk/tv/0/fleabag-just-posh-girls-kind-inverse-snobbery-threatens-creativity/ (accessed 28/08/2020).

Lee, D., 2019. 'Burning out, giving up or selling out? The performative burden of television production', paper presented at Leeds Media and Communication Research Seminar, 3rd March, University of Leeds.

Lemish, D., and Muhlbauer, V., 2012. '"Can't have it all": representations of older women in popular culture', *Women and Therapy*, 35, pp. 165–80.

Leonard, S., 2020. What Roseanne Barr meant to media studies, *Television and New Media*, 21(6), 596–601.

Levine, N., 2019. '10 Things You Never Knew About Phoebe Waller-Bridge', *BBC America*. Available at: https://www.bbcamerica.com/anglophenia/2019/05/10-things-you-never-knew-about-phoebe-waller-bridge (accessed 28/08/2020).

Lewis, M. M., 2014. *That's What She Said: Politics, Transgression, and Women's Humor in Contemporary American Television*, PhD thesis, Bowling Green State University, American Culture Studies.

Lewis, P., 2014. 'Postfeminism, femininities and organization studies: exploring a new agenda', *Organization Studies*, 35(12), pp. 1845–66.

Lewis, T., 2017. '*Chewing Gum's* Michaela Coel: "I enjoy making people uncomfortable"', *The Guardian*. Available at: https://www.theguardian.com/tv-and-radio/2017/jan/08/michaela-cole-enjoy-making-people-uncomfortable-chewing-gum-season-two (accessed 09/12/2017).

Littler, J. 2020. 'Mothers behaving badly: chaotic hedonism and the crisis of neoliberal social reproduction', *Cultural Studies*, 34(4), pp. 499–520.

Littlewood, J. and Pickering, M., 2005. 'Heard the one about the white middle class heterosexual father-in-law? Gender, ethnicity and political correctness in comedy', in: S. Wagg, ed. *Because I Tell a Joke or Two: Comedy, Politics and Social Difference*. New York: Taylor and Francis e-Library, pp. 290–310.

Liu, R., 2019. 'The making of a millennial woman', *Another Gaze*. Available at: https://www.anothergaze.com/making-millennial-woman-feminist-capitalist-fleabag-girls-sally-rooney-lena-dunham-unlikeable-female-character-relatable/ (accessed 28/08/2020).

Lockyer, S., 2010. 'Dynamics of social class contempt in contemporary British television comedy', *Social Semiotics*, 20(2), pp. 121–38.

Lockyer, S., 2015. 'An extra slice of Jo Brand', *Critical Studies in Television: The International Journal of Television Studies*, 10(2), pp. 118–28.

Logan, B., 2010. 'When did comedians get so middle-class?', *The Guardian*. Available at: https://www.theguardian.com/stage/2010/jul/21/comedy-middle-class (accessed 31/10/2023).

Lotz, A. D., 2017. *Portals: A Treatise on Internet-distributed Television*. Michigan: University of Michigan Library.

Lundy, A. D., 2018. 'Caught between a thot and a hard place: the politics of black female sexuality at the intersection of cinema and reality television', *The Black Scholar: Journal of Black Studies and Research*, 48(1), pp. 56–70.

Lusher, T., 2015. 'Julia Davis: "I like that really repressed stuff you can kick against"', *The Guardian*. Available at: https://www.theguardian.com/tv-and-radio/2015/dec/06/julia-davis-i-like-that-really-repressed-stuff-you-can-kick-against (accessed 16/11/2018).

Lury, K., 2005. *Interpreting Television*. London: Hodder Arnold.

Mahanty, S., 2020. 'Michaela Coel's *"I May Destroy You"* is the most exciting new TV series since *"Fleabag"*, *Elle*. Available at: https://www.elle.com/uk/life-and-culture/culture/a32807596/michaela-coel-i-may-destroy-you/ (accessed 28/08/2020).

Malik, S., 2002. *Representing Black Britain: Black and Asian Images on Television*. London: SAGE Publications.

Malone, N., 2017. 'The *Fleabag* Mystique', *The Cut*. Available at: https://www.thecut.com/2017/02/phoebe-waller-bridge-fleabag.html (accessed 28/08/2020).

Marghitu, S., 2018. '"It's just art": auteur apologism in the post-Weinstein era', *Feminist Media Studies*, 18(3), pp. 491–4.

Matthews, N., 2017. 'Netflix' *Chewing Gum's* Michaela Coel Gets Serious About Colorism', *DeenieMedia: Culture and Society*. Available at: https://www.deeniemedia.com/single-post/2017/04/04/Netflix-Chewing-Gums-Michaela-Coel-Gets-Serious-About-Colorism (accessed 09/12/2017).

Mayer, S., 2018a. 'The Varda variations: (re)introductions of the auteure in documenteur and beyond', *cléo: a journal of film and feminism*, 6(1). Available at: http://cleojournal.com/2018/04/11/varda-variations-documenteur/ (accessed 01/06/2020).

Mayer, S., 2018b. 'Literary celebrity, politics and the Nobel prize: the Nobel lecture as an authorial self-fashioning platform', in: J. Alexander and K. Bronk, eds., *(Extra)Ordinary?: The Concept of Authenticity in Celebrity and Fan Studies*. Leiden/Boston: Brill Rodopi, pp. 54–76.

McCabe, J., and Akass, K. 2007. *Quality TV: Contemporary American Television and Beyond*. London: I. B. Tauris.

McCann, H., 2017. '"A voice of a generation": girls and the problem of representation', in: M. Nash and I. Whelehan, eds., *Reading Lena Dunham's Girls: Feminism, Postfeminism, Authenticity and Gendered Performance in Contemporary Television*. London, UK: Palgrave Macmillan, pp. 91–104.

McCue, J. A., 2014. 'Empowering the Female Voice: Interdisciplinarity, Feminism, and the Memoir', *Journal of Integrated Studies*, 5(1), pp. 1–10.

McElroy, R., 2016. 'The feminization of contemporary british television drama: Sally Wainwright and red production', in: R. Moseley, H. Wheatley, and H. Wood, eds., *Television for Women: New Directions*. London and New York: Routledge, pp. 34–52.

McFarland, M., 2022. '"*Shining Vale*" creator on the horror of midlife: "depression and possession share similar symptoms"', *Salon*. Available at: https://www.salon.com/2022/03/20/sharon-horgan-shining-vale-salon-talks/ (accessed 21/01/2023).

McIntyre, A. P., 2022. *Contemporary Irish popular culture: transnationalism, regionality, and diaspora*. New York: Springer International Publishing.

McKenzie, S., 2019. 'The paradox of Phoebe Waller-Bridge', *The F Word*. Available at: https://thefword.org.uk/2019/12/the-paradox-of-phoebe-waller-bridge/ (accessed 07/10/2020).

McLean, G., 2004. 'Will *Nighty Night* change the sitcom for ever?', *The Guardian*. Available at: https://www.theguardian.com/culture/2004/apr/19/media.television (accessed 07/02/2019).

McLean, G., 2016. '*Catastrophe's* Sharon Horgan on making a splash with Merman', *The Guardian*. Available at: https://www.theguardian.com/media/2016/mar/13/sharon-horgan-catastrophe-clelia-mountford-merman (accessed 21/01/2023).

McRobbie, A., 2004. 'Post-feminism and popular culture', *Feminist Media Studies*, 4(3), pp. 255–64.

McRobbie, A., 2009. *The Aftermath of Feminism: Gender, Culture and Social Change*. London and California: SAGE Publications.

McRobbie, A., 2015, 'Notes on the perfect: competitive femininity in neoliberal times', *Australian Feminist Studies*, 30(83), pp. 3–20.

Medhurst, A., 2007. *A National Joke: Popular Comedy and English Cultural Identities*. London: Routledge.

Mellencamp, P., 1992. *High Anxiety: Catastrophe, Scandal, Age, and Comedy*. Bloomington: Indiana University Press.

Mijs, J., 2019. 'The gulf between the rich and poor is widening – we just can't see it', *The Independent*. Available at: https://www.independent.co.uk/voices/wealth-inequality-rich-poor-growing-gender-race-davos-a8745056.html (accessed 28/08/2020).

Miller, N., 1989. 'Changing the subject' in E. Weed, ed. *Coming to Terms: Feminism, Theory, Politics*. New York: Routledge.

Mills, B., 2005. *Television Sitcom*. London: British Film Institute.

Mills, B., 2009. *The Sitcom*. Edinburgh: Edinburgh University Press.

Mills, B., 2010. 'Being Rob Brydon: performing the self in comedy', *Celebrity Studies*, 1(2), 189–201.

Mills, B., 2013., 'What does it mean to call television "*cinematic*"?', in: J. Jacobs and S. Peacock, eds., *Television Aesthetics and Style*. New York: Bloomsbury Academic, pp. 57–66.

Mills, B., 2018. 'Comedy and the nation in *The Trip*' in: N. Marx and M. Sienkiewicz, eds., *The Comedy Studies Reader*. Texas: University of Texas Press, pp. 267–81.

Mills, B., and Horton, E., 2016. *Creativity in the British Television Comedy Industry*. Abingdon and New York: Routledge.

Mills, B. and Ralph, S., 2015. '"I think women are possibly judged more harshly with comedy": women and British television comedy production', *Critical Studies in Television*, 10(2), pp. 102–17.

Minor, L., 2023. 'Alma's not normal: normalising working-class women in/on BBC TV comedy' *Journal of British Cinema and Television*, 20(2), pp. 137–61.

Mittell, J., 2015. *Complex TV: The Poetics of Contemporary Television Storytelling*. New York: New York University Press.

Mizejewski, L., 2007. 'Queen Latifah, unruly women, and the bodies of romantic comedy', *Genders 1998–2013*. Available at: https://www.colorado.edu/gendersarchive1998-2013/2007/10/01/queen-latifah-unruly-women-and-bodies-romantic-comedy (accessed 28/08/2020).

Mizejewski, L., 2014. *Pretty/Funny: Women Comedians and Body Politics*. Austin: University of Texas Press.

Mizejewski, L., 2018. 'Kathleen Rowe Karlyn and feminist genres of laughter', *Jump Cut: A Review of Contemporary Media*, 58. Available at: https://www.ejumpcut.org/archive/jc58.2018/MizejewskiFeministCom/text.html (accessed 01/06/2020).

Mizejewski, L. and Sturtevant, V., eds., 2017. *Hysterical!: Women in American Comedy*. Austin: University of Texas Press.

Modleski, T., 1979. 'The search for tomorrow in today's soap operas: notes on a feminine narrative form', *Film Quarterly*, 33(1), pp. 12–21.

Moeschen, S., 2019. *The League of Extraordinarily Funny Women: 50 Trailblazers of Comedy*. Philadelphia, PA: Running Press.

Mooney, K., 2019. 'Why we're all obsessed with looking like Fleabag: first Phoebe Waller-Bridge's two-season show inspired lipstick and jumpsuit purchases. Now fans are getting her haircut', *Vox*. Available at: https://www.vox.com/the-goods/2019/6/10/18659673/fleabag-phoebe-waller-bridge-haircut-jumpsuit-red-wrap-dress (accessed 28/08/2020).

Monaghan, G., 2016. 'From poultry farming in Meath to talking turkey with HBO', *The Times*. Available at: https://www.thetimes.co.uk/article/from-poultry-farming-in-meath-to-talking-turkey-with-hbo-vkh3zmjg8 (accessed 21/01/2023).

Moran, C., 2011. *How to Be A Woman*. London: Ebury Press.

Moran, C., 2013. 'Caitlin Moran: why my sister and I wrote *Raised by Wolves*', *The Guardian*. Available at: https://www.theguardian.com/media/media-blog/2013/may/29/caitlin-moran-raised-by-wolves-sitcom (accessed 8/11/2019).

Moran, C., 2014. *How to Build a Girl*. London: Ebury Press.

Moran, C., 2019a. 'How much has life really changed for women since the Nineties?', *Stylist*. Available at: https://www.stylist.co.uk/life/caitlin-moran-how-to-be-a-woman-90s-vs-now-00s-sexism-feminism/276663 (accessed 18/12/2019).

Moran, C., 2019b. 'Caitlin Moran's celebrity watch: prepare for the inevitable Phoebe Waller-Bridge backlash', *The Times*. Available at: https://www.thetimes.co.uk/article/caitlin-morans-celebrity-watch-prepare-for-the-inevitable-phoebe-waller-bridge-backlash-rr87jnggw (accessed 28/08/2020).

Mountford, C., 2021. '"*This Way Up*" season 2: balancing comedy and poignancy', *CherryPicks*. Available at: https://www.thecherrypicks.com/stories/this-way-up-interview/ (accessed 21/01/2023).

Moylan, B., 2015. '*Catastrophe*: the romantic comedy that banned the words "I love you"', *The Guardian*. Available at: https://www.theguardian.com/tv-and-radio/2015/jun/22/catastrophe-rob-delaney-sharon-horgan-amazon-prime (accessed 21/01/2023).

Mumford, G., 2017. 'Samuel L Jackson criticises casting of black British actors in American films', *The Guardian*. Available at: https://www.theguardian.com/film/2017/mar/08/samuel-l-jackson-criticises-casting-of-black-british-actors-in-american-films (accessed 30/10/2023).

Munro, E., 2013. 'Feminism: a fourth wave?', *Political Insight*, 4(2), pp. 22–5.

Munro, E., 2014. 'Feminism: a fourth wave?', *The Political Studies Association*. Available at: http://www.psa.ac.uk/insight-plus/feminism-fourth-wave (accessed 16/02/2020).

Murdock, M, 1990. *The Heroine's Journey: Woman's Quest for Wholeness*. Boston: Shambhala Publications.

Murphy, C., 2013. 'Comedy star Sharon gets to rewrite history as *"Psychobitches"* Eva Peron and Cleopatra in new TV sketch show', *Independent.ie*. Available at: https://www.

independent.ie/regionals/herald/entertainment/around-town/comedy-star-sharon-gets-to-rewrite-history-as-psychobitches-eva-peron-and-cleopatra-in-new-tv-sketch-show-29277501.html (accessed 21/01/2023).

Myers, O., 2017. 'Michaela Coel is doing whatever the hell she wants', *Fader*. Available at: http://www.thefader.com/2017/04/04/michaela-coel-chewing-gum-season-two-interview (accessed 09/12/2017).

Negra, D., 2014. 'Claiming feminism: commentary, autobiography and advice literature for women in the recession', *Journal of Gender Studies*, 23(3), pp. 275–86.

Negra, D. and Holmes, S., 2008. 'Going cheap? Female celebrity in the reality, tabloid and scandal genres'. *Genders*, 48.

Neibaur, J., 2012. *Early Charlie Chaplin: The Artist as Apprentice at Keystone Studios*. Lanham, MD: Scarecrow Press.

Nelson, R., 1997. *TV Drama in Transition: Forms, Values and Cultural Change*. London: Palgrave Macmillan.

Newman, M. Z. and Levine, E., 2012. *Legitimating Television: Media Convergence and Cultural Status*. New York and London: Routledge.

Nicholson, R., 2009. '*Human Remains*: a macabre comedy masterpiece', *The Guardian*. Available at: https://www.theguardian.com/culture/tvandradioblog/2009/jul/17/human-remains-comedy-rob-brydon (accessed 26/10/2023).

Nicholson, R., 2010. '*Lizzie and Sarah*: has the BBC lost its nerve over this dark comedy?', *The Guardian*. Available at: http://www.guardian.co.uk/tv-and-radio/tvandradioblog/2010/mar/18/lizzie-sarah-bbc (accessed 07/02/2019).

Nicholson, R., 2016. 'An Interview with Julia Davis, the weird queen of British comedy', *Vice*. Available at: https://www.vice.com/en_uk/article/7bdgzz/julia-davis-british-comedy-nighty-night-jam-camping (accessed 16/11/2018).

Nochimson, M. P., 2019. *Television Rewired: The Rise of the Auteur Series*. Austin, TX: Texas University Press.

Nygaard T. and Lagerway, J., 2017. 'Liberal women, mental illness, and precarious whiteness in Trump's America', *Flow: A Critical Forum on Media and Culture*. Available at: https://www.flowjournal.org/2017/11/whiteness-in-trumps-america/?print=print (accessed 28/08/2020).

Nygaard T. and Lagerway, J., 2018. '*Broad City's* affable critique and the racial discourses of girlfriendship', *Flow: A Critical Forum on Media and Culture*. Available at: https://www.flowjournal.org/2018/03/broad-city-critique-girlfriendship/ (accessed 28/08/2020).

Nygaard T. and Lagerway, J., 2020. *Horrible White People: Gender, Genre, and Television's Precarious Whiteness*. New York: NYU Press.

O'Connor, A., 2017. 'Last night's *Catastrophe* featured the most Irish financial solution ever', *The Daily Edge*. Available at: https://www.dailyedge.ie/catastrophe-post-office-savings-account-3288167-Mar2017/ (accessed 21/01/2023).

Ofcom, 2015. *Public Service Broadcasting Annual Report 2015*. Available at: https://www.ofcom.org.uk/tv-radio-and-on-demand/information-for-industry/public-service-broadcasting/public-service-broadcasting-annual-report-2015 (accessed 07/02/2019).

Ofcom, 2018. 'Representation and portrayal on BBC television: thematic review'. Available at: https://www.ofcom.org.uk/__data/assets/pdf_file/0022/124078/report-bbc-representation-portrayal.pdf (accessed 23/11/2020).

O'Hagan, E. M., 2013. 'Feminists can be sexy and funny – but it's anger that changes the world', *The Guardian*. Available at: https://www.theguardian.com/commentisfree/2013/feb/26/feminists-sexy-funny-anger-changes-world (accessed 8/11/2019).

Orgad, S., and Gill, R., 2021. *Confidence Culture*. Durham, NC: Duke University Press.

Oyler, L., 2015. 'How to be Caitlin Moran', *Vice*. Available at: https://www.vice.com/en_us/article/4wbx9q/how-to-be-caitlin-moran-575 (accessed 18/12/2019).

Oyler, L., 2016. '"*Fleabag*" star Phoebe Waller-Bridge on "Unlikable" women and sexual validation'. *Vice*. Available at: https://www.vice.com/en_uk/article/gqk5q3/fleabag-star-phoebe-waller-bridge-on-unlikable-women-and-sexual-validation (accessed 10/11/2017).

Parker, R., 2018. 'Women writers campaign gathers pace', *Broadcast*. Available at: https://www.broadcastnow.co.uk/drama/women-writers-campaign-gathers-pace/5127172.article (accessed 02/01/2024).

Patterson, E., 2012. 'Fracturing Tina Fey: a critical analysis of postfeminist television comedy stardom', *The Communication Review*, 15(3), pp. 232–51.

Perkins, C. and Schreiber, M., 2019. 'Independent women: from film to television', *Feminist Media Studies*, 19(7), pp. 919–27.

Peroni, C., and Rodak, L., 2020. 'Introduction. The fourth wave of feminism: from social networking and self-determination to sisterhood', *Oñati Socio-Legal Series*, 10(1S), 1S–9S.

Peterson, A. H., 2017. *Too Fat, Too Slutty, Too Loud: The Rise and Reign of the Unruly Woman*. New York: Plume.

Petter, O., 2019. '*Fleabag* writer Phoebe Waller-Bridge reveals fear of being a "bad feminist"', *The Independent*. Available at: https://www.independent.co.uk/life-style/women/phoebe-waller-bridge-fleabag-bad-feminist-a8817151.html (accessed 28/08/2020).

Phillips, R. and Cree, V., 2014. 'What does the "Fourth Wave" mean for teaching feminism in 21st century social work?', *Social Work Education*, 33(7), pp. 930–43.

Pinedo, I. C., 2021. *Difficult Women on Television Drama: The Gender Politics of Complex Women in Serial Narratives*. London and New York: Routledge.

Piper, H., 2016. 'Broadcast drama and the problem of television aesthetics: home, nation, universe', *Screen*, 57(2), pp. 163–83.

Porter, L., 2005. 'Arts, tampons and tyrants: women and representation in British comedy', in: S. Wagg, ed., *Because I Tell a Joke or Two: Comedy, Politics and Social Difference* (2nd ed.). London and New York: Routledge, pp. 65–92.

Portwood-Stacer, L., 2013. 'Media refusal and conspicuous non-consumption: the performance and political dimensions of Facebook abstention', *New Media and Society*, 15(7), pp. 1041–57.

Press, J., 2018. 'Meet the dramedy queens: the women who built TV's new golden age', *The Guardian*. Available at: https://www.theguardian.com/tv-and-radio/2018/mar/05/meet-the-dramedy-queens-the-women-built-tvs-new-golden-age-derry-girls-insecure-catastrophe (accessed 04/09/2020).

Quirk, S., 2015. *Why Stand-up Matters: How Comedians Manipulate and Influence*. London and New York: Bloomsbury.

Quirk, S., 2018. *The Politics of British Stand-up Comedy: The New Alternative*. Basingstoke: Palgrave Macmillan.

Ralph, S., 2012. 'Lucy Lumsden: a new television auteur?', *Auteuse theory: a blog on women's cinema* (blog post). Available at: http://auteusetheory.blogspot.com/2012/07/lucy-lumsden-new-television-auteur.html (accessed 22/05/2019).

Ramachandran, N., 2020. 'Michaela Coel on turning down Netflix: "I was empowered and happy to have nothing"', *Variety*. Available at: https://variety.com/2020/tv/global/michaela-coel-netflix-queer-characters-1234718249/ (accessed 14/01/2021).

Ramaswamy, C., 2018. 'From fridging to nagging husbands: how *Killing Eve* upturns sexist clichés', *The Guardian*. Available at: https://www.theguardian.com/tv-and-radio/2018/oct/12/from-fridging-to-nagging-husbands-how-killing-eve-upturns-sexist-cliches (accessed 07/02/2019).

Raphael, A., 2009. 'There's no moral centre to *Pulling* because we don't have one!', *The Guardian*. Available at: https://www.theguardian.com/culture/2009/may/16/pulling-sharon-horgan-dennis-kelly (accessed 02/01/2024).

Read, B., 2018. 'With *Sally4Ever*, Julia Davis's signature comedy of discomfort lands stateside', *Vogue*. Available at: https://www.vogue.com/article/sally4ever-julia-davis-interview-hbo (accessed 16/05/2019).

Rees, J., 2004. 'A comic monster for our times', *The Telegraph*. Available at: https://www.telegraph.co.uk/culture/tvandradio/3614612/A-comic-monster-for-our-times.html (accessed 07/02/2019).

Renshaw, D., 2014. '*Nighty Night* box set review – a viciously funny, downright cruel comedy', *The Guardian*. Available at: https://www.theguardian.com/tv-and-radio/2014/nov/13/nighty-night-box-set-review-julia-davis (accessed 07/02/2019).

Rivers, N., 2017. *Postfeminism(s) and the arrival of the fourth wave: turning tides*. Basingstoke: Palgrave Macmillan.

Roberts, A., 2018. *The Double Act: A History of British Comedy Duos*. Gloucestershire: The History Press.

Robinson, J., 2016. 'The nasty women of TV comedy have arrived just in time', *Vanity Fair*. Available at: https://www.vanityfair.com/hollywood/2016/10/samantha-bee-obama-female-anger-tv-comedy (accessed 24/02/2021).

Rodan, D., Ellis, K. and Lebeck, P., 2019. *Disability, Obesity and Ageing: Popular Media Identifications*. Farnham and Burlington: Ashgate Publishing.

Rodgers, B., 2019. 'Contemporary TV shows are bringing out the unlikeable side of female leads', *Grazia*. Available at: https://www.grazia.co.in/people/contemporary-tv-shows-are-bringing-out-the-unlikeable-side-of-female-leads-4016.html (accessed 24/02/2021).

Rolinson, D. and Woods, F., 2013. 'Is *This England '86* and *'88*? Memory, haunting and return through television seriality', in: Fradley, M., Godfrey, S. and Williams, M., eds., *Shane Meadows: Critical Essays*. Edinburgh University Press: Edinburgh, pp. 186–202.

Rottenberg, C. 2013. 'The rise of neoliberal feminism', *Cultural Studies*, 28(3), pp. 418–37.

Rowe, K., 1995. *The Unruly Woman: Gender and the Genres of Laughter*. Texas: Texas University Press.

Rowe, K., 2017. 'Foreword' in: L. Mizejewski and V. Sturtevant, eds., *Hysterical!: Women in American Comedy*. Austin, TX: University of Texas Press, pp. vvii–ix.

RTS Media. 2018. 'ITV launches Comedy 50:50 initiative for female writers', *Royal Television Society*. Available at: https://rts.org.uk/article/itv-launches-comedy-5050-initiative-female-writers (accessed 08/05/2019).

Russo, M., 1994. *The Female Grotesque: Risk, Excess and Modernity*. New York: Routledge.

Saha, A., 2017. *Race and the Cultural Industries*. Malden, MA: Polity Press.

Sally, L., 2021. *Neo-Burlesque: Striptease as Transformation*. New Brunswick, NJ: Rutgers University Press.

Schaffer, G., 2016. 'Fighting Thatcher with comedy: what to do when there is no alternative', *Journal of British Studies*, 55(2), pp. 374–97.

Schniedermann, W., 2020. 'Precarious mobility: vagrancy in American pop culture', in: W. Lenz, ed., *Poverty in American Popular Culture: Essays on Representations, Beliefs and Policy*. Jefferson, MC: McFarland, pp. 161–78.

Sconce, J., 2014. 'Explosive apathy', in: C. Perkins and C. Verevis, eds., *B Is for Bad Cinema: Aesthetics, Politics, and Cultural Value*. Albany, NY: State University of New York Press, pp. 21–42.

Scott, D., 2020. 'Michaela Coel says this is why she turned down $1m Netflix deal', *Cosmopolitan*. Available at: https://www.cosmopolitan.com/uk/entertainment/a33231581/michaela-coel-i-may-destroy-you-netflix/ (accessed 14/01/2020).

Seale, J., 2012. 'Rich in laughs: how Sky took over British comedy', *The Radio Times*. Available at: https://www.radiotimes.com/news/2012-02-15/rich-in-laughs-how-sky-took-over-british-comedy/ (accessed 16/11/2018).

Seaton, W., 2018. *The Labour of Feminist Performance: Postfeminism, Authenticity, and Celebrity In Contemporary Representations Of Girlhood On Screen*. PhD thesis, Keele University.

Sedgwick, C., 2024. *Inequality in Contemporary Stand-Up Comedy in the UK*. London: Palgrave Macmillan.

Shields Dobson, A. and Kanai, A., 2019. 'From "can-do" girls to insecure and angry: affective dissonances in young women's post-recessional media', *Feminist Media Studies*, 19(6), pp. 771–86.

Shifman, L., and Lemish, D., 2010. 'Between feminism and fun(ny)mism', *Information, Communication and Society*, 13(6), pp. 870–91.

Shifman, L. and Lemish, D., 2011. '"Mars and Venus" in virtual space: post-feminist humor and the internet', *Critical Studies in Media Communication*, 28(3), pp. 253–73.

Simmons, J. and Rich, L. E., 2013. 'Feminism ain't funny: woman as "fun-killer," mother as monster in the American sitcom', *Advances in Journalism and Communication*, 1(1), 1–12.

Skeggs, B., 2009. 'The moral economy of person production: the class relations of self-performance on "reality" television', *The Sociological Review*, 57(4), pp. 626–44.

Smith, A., 2011. 'Femininity repackaged: postfeminism and *Ladette to Lady*', in: M. Waters, ed. *Women on Screen: Feminism and Femininity in Visual Culture*. London: Palgrave Macmillan, pp. 153–66.

Sobott-Mogwe, G., and Cox, D., 1999. 'Laughter and the Medusa: an interview with Jo Brand', *Journal of Gender Studies*, 8(2), pp. 133–40.

Steinmetz, K., 2020. 'She coined the term "intersectionality" over 30 years ago. here's what it means to her today', *Time Magazine*. Available at: https://time.com/5786710/kimberle-crenshaw-intersectionality/ (accessed 23/11/2020).

Stolworthy, J., 2017. 'Riz Ahmed warns parliament that a lack of diversity in TV is leading people to Isis', *The Independent*. Available at: http://www.independent.co.uk/arts-entertainment/tv/news/riz-ahmed-warns-parliament-that-lack-of-diversity-in-tv-leads-people-to-isis-a7610861.html (accessed 09/12/2017).

Stott, A., 2005. *Comedy (The New Critical Idiom)*. London: Routledge.

Strange, N., 2011. 'Multiplatforming public service: The BBC's "bundled project"', in: J. Bennett and N. Strange, eds., *Television as New Media*. Durham: Duke University Press.

Strangelove, M., 2015. *Post-TV: Piracy, Cord-Cutting, and the Future of Television*. Toronto: University of Toronto Press.

Swift, H. J. and Steeden, B., 2020. 'Exploring representations of old age and ageing', *Centre for Ageing Better: Literature Review*. Available at: https://www.ageing-better.org.uk/sites/default/files/2020-03/Exploring-representations-of-old-age.pdf (accessed 10/02/2021).

Swink, R. S., 2017. 'Lemony Liz and likable Leslie: audience understandings of feminism, comedy, and gender in women-led television comedies', *Feminist Media Studies*, 17 (1), pp. 14–28.

Tally, M., 2016. *The Rise of the Anti-Heroine in TV's Third Golden Age*. Newcastle-upon-Tyne: Cambridge Scholars Publishing.

Tasker, Y. and Negra, D., 2007. 'Introduction: feminist politics and postfeminist culture', in: Y. Tasker and D. Negra, eds., *Interrogating Postfeminism: Gender and the Politics of Popular Culture*. Durham, NC and London: Duke University Press, pp. 1–25.

Tasker, Y., 2018. 'Women and...(the canon?): picturing and positioning the woman filmmaker'. Conference paper. *Doing Women's Film and Television History IV: Calling the Shots – Then, Now, and Next*, University of Southampton, 23–25 May 2018.

Tate, G., 2015a. 'Meet Michaela Coel: the rising star behind *Chewing Gum*, E4's new drama about London estate life', *Evening Standard*. Available at: https://www.standard.co.uk/lifestyle/london-life/meet-michaela-coel-the-rising-star-behind-chewing-gum-e4s-new-drama-about-london-estate-life-a2950646.html (accessed 04/04/2020).

Tate, G., 2015b. 'Sharon Horgan: "It's hard to stay in love when you've got kids"', *The Telegraph*. Available at: https://www.telegraph.co.uk/culture/tvandradio/11354674/sharon-horgan-interview-catastrophe-channel-4.html (accessed 21/01/2023).

The Herald, 2015. 'TV review: *Raised by Wolves* was a bloody mess'. *The Herald*. Available at: https://www.heraldscotland.com/arts_ents/13206012.tv-review-raised-by-wolves-was-a-bloody-mess/ (accessed 8/11/2019).

Tomsett, E., 2023. *Stand-up Comedy and Contemporary Feminisms: Sexism, Stereotypes and Structural Inequalities*. London, New York and Dublin: Bloomsbury.

Topshop Blog, 2018. 'Why you need to meet Caitlin Moran', *Topshop Blog*. Available at: https://www.topshop.com/blog/2018/07/why-you-need-to-meet-caitlin-moran (accessed 18/12/2019).

Traister, R., 2018. *Good and Mad: The Revolutionary Power of Women's Anger*. New York: Simon and Schuster.

Tucker, E., 2015. 'Neville Brody designs bespoke typefaces for Channel 4 rebrand', *Dezeen*. Available at: https://www.dezeen.com/2015/09/30/neville-brody-bespoke-typefaces-channel-4-rebrand-4creative-jonathan-glazer-dblg/ (accessed 18/12/2019).

Tully, M., 2018. *Trainwreck Feminism: Women, Comedy and Postfeminist Culture*, PhD thesis, University of Iowa.

Tyler, I. and Bennett, B., 2010. '"Celebrity chav": Fame, femininity and social class', *European Journal of Cultural Studies*, 13(3), pp. 375–93.

Valinoti Jr, R., 2010. *Another Nice Mess - the Laurel and Hardy Story*. Duncan, OH: BearManor Media.

Wagg, S., 1998. 'Punching your weight. Conversations with Jo Brand' in: S. Wagg, ed. *Because I Tell a Joke or Two: Comedy, Politics and Social Difference*. London and New York: Routledge, pp. 111–36.

Wahlquist, C., 2016. 'Germaine Greer tells Q&A her trans views were wrong, but then restates them', *The Guardian*. Available at: https://www.theguardian.com/books/2016/apr/12/germaine-greer-tells-qa-her-trans-views-were-wrong-but-then-restates-them (accessed 8/11/2019).

Walker, N. A., and Dresner, Z., 1998. 'Women's humor in America', in: N. A. Walker, ed. *What's So Funny?: Humor in American Culture*. Wilmington, DE: Scholarly Resources, pp. 171–84.

Wallace, M., 1978. *Black Macho and the Myth of the Superwoman*. New York: The Dial Press.

Wallace, R., 2018. *Mockumentary Comedy: Performing Authenticity*. London: Palgrave Macmillan.

Walker, S., 2016. 'Crying wolf: millionaire leftie luvvie Caitlin Moran fails in bid to raise cash for new series of *Raised By Wolves*', *The Sun*. Available at: https://www.thesun.co.uk/tvandshowbiz/2227624/millionaire-leftie-luvvie-caitlin-moran-fails-in-bid-to-raise-cash-for-new-series-of-raised-by-wolves/ (accessed 8/11/2019).

Walker, T., 2012. 'Morgan Freeman: why black actors quit Britain', *The Telegraph*. Available at: https://www.telegraph.co.uk/culture/film/film-news/9413115/Morgan-Freeman-Why-black-actors-quit-Britain.html (accessed 30/10/2023).

Walters, S. D., 2017. 'Lesbian request approved: sex, power and desire in *Orange is the New Black*', in: M. Buonanno, ed. *Television Antiheroines: Women Behaving Badly in Crime and Prison Drama*. Bristol and Chicago: Intellect, pp. 199–216.

Wanzo, R., 2016. 'Precarious-girl comedy: Issa Rae, Lena Dunham, and abjection aesthetics', *Camera Obscura: Feminism, Culture, and Media Studies*, 31(2), pp. 27–59.

Watson, E., Mitchell, J. and Shaw, M. E., 2015. *HBO's Girls and the Awkward Politics of Gender, Race, and Privilege*. Lanham, MA: Lexington Books.

Webley Adler, K., 2022. 'Sharon Horgan on writing women who are "funny and strong and f*ck up every day"', *Elle*. Available at: https://www.elle.com/culture/movies-tv/a42170146/sharon-horgan-bad-sisters-interview/ (accessed 02/01/2024).

Webster, G., 2019. 'The irresistible rise of Phoebe Waller-Bridge', *Medium*. Available at: https://medium.com/@guywebster_71417/the-irresistible-rise-of-phoebe-waller-bridge-e90a5208b5c3 (accessed 28/08/2020).

West, C., 2012. 'Mammy, Jezebel, Sapphire, and their homegirls: developing an 'oppositional gaze' toward the images of black women', in: J. C. Chrisler, C. Golden, and P. D. Rozee, eds., *Lectures on the Psychology of Women* (4th ed). Long Grove, IL: Waveland Press, pp. 286–99.

Weissmann, E., 2012. *Transnational Television Drama: Special Relations and Mutual Influences between the US and the UK*. Abingdon and New York: Palgrave Macmillan.

Wheatley, H., 2016. *Spectacular Television: Exploring Televisual Pleasure*. London and New York: I. B. Tauris.

Whelehan, I., 2000. *Overloaded: Popular Culture and the Future of Feminism*. London: Women's Press.
Williams, M., 2017. '"I kinda prefer to be a human being": Roseanne Barr and defining working-class feminism and authorship', in: R. Samer and W. Whittington, eds., *Spectatorship: Shifting Theories of Gender, Sexuality, and Media*. Texas: University of Texas Press, pp. 107–24.
White, P., 2016. 'Caitlin Moran slams lack of working class comedies', *Broadcast Now*. Available at: https://www.broadcastnow.co.uk/caitlin-moran-slams-lack-of-working-class-comedies/5108428.article (accessed 8/11/2019).
White, P., 2019. 'Sky strikes first-look distribution deal with Sharon Horgan's 'Catastrophe' co-producer Merman TV', *Deadline*. Available at: https://deadline.com/2019/12/sky-strikes-first-look-deal-with-catastrophe-co-producer-merman-tv-1202800222/ (accessed 21/01/2023).
White, P. W., 2021. 'Michaela Coel 'noodling" ideas as HBO eyes new projects from "*I May Destroy You*" Creator', *Deadline*. Available at: https://deadline.com/2021/02/hbo-eyeing-new-projects-michaela-coel-i-may-destroy-you-noodling-1234691702/ (accessed 24/02/2021).
White, R., 2010. 'Commentary and criticism: women, humour, and feminism', *Feminist Media Studies*, 10(3), pp. 353–67.
White, R., 2012. 'Women are angry! *Lizzie and Sarah* as feminist critique', *Feminist Media Studies*, 13(3), pp. 415–26.
White, R., 2014. 'Funny old girls: representing older women in British television comedy', in: I. Whelehan and J. Gwynne, eds., *Ageing, Popular Culture and Contemporary Feminism: Harleys and Hormones*. Abingdon and New York: Palgrave Macmillan, pp. 155, 171.
White, R., 2015. '*Miranda* and *Miranda*: feminism, femininity and performance', in: C. Nally and A. Smith, eds., *Twenty-first Century Feminism: Forming and Performing Femininity*. New York and Basingstoke: Palgrave Macmillan, pp. 119–39.
White, R., 2018. *Television Comedy and Femininity: Queering Gender*. London and New York: I. B. Tauris.
Whitson, J., Simon, B. and Parker, F., 2021. 'The missing producer: rethinking indie cultural production in terms of entrepreneurship, relational labour, and sustainability', *European Journal of Cultural Studies*, 24(2), pp. 606–27.
Wilson, J., 2020. '*I May Destroy You's* Michaela Coel rejected Netflix's $1 Million offer in favor of the BBC because of ownership', *Forbes*. Available at: https://www.forbes.com/sites/joshwilson/2020/07/07/i-may-destroy-yous-michaela-coel-rejected-netflixs-1-million-offer-in-favor-of-the-bbc-because-of-ownership/?sh=16f152031fc7 (accessed 14/01/2021).
Wiseman, E., 2016. '*Catastrophe* creator Sharon Horgan on why real life is the key to her success', *Stylist*. Available at: https://www.stylist.co.uk/people/sharon-horgan-interview-the-real-deal-pulling-catastrophe-pulling-tv-talent/25606 (accessed 21/01/2023).
Wood, H., 2019. 'Fuck the patriarchy: towards an intersectional politics of irreverent rage', *Feminist Media Studies*, 19(4), pp. 609–15.
Woods, F., 2015, 'Girls talk: authorship and authenticity in the reception of Lena Dunham's *Girls*', *Critical Studies in Television*, 10(2), pp. 37–54.

Woods, F., 2016. *British Youth Television: Transnational Teens, Industry, Genre*. Basingstoke: Palgrave Macmillan.

Woods, F., 2017. 'Streaming British youth television: online BBC three as a transitional moment'. *Cinema Journal*, 57(1), pp. 140–6.

Woods, F., 2019. 'Too close for comfort: direct address and the affective pull of the confessional comic woman in *Chewing Gum* and *Fleabag*', *Communication, Culture and Critique*, 12(2), pp. 194–212.

Woodward, K. M., 1999. 'Introduction', in: K. M. Woodward, ed., *Figuring Age: Women, Bodies, Generations*. Bloomington: Indiana University Press, pp. ix–xxix.

Woods-Giscombé, C. L., 2010. 'Superwoman schema: African American women's views on stress, strength, and health', *Qualitative Health Research*, 20(5), pp. 668–83.

Wrenn, M. V. and Waller, W., 2021. 'Feminist institutionalism and neoliberalism', *Feminist Economics*, 27(3), 51–76.

Yates, C., 2015. *The Play of Political Culture, Emotion and Identity*. Basingstoke: Palgrave Macmillan.

Yates, R., 2017. 'Reggie Yates meets *Chewing Gum* creator Michaela Coel: "I never saw my life represented on TV"', *Radio Times*. Available at: http://www.radiotimes.com/news/2017-01-12/reggie-yates-meets-chewing-gum-creator-michaela-coel-i-never-saw-my-life-represented-on-tv/ (accessed 04/04/2020).

Young, M., 2017. 'Introduction: bad girls in popular culture', in: M. Young and J. A. Chappell, eds., *Bad Girls and Transgressive Women in Popular Television, Fiction, and Film*. Basingstoke: Palgrave Macmillan, pp. 1–12.

Youngs, I., 2019. '*Fleabag* at the Emmys: how America fell in love with a "dirty" British comedy', *BBC News*. Available at: https://www.bbc.co.uk/news/entertainment-arts-49794823 (accessed 30/10/2023).

You Magazine, 2021. 'Sharon Horgan: "Motherhood? I'm a tight-fisted ballbreaker!"'. Available at: https://www.you.co.uk/sharon-horgan-interview-2021/ (accessed 21/01/2023).

Zimmerman, T., 2017. '#Intersectionality: The Fourth Wave Feminist Twitter Community', *Atlantis: Critical Studies in Gender, Culture and Social Justice*, 38(1), pp. 54–70.

Zeisler, A., 2016. 'Pondering our mad futures with the British columnist Caitlin Moran', *The New York Times*. Available at: https://www.nytimes.com/2016/12/05/books/review/moranifesto-caitlin-moran.html (accessed 18/12/2019).

Index

abject/abjection, 50, 80, 113, 127
Absolutely Fabulous, 33, 47–8, 57
activism, 16, 18, 46, 74, 109–10, 142
agency, 20, 87, 94, 114, 117, 134–5
Aherne, Caroline, 62, 88
ambivalence, 4–6, 42, 72, 81, 98–9, 126, 138, 146
anger, 16, 32, 34–5, 83
'Angry Black Woman', 103, 112
art
   high, 43, 56, 144
   low, 43, 56, 107, 144
authenticity, 29, 65, 89
autobiographies, 50, 95, 130
autonomy, 69, 135

backlash, 46, 73, 77, 96, 98, 146
Ball, Lucille, 9, 12, 21, 112
Banet-Weiser, Sarah, 2, 46, 53
Barr, Roseanne, 9–10, 19, 109–10
Bea, Aisling, 73, 128, 133
Black British, 103–5, 110, 119, 146
Black feminists, 14, 74, 118
Black women, 7–8, 14, 102–4, 111–13, 118, 125
brand of feminism, 83, 86, 93, 95
Brand, Jo, 24–5, 32
Broad City, 50, 67, 84

carnival, 5, 10, 124
carnivalesque, 24, 124, 143
cinematic, 12, 20, 55–6
class differences, 71, 113, 114

class politics, 6, 54, 65, 145
Clifford, Sian, 61, 67
collaboration, 19–20, 22, 29, 33–4, 66–7, 128, 141
collectivity, 66, 124, 139
commissioners, 36–7, 39, 94, 98
communities, 49, 66, 95, 115
confessional, 50, 61, 72, 77, 144
confidence, 68, 75, 137–8
Coogan, Steve, 27, 51
Cooper, Daisy May, 62
Crazy Ex-Girlfriend, 41, 67
creative workers, 37, 67, 79, 142
creativity, 9, 70, 98, 130–1, 134, 138
cringe, 28, 31, 42–4, 108, 123
   comedy, 28, 109, 144

Dear Joan and Jericha, 44, 51
Delaney, Rob, 122–3, 134–5
Derry Girls, 88, 94
diversity, 3, 15, 22–3, 30, 64, 72, 75, 87, 103–4, 106, 137
dramedy, 60–1, 144
Dunham, Lena, 6, 42, 45, 52, 54, 56, 60, 79, 94, 97–9

Éclair, Jenny, 24, 32
edgy, 2, 6, 29, 38, 40, 53, 65, 146
emergent feminisms, 16–18, 58, 148
empowerment, 17, 35, 68, 117
entrepreneur, 128, 131, 134, 138
entrepreneurship, 135–6, 138
ethnicity, 13, 23, 139

feminine, 12, 20, 45, 56, 60, 69, 75, 82, 93, 134, 136, 143–4
  humour, 57, 133–4
Fey, Tina, 12, 42, 52, 79, 82, 84, 95
Ford, Jessica, 56, 109
Friedman, Sam, 24, 62, 145
friendship, 67, 80, 102, 133

Gill, Rosalind, 17, 42, 137
Glazer, Ilana, 50, 58
Gray, Frances, 9, 24, 29, 45
grotesque, 2, 23, 29, 32, 42, 44–6, 48, 111–14, 118

Hart, Miranda, 64–5
  Miranda (TV series), 47, 64–5, 92, 113
Horrible White People (book), 15, 58, 67
Horton, Erica, 19, 39
Hughes, Sarah, 40–1, 47, 51
Hynes, Jessica, 33–4, 38, 44, 48, 51, 58

Ilott, Sarah, 13
inclusive, 74, 77, 81, 103
individualism, 17, 66, 113, 126, 135, 138
inequality, 14, 24, 58, 106
Insecure, 50, 67, 103
internet, 45, 73, 96, 109
intersectionality, 14–15, 17, 26, 54, 74, 81, 97, 109, 110, 118, 124–5, 139, 141–2
Ireland, 128–9, 132, 134, 137, 139, 141
Irish, 3–4, 8, 122, 125, 128–9, 137, 139
  showrunner, 121, 127, 139
I Love Lucy, 21, 112

Jacobson, Abbi, 49, 58
Jones, Ruth, 32, 39, 51, 58
Jones, Vicky, 20, 55, 66

Killing Eve, 40–1, 55, 60
Khan, Guz, 59, 86

labour, 3–4, 8–9, 20, 28, 34, 62, 88, 121, 131, 137–8, 143
  invisible, 19, 98

Lagerway, Jorie, 15, 58, 67, 144
Larson, Sarah, 21, 40–1, 43
legitimation, 26, 51, 56, 59
Lockyer, Sharon, 71
Lumsden, Lucy, 38–9, 52

McGee, Lisa, 88, 127
McRobbie, Angela, 45, 147
Medhurst, Andy, 25
memoir, 12, 79, 82–3
Mermade, 8
Merman, 131–4, 136
messiness, 4, 45, 54, 66, 68–9, 77, 143
messy, 4–5, 76, 84–5, 96, 121, 123, 138, 141
Me Too, 16, 142
Midlands, 86–9, 91–3, 95, 145
  West, 80, 86–7
millennial, 50, 54, 61, 102
Mills, Brett, 13, 19, 28–30, 37–8, 43, 108, 133
minority, 21, 25, 47, 118
Miranda, 47, 64–5, 92, 113
Miss Piggy, 10, 80, 91
Mizejewski, Linda, 11, 13, 20, 33, 77, 113
monologues, 2–3, 25, 73, 118
Morgan, Diane, 124
Morris, Chris, 27–8, 33, 51
motherhood, 90, 92–3, 121, 123–4
Mountford, Clelia, 8, 132–6
music-hall, 23–5

national, 3, 18, 22, 60, 104–5, 128, 148
  fixation, 6, 54
  identity, 86, 139, 147
nationality, 3, 127, 129
nations, 22, 128
Negra, Diane, 82–3, 86, 93, 95, 97
neoliberal, 14–16, 46, 61, 66–9, 76–7, 90, 130, 135, 138–9
Nygaard, Taylor, 15, 58, 67, 144

online, 14, 22–3, 45–6, 64, 74, 77, 148
  feminism, 53, 118
  spaces, 35, 73

oppression, 14, 74, 83, 109, 148
Orgad, Shani, 137–8
O'Shaughnessy, Barunka, 20, 51, 136

parody, 10
parodying, 70
patriarchy, 82–3, 85, 114, 126
Pepperdine, Vicki, 20, 44, 51–2
Pile, Victoria, 58
Poehler, Amy, 21, 60, 84
popular culture, 4, 12, 83, 110, 146
Porter, Laraine, 24, 32
Portwood-Stacer, Laura, 46, 72
postfeminism, 16–18, 45, 58, 68, 76, 135, 139, 146–7
postfeminist, 12, 16–18, 29, 48, 66, 75–7, 81, 135, 138–9, 146–7
  comedy, 18
  culture, 44, 58, 68, 126, 147
  ideals, 45, 71, 76
precarious-girl comedy, 50, 57–8
precarity, 138, 146
prestige, 5, 7, 39, 53
privilege/privileged, 14-15, 17, 37, 45, 63–4, 70, 71–2, 95, 112, 123, 126
production company, 55, 106, 122, 132–3, 138
public service broadcasters, 39, 58, 105, 117

quality television, 22, 38–9, 56

racism, 7, 24, 33
racist, 97, 109
RADA, 55, 67
Ralph, Sarah, 13, 37–8, 133
regional, 38, 63, 80, 88, 124, 145
Roseanne, 10, 21, 47, 109–10
Russo, Mary, 32

Schuster, Saskia, 37–8
semi-autobiographical, 5, 41, 53, 72, 81–2, 101, 128, 143, 148
  comedies, 6, 28, 49–50, 80

sexism, 16, 18, 24, 41, 83, 96
showrunners, 21, 39, 56, 103, 148
sisterhood, 51, 65, 133, 149
social class, 10, 23, 33, 54, 70, 80, 141, 145–6
social media, 14, 35, 43, 45–6, 72, 118, 148
solidarity, 14, 32, 117, 139, 148
spectacle, 10, 56, 69, 84, 98, 112, 123, 126, 138
stand-up, 9, 11, 24–5, 32, 62, 103, 136
stardom, 15, 43, 71, 128, 131, 139
stereotypes, 22–4, 47–8, 52, 70, 87, 102, 104, 109, 112–13, 118, 123, 125–6

technology, 17–18, 45, 147–8
teenagers/teens, 80–1, 82, 83, 107, 129, 130, 145
teen TV, 108
theatre, 23, 55, 63, 101, 107, 144
trainwreck feminism, 58
trainwrecks, 58, 68
transnational, 14, 22, 45, 59, 121, 128, 131, 144
Twitter, 14, 34–5, 94, 122

UK TV industry, 15, 19, 26, 105–6
underrepresented, 44, 48, 74, 80, 102, 104, 115, 145–6
unlikability, 57
unlikeable, 4, 54, 57, 125

Wallace, Nellie, 23, 25
Walsh, Holly, 20, 124, 134, 136
White, Rosie, 11–12, 34, 44, 46, 48, 64
whiteness, 15, 44, 58–60, 97, 115, 125
Willan, Sophie, 62, 145
Wood, Victoria, 18, 24–5, 33, 87
Woods, Faye, 7, 12, 57, 59–60, 73, 89, 101, 108

EU Authorised Representative:
Easy Access System Europe Mustamäe tee 50, 10621 Tallinn, Estonia
gpsr.requests@easproject.com

Printed and bound by CPI Group (UK) Ltd, Croydon, CR0 4YY
15/03/2026
02071756-0009